Nonviolent Political Economy

Nonviolent Political Economy offers a set of theoretical solutions and practical guidelines to build an economy of nonviolence which implies a social state of peacefulness, involving minimal violence and minimal destruction of nature.

The book provides renewed reflections on heterodox economics, ecological economics, anthropology, Buddhism, Gandhianism, disarmament, and business ethics, as well as innovative initiatives such as Blue Frontiers. It also sets out feasible solutions to transform societies that have suffered prolonged conflicts such as Syria, Iraq and Kurdistan. Bringing together authors from around the world, this collection includes new perspectives on the abolition of profit and debts; disarmament and reconciliation; obliteration of the consumer society; expansion of collective property; Buddhist and Gandhian economies; small-scale and artisanal production, the increasing use of clean energies; a gradual reduction in the human population; self-organized collective action; political processes closer to direct and radical democracy, and anarchy.

Discussing cutting-edge developments, this book provides valuable tools to build alternatives to the prevailing models of (violent) political economy. It will be of great interest to a public of critical citizens, students and researchers from a range of disciplines and backgrounds, and all those seeking to understand the fundamental concepts of nonviolent political economy.

Freddy Cante is a Full Professor at the School of Political Science, Government and International Relations, at Universidad del Rosario, Colombia. He is a founding member of the International Consortium for Research on Violence and of the interdisciplinary group JANUS, for the study of peace and conflicts. His research focuses on welfare economics, public choice, social choice, collective action, nonviolent political action, and in the political economy of nonviolence.

Wanda Tatiana Torres is a Political Scientist and Internationalist from Universidad del Rosario, Colombia. As a Chevening scholar, she is a current candidate for a Masters of Science in Global Politics at The London School of Economics and Political Science. She is also a former researcher at the Regional Center for Strategic Security Studies (CREES), at the National War College in Bogota, Republic of Colombia and an International Advisor to the Command of the National Colombian Army.

Routledge Frontiers of Political Economy

For more information about this series, please visit: www.routledge.com/books/series/SE0345

Nonviolent Political Economy

Theory and Applications

**Edited by
Freddy Cante and Wanda Tatiana
Torres**

Routledge
Taylor & Francis Group

LONDON AND NEW YORK

First published 2019 by Routledge

2 Park Square, Milton Park, Abingdon, Oxon, OX14 4RN
605 Third Avenue, New York, NY 10017

Routledge is an imprint of the Taylor & Francis Group, an informa business

First issued in paperback 2020

British Library Cataloguing in Publication Data
A catalogue record for this book is available from the British Library

Library of Congress Cataloging-in-Publication Data
A catalog record has been requested for this book

ISBN: 978-1-138-50284-0 (hbk)
ISBN: 978-0-367-72718-5 (pbk)

Typeset in Bembo
by Taylor & Francis Books

Contents

Illustrations

Figures

Tables

Contributors

Freddy Cante is Ph.D. in Economic Sciences at the National University of Colombia and Full Professor at the School of Political Science, Government and International Relations at Universidad del Rosario (since 2008). His areas of research include: welfare economics, public choice, social choice, collective action, nonviolent political action, and political economy of nonviolence. Cante is a former Advisor to the Mayor of Bogota, Antanas Mockus (2002 and 2003) in the design of collective civil resistance actions; founding member of the International Consortium for Research on Violence (since 2013) and of the interdisciplinary group JANUS, for the study of peace and conflicts. Cante is co-editor of *The Handbook of Research on Transitional Justice and Peace Building in Turbulent Regions*.

Wanda Tatiana Torres is a Political Scientist and Internationalist from Universidad del Rosario, Colombia. Torres is a former research assistant to Professor Cante at the Political and International Studies Group, Universidad del Rosario. As a Chevening scholar, she is a current candidate for an M.Sc. in Global Politics at The London School of Economics and Political Science. She is an alumna from the William J. Perry Center for Hemispheric Defense Studies at the National Defense University, located in Washington D.C., United States of America. Torres is also a scholar from the George C. Marshall Center – European Center for Security Studies, located in Garmisch-Partenkirchen, Germany. Also, Torres is a former researcher at the Regional Center for Strategic Security Studies (CREES), at the National War College in Bogota, Republic of Colombia and an International Advisor to the Command of the National Colombian Army.

Tilman Bauer is a Peace Researcher and Doctoral Candidate at Aalto University School of Business, Helsinki, Finland. Tilman Bauer, originally from Finland and Germany, researches the relationship between business and peace as a doctoral candidate at Aalto University School of Business in Helsinki, Finland. He explores a new paradigm for business thinking where ethical business can foster holistic peace in society. In 2018, he led the Aalto Doctoral Student Association. He previously worked as assistant to the CEO at Autarkia GmbH, which organizes the Green World Tour event series bringing sustainability into the mainstream. He has completed three masters' degrees in Peace Studies, Business Management, and Sustainability.

Marco Paulo Vianna Franco is a researcher and professor at the School of Government of João Pinheiro Foundation, in Belo Horizonte, Brazil. He is currently a Ph.D. candidate in Economics at the Center for Development and Regional Planning of the Federal University of Minas Gerais. His research interests include ecological economics, political economy of the environment, political ecology, methodology of economics and history of ecological economic thought.

Gábor Kovács (Ph.D.) is an assistant professor at the Business Ethics Center of the Corvinus University of Budapest. He defended his doctoral thesis 'The Value-orientations of Christian and Buddhist Entrepreneurs' in 2017. He made his undergraduate studies in economics and management. He received his master's degree in Buddhist studies from the Budapest Buddhist University in 2010. He has participated in research projects of the Business Ethics Center about the ethical value-orientations and the ecological value-orientations of Hungarian entrepreneurs. He is currently researching on Buddhist economics, and the role of spirituality in business. He is the secretary of the Hungarian Bhutan Friendship Society since its foundation in 2011. He is a member of the Pali Translation Group that aims at the translation of Buddhist Scriptures from the Pali Canon to Hungarian language since 2008.

Lucas Ferreira Lima, is a Doctoral candidate in Economic Development at the Institute of Economics of the University of Campinas, Brazil. He is a University Professor of Faculdades Metropolitanas Unidas (FMU) Educational Complex in São Paulo. Ferreira Lima is an Economist from Federal University of Uberlandia. Master in Economic Development, Institute of Economics of the University of Campinas. Member of the International Society of Ecological Economics (ISEE). His interests and researches are focused on ecological economics, sustainable development, territorial public policies, rural development policies and organic production.

Carlos Eduardo Maldonado, is Full Professor of Epistemology, Complexity Science, Logic and Ethics at the School of Medicine in Universidad del Bosque, Bogota – Colombia. Maldonado obtained his Ph.D. in Philosophy from KU Leuven (Belgium). He has been a distinguished visiting scholar at Pittsburgh University (EE.UU.); at the Catholic University of America (Washington, D.C.) as a as Visiting Research Professor; and as an Academic Visitor at the Faculty of Philosophy, in Cambridge University (United Kingdom). He has been acknowledged with the "Distinction to the Merit" by the Universidad Nacional Mayor de San Marcos, Lima, Peru, for his contributions to philosophy and complexity. He is also a Research Senior at Colciencias. In 2017, he was entitled as a Distinguished Visiting Professor by Universidad Nacional Autónoma de Nicaragua. Maldonado is a Senior Member of the The Institute of Electrical and

Electronics Engineers (IEEE) and an Honorary Doctor *Honoris Causa*, University of Timisoara (Rumania), 2015.

Kozo Torasan Mayumi is a Full Professor at Tokushima University and currently an editorial board member of *Ecological Economics, International Journal of Ecological Economics and Statistics, Journal of Economic Structures, Ecosystem Services, Romanian Journal of Economic Forecasting*, and *Theoretical and Applied Economics*. Mayumi is alumni from the Graduate School of Engineering at the Department of Applied Mathematics and Physics of Kyoto University. Between 1984 and 1988 he studied Bioeconomics at Department of Economics of Vanderbilt University under Professor Nicholas Georgescu-Roegen's supervision. Since then, Mayumi has been working in the field of energy analysis, ecological economics and complex hierarchy theory.

Together with Dr. Mario Giampietro and other three researchers Mayumi started a biennial international workshop (Advances in Energy Studies) starting 1998 in which many distinguished scholars in the field of energy analysis took part. He is one of the five general editors of *The International Encyclopedia of Environment and Society* to be published from Wiley-Blackwell. Mayumi is the first recipient of Georgescu-Roegen Awards (Unconventional Thinking Category) at the 13th Delhi Sustainable Development Summit in 2013.

Mayumi's works include the following books: (1) *The Origins of Ecological Economics: The Bioeconomics of Georgescu-Roegen*. London: Routledge, 2001; (2) *The Jevons Paradox and the Myth of Resource Efficiency Improvements*, The Earthscan, 2007 (with John Polimeni, Mario Giampietro and Blake Alcott); (3) *The Biofuel Delusion: The Fallacy of Large Scale Agro-Biofuel Production*, The Earthscan, 2009 (with Mario Giampietroz); (4) *The Metabolic Pattern of Societies: Where Economists Fall Short*, Roultedge, 2011 (with Mario Giampietro and Alev Sorman); and (5) *Energy Analysis for a Sustainable Future: Multi-Scale Integrated Analysis of Societal and Ecosystem Metabolism*, Routledge, 2012 (with Mario Giampietro and Alev Sorman).

Nathalie Mezza-García is a Ph.D. candidate at the Centre for Interdisciplinary Methodologies at the University of Warwick, United Kingdom, and a Rodolfo Llinás, Fundación CEIBA, Doctoral Fellow. Her research explores how can human societies politically self-organize using internet-based technologies and artificial intelligence. Through the lenses of complexity science and clear influences of anarchistic and utopian thinking, her work also explores elements of freedom, networks and surveillance in the solar stage of a transhuman civilisation.

Guillermo Díaz Muñoz is a Professor and Researcher at the Interdisciplinary Center for Training and Social Engagement (CIFOVIS), ITESO – Universidad Jesuita de Guadalajara, México. Díaz Muñoz obtained his PhD in Scientific and Social Studies, ITESO. He is a member of the Basic Academic Unit of "Social

Economy and Dignified Labour" at CIFOVIS, where he has worked as a coordinator and researcher. His research focuses on social education, popular education, social ethics, citizen building, democratic governability, sustainable regional development, *buen vivir*, and solidarity economy. His most renowned work has explored social movements, territorial citizen alternatives, development alternatives, regional organizations and "buen vivir". Díaz has been a member of the Research Committee at ITESO and he is a current member of the National Researchers System (SNI), National Council for Research and Technology, where he is responsible for the "Solidarity Economy and Alternative Food National Thematic Network".

Michael N. Nagler, is Professor Emeritus of Classics and Comparative Literature at the University of California, Berkeley, United States. He is a founding member of the Peace and Conflict Studies Program at UC. Nagler is Founder and President of the Metta Center for Nonviolence (www.metta center.org) and author of *Our Spiritual Crisis, The Nonviolence Handbook,* and *The Search for a Nonviolent Future*, which received a 2002 American Book Award. *Search* and the *Handbook* have been translated into Arabic, Italian, Spanish, Korean, Croatian, and other languages. Other writings of his have appeared in the *Wall Street Journal* among other venues, and he has spoken and written about nonviolence, meditation, and world peace for more than thirty years at campuses, public venues, and the UN and co-hosts *Nonviolence Radio* bi-weekly with Metta's Executive Director, Stephanie Van Hook at KWMR, out of Point Reyes Station, CA.

Among other awards, he received the Jamnalal Bajaj International Award for Promoting Gandhian Values Outside India in 2007. Michael is a student of Sri Eknath Easwaran, Founder of the Blue Mountain Center of Meditation (www.bmcm.org). He has lived at the Center's ashram in Marin County since 1970 and does presentations at their workshops on passage meditation. He is currently finishing a book, *The Third Harmony,* and a major documentary film with the Fund for Sustainable Tomorrows, both dealing with nonviolence and the "new story" of reality and human nature.

Silvia Nicola is currently a PhD student at the Freie Universität Berlin, where she deals with the role of external actors in the "Breaking and Making of States" based on a structured focused comparison of Iraqi-Kurdistan and Kosovo. Further, she holds an M.A. (2016) in Military Studies from the University of Potsdam (Germany) and a B.A. (2012) in Political Science from the Freie Universität Berlin (Germany) and the University of Granada (Spain). Ms. Nicola specialized on post-conflict transformation, security and energy policies and regionally on the Middle East and the Balkans.Ms. Nicola is currently working as a research associate at the Felsberg Institute (Germany) and also as a policy consultant on matters related to migration and disporas. Furthermore, she is a member of The German Middle East Studies Association for Contemporary Research and Documentation (DAVO).

James F. Powers is a Senior Fellow for the US Special Operations Command's Joint Special Operations University, located on MacDill Air Force Base, Tampa, Florida. His specific research/teaching areas encompass combating violent extremism and terrorism, inter-ministerial collaboration & coordination, and homeland security.

Magnus Treiber is a Professor at the Institute of Social and Cultural Anthropology, Ludwig-Maximilians-Universität (LMU) in Munich, Germany. He is affiliated to The Felsberg Institute, located in Germany. He teaches anthropological methods and theory as well as economic anthropology. As a researcher on transnational migration from North-East Africa, he is particularly interested in social and cultural discourses on and effects of global asymmetries.

Stéphane Valter is an Assistant Professor in Arabic language and civilization at Normandy University (Le Havre) – France. Valter holds a PhD in Political Science, Institut d'études politiques, Paris France. Valter's fields of research focus on ideological and political issues in the contemporary Arab world, Syrian nationalism, sectarianism in the Middle East, national identities (in the ME and for Muslims living in the West), religion and authoritarianism. Valter has been an administrative / scientific secretary at the Institut Français d'Études Arabes de Damas (IFEAD, Syria, 1992–1997), scientific assignment granted by the Centre National de la Recherche Scientifique (2016–2017) at the Centre d'Etudes et de Documentation Économiques, CEDEJ (Cairo).

Acknowledgments

The book that the reader is about to enjoy is the result of a great research effort, of academic seduction to attract partners to this intellectual enterprise, and of a demanding editing work. Our greatest thanks are, precisely, to all the authors who have given their contributions to building this collective text, and to the various members of Routledge publishing house who believed in this project since mid-2016, when we developed the first proposal.

We are immensely grateful to a number of people who have made this collective work possible. In particular, we would like to thank members of the Universidad del Rosario (the oldest university in Colombia). They are the main academic leaders of the University: Rector Alejandro Cheyne, and Vice-Rector Stéphanie Lavaux. They have prioritized the study of peace and conflict in the University and have organized the JANUS interdisciplinary group to investigate these topics. We would like to acknowledge the enormous support of the directives at the School of Political Science, Government and International Relations of Universidad del Rosario. Special thanks to our former Deans Eduardo Barajas and Mónica Pachón, as well as to the current Dean Julio Londoño Paredes, also to professor Arlene Tickner who leads the Political and International Studies Group. We would also like to make a special acknowledgement to James Powers, who devoted his time to the revision and betterment of this work, particularly during the initial stages of drafting and redrafting the proposal.

For the invaluable work of reviewing the content and form of the various chapters of this book, we are grateful to the following teachers: Thomas Green, Oscar Palma, Mauricio Jaramillo, Andrés Sampayo, and Andrés Galindo. Special thanks to our friend Jaime Villamil, and to our colleague Sonya Scott.

And we are also very grateful to the students: Natalia Andrea Puerto, Manuela Borrero, Anamaría Carmona, and Carolie Van Oostrum. They contributed greatly to the form of the articles.

Foreword

Two important words enriching each other. 'Nonviolent' easily becomes bla-bla, and 'economy' is too general. But, does 'nonviolent' make a difference for the better to the economy? And vice versa, can 'economy' make 'nonviolent' more positive, beyond resistance to evil?

Let us start with 'economy', here conceived of as a cycle with three poles: Nature, Production, Consumption. And three processes: Extraction from Nature, Distribution from Production to Consumption, and Pollution from Production-Consumption back to Nature. The cycle flow is in that order: Nature–>Production–>Consumption–>Nature.

A simple summary of the economy: humans extract resources from nature, produce-process for (intermediate and final) consumption, and sends what they cannot consume back to nature (but economists, like dishonest book-keepers, left out the Nature part). And we want it all to be nonviolent!

'Do no harm!', the negativism of *non*violent, is no answer. 'Peace', 'peaceful' include positive peace, so *Peace Economics* is the title for my book (Transcend University Press, 2012) with 'do good!'.

Let us now complicate the issue by introducing money, 'greasing', speeding up the cycle at the Distribution link. Not only consumable products in return for labor or other products; anything in return for anything, at the same price. The general flow of money is contrary to the cycle flow: there is monetized consumer demand (and producer supply to stimulate demand), to be met by monetized producer supply, to be met by resources from nature. We notice that consumers pay for products – goods and services – producers pay for resources, and nobody pays nature; it is not only extracted, but exploited. Violence.

Money takes on its own life, generalized to 'financial objects', including complex 'derivatives'. Added to the 'real economy' for end consumption then there is a 'finance economy' for buying and selling of financial objects, with no end consumption. It just goes on and on.

Nonviolence to nature as non-depletion and non-pollution is not good enough; only negative peace. Positive peace with nature would enhance nature, cater to nature's need for diversity and symbiosis, increase the diversity of biota and abiota, stimulate photosynthesis and other syntheses enriching nature. A model is forestry, clearing to improve the access of plants, trees, animals to sun and (not too much) water. This is also done in animal parks as opposed to the very violent zoos with cages, etc. They should be forbidden, right away.

But the basic violence is slaughter, for food. Let nature yield its fruits voluntarily. A nonviolent economy is vegetarian and beyond.

Does this limit extraction to the 'sustainable', reproducible? 'Sustainable', *status quo,* is not good enough, 'enhanceable' is the word. A better nature will offer more to extract, and reduce nature's violence, drought-flooding-tsunamis-earthquakes. A nature at ease with itself and humans, without being tamed like we tame animals. Plowing furrows for monocrop seeds, remedying lost diversity with manure and poison, is violence. Permaculture, diverse, symbiotic, is nonviolent. That nature is enriched and offers more and better fruits.

We move on to Production-Distribution-Consumption with humans all over, but with no Protagoras 'man is the measure of all things'. Our discourse for the economy certainly also includes nature a 'measure'.

The argument would be the same. Not to do harm to human beings is to meet their basic needs, to stay alive, and for water and food, clothing and shelter, health, and education to relate to others. Not good enough, we want both the real and the finance economy also to do good to humans, to enhance them, not only not to do harm. Too modest. Or, a discourse advanced by not very modest people wanting to protect an economy serving elites, not people, with some minor modifications?

Cooperation, not competition? Both, competition is fun, like in sports, games as long as losing does no real harm. A false dichotomy.

Dialogue is the key, between consumers and producers. Consumers having a say in what is produced would also be in the interest of the producers. *Diversity is another key*, individual consumers differ.

Instead of producers doing 'market studies', they should enter into dialogue with people. They might discover that instead of cars that all look alike and are the same except for class geared to class society, people want slower, less risky cars, more like Tivoli cars. And computers that save automatically, erasing being a decision.

Instead of spying on people to offer packages geared to their demand 'profiles', let people express individual wishes and meet them. Humans seem today to be increasingly individualist and diverse; and they want to be in command as subjects, not manipulated as objects.

In short, equality between the Production and Consumption poles, like between them and the Nature pole. But the cycle itself should also be nonviolent: a cycle with the three poles in three different continents is violent by being beyond control, even comprehension. Contract the cycle to the regional-state-provincial-local levels, to facilitate dialogues on equal terms. An argument for localism.

Distribution uses long chains for products to reach consumers, even across regional and state borders; transport at the expense of Nature, fees for the consumers. Again, an argument for localism.

Finance economy for nonviolent investment; not derivative chains for speculation at the expense of many. To be forbidden, right away.

In a nonviolent economy consumption not only makes no harm but is a delight, like meetings in virtual space, or driving at no risk. Or, by making drinking and eating more delightful. To quench thirst water does the job, straight down. But anything with taste should stay some time in the mouth, near the taste and smell buds. Chew slowly, and no violence by 'washing it down'. Nonviolent quantities of good wine and juices are for tasting and smelling, not for washing. *Bon apétit!*

Johan Galtung
Transcend International: A Peace
Development Environment Network

Preface

In George Orwell's classic novel, *1984*, individuals had a completely false vision of the world due to the sinister manoeuvres of the Minister of Truth. Symptomatically, on a large sign inscribed on the white pyramid of the aforementioned ministry, the following official slogans of the Party were read: "war is peace, freedom is slavery, ignorance is strength".

Sadly, we are suffering from a similar deception, largely caused by mainstream ideologues (conventional economists alive or deceased) and by men of action (politicians and businessmen). Among the dominant teachings that stand out are affirmations that have become part of mainstream beliefs, namely: economic growth is a symptom of good health of the economy; the invisible hand of the competitive market transforms private vices into public virtues; selfishness and violent competitions are the engines of biological evolution and economic progress; more is better than less; and salvation is possible by ostensibly increasing public and private expenditures. However, we believe that the solution to all our problems lies in the sleepless technical progress. At the extremes of greater cynicism, either the reality of global warming is denied or some powerful states and enterprises want to hide it by saying this is a consequence of economic progress and good business.

In contrast to fallacious theories and obscure concepts, there are remarkable contributions of some heretical and heterodox authors, authentic social scientists and universalist thinkers, who have shed light on certain issued for a long time. Their aim is to (re)think the world in reverse of what orthodox and conventional scholars have taught us. The anthropologist Marshall Sahlins (2008) shows that the dominant models of conventional economics have portrayed a world in the image and likeness of the selfish and competitive bourgeois. He argues that the most serious and rigorous investigations in the empirical field show that human beings and animals are social beings that have developed mutual aid and cooperation; he argues that anarchy is not violence, and that thinking "we are not part of nature" is another erroneous assumption; as it is a thought as unnatural and absurd as that of supposing that we are mind without a body, and reason without emotions.

The philosopher Jon Elster (2000) proposes a *suggestive constraint theory* and shows the benefit of spending fewer resources and imposing certain restrictions (such as the voluntary deprivation of resources) in the design of political constitutions, in consumption and, even, in artistic creativity. Contrary to conventional wisdom, economists like Kenneth Boulding (1966), Nicholas Georgescu-Roegen (1975), E. J. Mishan (1993), Ernst Friederich Schumacher (1973) and Serge Latouche (2010) proved that growth and opulence are extremely harmful to humanity and nature, that it is preferable not to grow, and that it is more sensible to tend for a decreasement.

In open opposition to the conventional economists who have defended selfishness and utilitarianism, and who have naively or maliciously assumed that the market originated in voluntary transactions and without the State's intervention, great social scientists like Kenneth Boulding (1973), Poitr Kropotkin (2014), Marcel Mauss (1990), Elinor Ostrom (1991), Karl Polanyi (2001) and even Adam Smith (2011) have shown that, like other creatures of nature, human beings have instinct behaviours of love and support, that people cooperate conditionally in environments of reciprocity, and that, sometimes, we are unconditional lovers with enormous gestures of magnanimity.

Some lovers of freedom and passionate researchers like Karl Popper (2011) states that, contrary to what conventional thinkers taught us, democracy does not consist so much in voting for this or another representative. Quite the contrary, that there is a permanent exercise in which citizens demand accountability from their rulers, a strong sense of citizen control, and the imminent alternative to overthrow governments without violence when those who govern are proven to be corrupt or inept. In frank opposition to the legitimization of hierarchies and the propagation of habits of blind obedience, thinkers such as Étienne de La-Boétie (2012), Stanley Milgram (1974), and Phillip Zimbardo (2008) illustrate the enormous dangers to freedom of acquiescence and lack of sensitivity to the suffering of victims. There is also a political economy of anarchism. Contrary to the harmful deification of the selfish individual, competition, arbitrariness and State violence (including the various state interventions of capitalism and socialism), anarchism show attributes of human society, such as cooperation and spontaneous mutual help, the possibility of confederations of autonomous commonalities, the commons as an appropriate form of appropriation of resources, the abolition of the petty borders imposed by the nation states and the non-violent social revolutions of anarchy. The work of Rob Knowles (2004) represents an excellent historical example of these features.

Accordingly, Nonviolent Political Economy (NPE) encompasses the study of the complex relations and interactions among political, economic, ideological, and organizational power that do not generate devastating and/or harming impacts on nature and human life. It invites reflection on heterodox streams of social and economic thought to generate some modalities of self-organized collective action used to promote the preservation of commons. NPE accepts sacrificing widely-accepted opulence and economic growth to preserve nature and promote welfare based on a good quality of life. In this regard, NPE challenges traditional streams of the economy and invites its main representatives to rethink old scenarios from a wider perspective. Nonviolent action is a non-destructive power, a force that promotes diverse pedagogic, political, economic, and social transformations towards a more peaceful social order.

The main features and some important components of a nonviolent economy (discussed and explained herein) are depicted in the following table:

Table I.1 A framework of nonviolent political economy

Relationship	Concept	Theory of Reference
Between human being nature	Production	Bioeconomics and Degrowth, Ecological Economics, Buddhist Economy, Economic Theory of Leisure
	Appropriation	Gandhian and Buddhist Economy, Commons, Economics of Giving, Political Economy of Love
	Welfare	Universal welfare including nature and human beings
Social Relations	Distribution	Non-possessive individualism, Altruism and Reciprocity, Solidarity Economies
	Exchange	Fund-flows model, Free Money and abolition of debts
	Consumption	Enjoyment of life, *buen vivir*.
	Decisions and Choices	Radical Democracy, Anarchism, Self-organized collective action, Complexity and Free will
	Security and Conflict Resolution	Nonviolent Political Action, Civilian Post-military systems of defense

Source: Table designed by the authors

The methodological approach of NPE implies the abandonment of metaphysical models of the conventional neoclassical economy including rational choice and accepting the consequent realities of uncertainty, complexity and emotions; and the adoption of realistic assumptions about human behaviour (including experiments and fieldwork). A challenging task is the abandonment of deterministic models of behaviour (simplistic sceneries of certainty and risk) and the consequent adoption of non-deterministic models (open to uncertainty, complexity and freedom of will).

The select group of scholars who contributed to this collective book offer some guidelines and key components for considering an economy of nonviolence. As the reader may note, they offer some proposals against conventional economic thinking, while some others go beyond to rescue heresies and creative ideas of conventional economists.

In this book we offer two perspectives of NPE, namely: free and quixotic horizons, which consist of theoretical proposals as suggested in the table, in order to show what is possible to do to generate a nonviolent economy. Moreover, some perspectives adjusted to the gloomy spirit of economists try to resolve violent conflicts in turbulent countries such as Iraq and Syria, and to address the issue of security and disarmament in the world in the short term.

About the book

After fifteen years of research and teaching in the field of nonviolent political action, and of practical learning as an advisor to the Mayor of Bogotá, Antanas Mockus, in policies of nonviolent civil resistance, Professor Freddy Cante met again on the road with one of its most outstanding students, Wanda Tatiana Torres. Both, Cante and Torres recognized that very little has been done about the nonviolent economy. This is the genesis of the main theme for this book.

Both authors believe that this project will leave an imprint on future generations. This book is designed to fill a gap in the study of the economy from an interdisciplinary perspective. This is an invitation to think further and to explore new and much-needed approaches to better serve the global community. Not everything is lost, and still, there is still plenty of work to do.

Bibliography

Boulding, K. (1966). The Economics of the Coming Spaceship Earth. In H. Jarret, *Environmental Quality in a Growing Economy*. Baltimore, MD: Johns Hopkins University Press, pp. 3–14.

Boulding, K. (1973). *The Economy of Love and Fear*. New York: Wadsworth Publishing Company.

Elster, J. (2000). *Ulysses Unbound*. New York: Columbia University Press.

Georgescu-Roegen, N. (1975). Energy and Economic Myths. *Southern Economic Journal*, 347–381.

Knowles, R. (2004). *Political Economy from Below: Economic Thought in Communitarian Anarchism, 1840–1914 (New Political Economy)*. New York USA: Routledge.

Kropotkin, P. (2014). *Mutual Aid: A Factor in Evolution*. New York: Dancing Unicorn Books.

La-Boétie, E. (2012). *On Voluntary Servitude*. Indianapolis, IN: Hackett.

Latouche, S. (2010). Degrowth. *Journal of Cleaner Production*.

Mauss, M. (1990). *The Gift: Forms and Functions of Exchange in Archaic Societies*. London: Routledge.

Milgram, S. (1974). *Obediency to Authority*. New York, NY: Harper and Row.

Mishan, J. (1993). *The Cost of Economic Growth*. London: Praeger.

Orwell, G. (1949). *Nineteen Eighty-Four*. London: Secker & Warburg.

Ostrom, E. (1991). *Governing the Commons: The Evolutions of Institutions for Collective Action*. Cambridge, MA: Cambridge University Press.

Polanyi, K. (2001). *The Great Transformation: The Economic and Political Origins of our Time*. Boston, MA: Beacon Press.

Pope-Francis. (2015). *Laudato Si – On Care for Our Common Home*. Vatican City: Editrice Vatican Libreria.

Popper, K. (2011). *The Open Society and Its Enemies*. London: Routledge.

Sahlins, M. (2008). *The Western Illusion of Human Nature*. Chicago, IL: Prickly Paradigm Press.

Schumacher, E. (1973). *All the Small is Beautiful*. New York: Harper & Collins.

Smith, A. (2011). *Theory of Moral Sentiments*. London: Gutenberg Publishers.

Zimbardo, P. (2008). *The Lucifer Effect*. New York: Random House.

Introduction

Nonviolent political economy: a research and teaching agenda

Freddy Cante and Lucas Ferreira Lima

Introduction

The history of modern economics is a history of hackneyed formulas (investment, productivity, profitability, opulence, growth, etc.), of a persistent recourse to purely technological solutions and the creation of markets for everything that exists, and an unhealthy faith in chimeras like the invisible hand. It is disturbingly similar to the tragicomedy of Beckett (1982), in which some unfortunate beings, trapped in a futile routine of extreme absurdity and misery, wait for their savior Godot – who is a savior who never arrives.

Our objective, with this introductory article, and with the book on non-violent political economy, is to suggest a horizon of research, teaching and even action. This will revive some forgotten perspectives and also offer some new ones, in order to propose another kind of economy. The idea is to escape from the absurdity and violence in which traditional economic thought has plunged the world, and to do so before it is too late.

The violence of conventional economic thinking

Nearly a century ago, in Oklahoma in the midst of the economic crisis of the 1930s, the farmers lost their land because they were indebted to the banks, and due to an ecological disaster known as the dust bowl, and they were forced to move to California (an expected Earthly paradise that transpired to be a hell of brutal competition). In a fragment of the extraordinary reflective narrative of Steinbeck the violence and absurdity of the modern economy is described thus:

> And the owner men explained the workings and the thinkings of the monster that was stronger than they were. A man can hold land if he can just eat and pay taxes; he can do that. Yes, he can do that until his crops fail one day and he has to borrow money from the bank. But – you see, a bank or a company can't do that, because those creatures don't breathe air, don't eat side-meat. They breathe profits; they eat the interest on

money. If they don't get it, they die the way you die without air, without side-meat. It is a sad thing, but it is so.

(Steinbeck 2002, p. 31)

Recent figures from Credit Suisse indicate that we can update Steinbeck's reflection by drawing a portrait of the current pyramid of global inequality. At the apex of this great pyramid is located 0.7% of the global population (violent opulent monsters who breathe profit), each of whom possesses over US $ 1,000,000, and who own 45.6% of the world's wealth. Below them lie their closest residents of the neighborhood of privilege, their closest allies and accomplices (monstrosities that also consume profit and interests): they comprise 7.5% of the world population, have fortunes between US $ 100,000 and a million dollars, and possess 40.6 % of the world's wealth. In the middle zone appear the so-called middle classes (who would be better called "well-off" proletarians). Their riches that are between US $ 10,000 and US $ 100,000, reach 18.5% of the population and have a meager 11.5% of the wealth. Then, in the wide lower area of the pyramid are the poorest: those who have insufficient funds to survive decently. Their meagre wealth ranges from a few cents, up to US $ 10,000; although these are 73.2% of the world's population they only possess 2.4% of the wealth (Credit-Suisse 2016).

This portrait could be made even more grotesque due to the colossal economic power of the truly rich that is evidenced in a recent report thus:

The gap between the really rich and the merely rich continues to widen, as fortunes soar to new heights. A record 2,208 billionaires made Forbes' 32 annual ranking of the world's billionaires. Altogether they are worth a record $9.1 trillion, up 18% from a year ago. The 20 richest people on the planet are worth a staggering $1.2 trillion, a sum roughly equivalent to the annual economic output of Mexico. In aggregate, they may represent less than 1% of total billionaires but their riches amount to 13% of the total fortune of all billionaires worldwide.

(Forbes 2018)

They have made these fortunes thanks to inheritances, monopolies and nepotism; they manage empires of marketing, finance and information technology, and they marshal masses of consumers and users through algorithms and advertising. They are the owners of the big commercial empires, such as Microsoft, Facebook, Amazon, Google, Berkshire Hathaway, Zara, Wal-Mart, etc.

From different shores, two scholars give clues that help us to understand this portrait of violence and inequality. Baker (2008) even contends that those who control information, money and advertising have a power that surpasses that of the Leviathans of the last century (the totalitarianisms of Stalin, Hitler, Mussolini, and Mao, and the authoritarianism as those of Franco and Pinochet), and makes them more monstrous Behemoth. Macpherson (2010), meanwhile, shows that market competition is a real war in which the strongest imposes their law, demonstrating that greedy individual cravings for possessions are the main obstacles to any movement towards a democracy.

The so-called middle classes, who are part of the consumerist society, seem to find the meaning of life in extravagant consumer experiences (Patel 2012), and they are generally obese and over-feed. They are consumers of meat-intensive diets (in turn intensive in grain crops and in water expenditure), and are slaves of the financial system, because they borrow to dress fashion, travel, have cars, and all kinds of electronic devices for home life and active partici-pation in social networks. In the underworld the poorest and starving, undernourished and frustrated, barely survive. In extreme cases of misery, they are the most likely to suffer a slow and painful death by not having access to food: by 2016, about 108 million human beings were experiencing food crisis, and were even on the verge of famine (FSIN 2017).

The current situation, with its inequalities and injustices, its manipulation and control of thought, and its enormous ecological calamities is more tremendous than that narrated by Steinbeck, and has clear symptoms of market totali-tarianism. It resembles the one illustrated in the novel *Mengele Zoo* (Nygardshaug 2014), and the totalitarian social engineering experiments of Huxley (1932) and Orwell (1949).

Various distributive schemes have been proposed in this context: liberal and social democratic, the big socialist projects based on a dash for growth, and by a world that remains determined to follow the path of economic development and expansion of the market society. These have all involved global violence, and sometimes apocalyptic violence.

Naomi Klein (2014) has enumerated the results of the global warming that we are already suffering: extreme climatic variations, accelerated disappearance of animal and plant species, expansion of deserts across extensive planetary geographies and floods in other large portions of the planet: she sees these as the collective result of the extraction and combustion of fossil fuels since the industrial revolution.

Then there are the threats of nuclear weapons. Schelling, an ideologue of the cold war, and Aumann, an architect of preventive war, have said that the last decades have been miraculously lived, because, since Hiroshima and Nagasaki, there has existed a kind of taboo against the use of such weapons. Nevertheless, the empirical evidence shown by shows the gigantic growth of destructive power that increases the possibility of destruction: there are currently about 27,000 nuclear weapons in the world, and 50 ordinary bombs are enough to end the life of 200 million human beings (New-internationalist 2008).

There are two facets of conventional economics, namely: classical political economy (Smith, Ricardo, Malthus, Marx and J.S. Mill) which offers broad approaches to social conflict (class struggle, exploitation, freedom, alienated work, commodity fetishism, etc.), but which still exhibits ignorance or sim-plistic view of nature in its models; then there is neoclassical theory, with views about market and collective choice without politics (overlooking social conflict and power), and with the suppression of nature (via its production function which recognizes only two productive factors, work and capital) or, at best, its trivialization of it (via a production function that links labor, capital and land, but which retains the unlikely assumption that nature can be replaced by capital and labor),and to this is added the pedantic and prolonged indifference to criticism and alternative approaches (Daly 1999). Other simplistic approaches include cost-benefit analysis, and compensation prices to supposedly repair damages to nature which are euphemistically denominated as externalities (these views are typical of environmental economics).

Contemporary market-functional economic models are not only dominant but also tend to promote markedly destructive patterns of behavior such as productivism, consumerism, accumulation and speculation. In the last mid-century capitalism has become more violent, due to the neoliberal offensive. In the field of practice, F. Hayek, M. Friedman (and his entire Chicago boys' club, and related economists such as J. Sachs) both helped to devise fierce neoliberal policies (condensed into the so-called Washington Consensus), at the behest of fearsome dictatorships such as that of Pinochet in Chile, and of authoritarian technocratic interventions in Poland, South Africa, Argentina, the same United States, Iraq, etc., as Klein has shown (2008). We need to remember Hayek's admission about the ultimate choice implied in his thought:

> Liberalism and democracy, although compatible, are not the same. The first is concerned with the extent of governmental power, the second with who holds this power.
>
> (Hayek 1966, p. 111)

This implies (to neoliberal economists, at least) that under a dictatorship there can be economic freedom and respect for private property, which is what is important for the good health of markets.

Neoliberal economists like Hayek have tried to establish two influential ideas. First, everything has a price, for everything there is a market. This has allowed neoliberals like G. Becker, M. Friedman, J. Buchanan, R. Coase (all members of the Mont Pelerin group founded by F. Hayek, and winners of the Nobel Prize in Economics), to make market models with which to theorize about family, politics, consensus, the rights to generate externalities and the sale of licenses to emit greenhouse gases, etc. Second, the market allows voluntary exchanges, and is an empire of freedom, redistributive policies and social justice initiatives are dangerous and counterproductive (Hayek 1988, Nozick 1974).

Conventional economic thought is excessively violent because it is extremely restricted (that is, it has a very simplified and narrow view of the human being and ignores nature), it is also anthropomorphic and anthropocentric. Conventional political economy is largely a functional knowledge that primarily serves economically and politically dominant classes (capitalists, rentiers, military, administrators, etc.), and consequently promotes highly destructive human actions that generate social and environmental damage. They also favor some centers of military, political and economic power (United States, Europe,

China, etc.). Here it is pertinent to remember, as (Hagemann, Kufenko and Raskov 2016), that many great economists (especially scholars of game theory, such as Oskar Morgenstern, John von Neumann, Michael Intriligator, John Nash, Thomas Schelling, J.K. Arrow, H. Simon and Steven Brams) have often worked in the service of military powers like the United States. Nevertheless, there are some authors who have made significant contributions to the study of economic aggregates, collective action, social choice and welfare, and governance of the common pool resources, such as Keynes (1990), Arrow (1963), Schelling (2006), Ostrom (1991), Sen (2009, 2017), but their models are rooted in neoclassical theory.

The idea of nonviolent economy

A nonviolent economy would be equivalent to a state of peacefulness, with minimal violence between human beings, and with a minimal destruction of nature. It would have the following fundamental features: the abolition of profit, achieved through a massive campaign of civil disobedience for non-payment of debts and taxes and implementation of solidarity economics; total disarmament (including the abandonment of weapons of mass destruction, as well as personal arms); the limitation of consumption to serve dignified and frugal subsistence, without the conspicuous consumption of positional goods and services, luxuries and excesses; a genuine leisure or free time, achieved through the eradication of drudgery; an expansion of collective property (common property) and a concomitant reduction of private property (thanks to the abolition of inheritance, and the significant reduction of positional assets); simple, small-scale and artisanal production (intensive in the human effort and expenditure of endosomatic energies it would require), and an increasing use of clean energies (mainly solar and wind); a gradual, but significant, reduction in the human population; an abolition or, at least, a neutralization of the political class (rulers, military, clergy, intellectuals, administrators, etc.), which would be compatible with political processes closer to direct and radical democracy, and with anarchy.

This state of peacefulness would not be equivalent to the famous stationary state dreamed of by economists such as Mill, with its population and consumption stabilized after a period of remarkable economic growth (Mill 1885, pp. 595–597). Even this would demand a radical change in values and ideologies in the direction that J. S. Mill aptly suggested: instead of the extreme and violent competition (of crushing, damaging and exterminating others, and of destroying nature), a nonviolent economy implies an intensive coexistence in cooperation and fraternity, and this implies, in turn, a suppression of the most predatory economic activities (such as extraction and combustion of fossil fuels, a large part of mining, and livestock and agro-industry), and an eradication of parasitic activities based on the exploitation of others.

Might it be possible to derive fundamental elements of an economic theory of nonviolence or a nonviolent political economy (NPE) from the partial contributions or the total work of some of the most heterodox, radical and creative economists (and other social thinkers)? Some ideas about nonviolent economies from authors partially rooted in conventional economic theory do exist, but one of the great contributions of those who propose an NPE would be to shed conceptual light on the generation of social relations of appropriation, productive transformation, distribution, exchange, consumption, enjoyment of life or well-being, and to processes individual and collective choice that meet at least three requirements, namely: inclusion, non-violence and free will.

Inclusion implies the suppression of, or significant reduction of, the most petty entry barriers that exclusive groups such as families, communities, unions, parties and nations may have, although this requires continuing research on the impurities of public goods and (as a resource to reduce congestion) the invention of clubs. Some successes have been made in this direction, as Buchanan (1965) and Tiebout (1956) have shown. Inclusion also requires going beyond humanistic cosmopolitanism, promoting a well-being that encompasses all living beings and nature in the perspective of Francis of Assisi (Pope Francis 2015). Obviously, inclusion makes sense in long-term horizons, including not only present but also future generations. The father of the bioeconomics concept, Georgescu-Roegen, emphasized "minimizing the rate of remorse", because an expensive taste, or an excess of consumption, implies an intertemporal rate of preference for the present (and exclusion of the future generations). Because of our greed we, directly and indirectly, kill other living beings (humans, animals and plants) in both the present and the future.

Economic non-violence means conceiving necessary transformations that can generate a drastic reduction of direct and structural violence in the sphere of social relations, and subsistence economic processes with minimal levels of destruction and depredation. This includes promotion of organic agriculture and small-scale economies, in the perspective of authors such as Schumacher (1973). The teachings of nonviolence present in Ghandian thought, in Buddhism, in Christianity, in environmentalism, in the ancestral wisdom of indigenous peoples, and in many other perspectives of nonviolence, can be crucial sources for this research.

A libertarian choice, full of free will, is a type of action open to originality, surprise and that cannot be foreseen or controlled by any center of power. There is a harmful pretension to knowledge that consists of totalitarian engineering projects that seek to domesticate living beings (including humans) and the rest of nature, which imply high levels of control, which is possible in deterministic and rational environments (such as the certainty and the risk). Uncertainty, understood as a radical ignorance of the future (which does not allow the calculation of probabilities, not being able to list future events, much less to weigh their possible occurrence), is a favorable environment for free will.

Extended approaches to the conflict

At the end of the 1980s, the influential social scientist Ralf Dahrendorf (2007) argued that modern social conflict has consisted of a tension between two revolutions. The first of these is the industrial revolution (originating in

England) that, from innovation and technical change, has allowed progress in the productive forces, and which has driven an improvement in living conditions (thanks to increased personal and collective income), and which has resulted in a colossal growth of the population and the expansive universe of goods and services. Dahrendorf's second revolution second was the French Revolution (the mother of socialism and social democracy), which consisted of a social struggle to promote a just distribution of income and wealth, and some democratization of property. Dahrendorf did not hesitate to criticize Latin American socialist experiments such as Cuba and Nicaragua, for their emphasis on justice and blatant neglect of economic growth. He showed that the staunch liberals find in economic growth the healing of all evils, while the socialists of diverse tendencies must promote redistributive policies without ceasing to grow their economies.

Walter Benjamin (2009), in a historical reflection on wars and peace processes showed that, in the best of cases, the warlike conflict between men (social conflicts) could be ended, but that the economic progress consists in a perpetual war of the human being against nature. Even socialists sinned, therefore, by assuming that natural resources are available infinitely and freely. Seven decades after the Second World War we can see the enormous ecological damage caused by the wave of material progress, and emerging conflicts over water can already be noticed, as well as forced displacement due to the climate change generated by growth. Benjamin, in addition, was correct to argue that a fully restorative justice is not feasible (it is impossible to resuscitate corpses), and that (looking towards the future), the current generations are victimizers of their offspring and violent destructors of nature (whether due to brutal greed to an exaggerated preference for the present).

For the last 250 years, conventional economic theory (as enshrined in the classics of political economy and neoclassical economics), has been limited to offering dissimilar solutions for what Dahrendorf called modern social conflict. The only honorable exceptions are, to a certain extent, the physiocrats, notably Georgescu-Roegen and other scholars of the bioeconomy and ecological economics (Georgescu-Roegen 1971, Daly, 1974, Daly and Farley 2011: Martinez-Alier and Schlupman 1987, Mayumi 2001). Then there are the authors who, very timidly, discuss the costs and limits of growth, and population expansion as (Carson 1962: Ehrlich 1968; Hardin 1968; Mishan 1993), and the paradigmatic work of the Club of Rome's: *Limits to Growth* (Meadows, Meadows, Randers and Behrens, 1972).

As brilliantly exposed by Polanyi (2001) classics like those of Smith (1776) and Ricardo (1817) and later, the neoclassical economists, have worked to legitimize the violence of capitalism (abolition of communal properties, forced displacement of peasants to the cities), and they have defended a world of mercantile competition without remnants of kindness (paternalism towards the poor), and without major restrictions against speculation and the strategic manipulation of prices (downward flexible salaries for employees, unlimited profits for owners), a rude competition without morality or social preferences.

The rebel Marx (2010), and his twentieth century followers such as Kalecki (1971), Sraffa (1960) and Parijs (1997) have examined the following shared themes: the exploitation of man by man and the radical solutions to it, such as socialism and communism; the class struggle that is hidden in the Keynesian macro-economy; a neo-Ricardian and Marxist questioning of the neoclassical function of production, showing that capital originates in preterit work; and a basic income proposal (universal, dignified and unconditional salary) that, based on the conciliatory spirit of Keynes (1990) and Rawls (1971), offers a capitalist path towards socialism (a kind version of the Pareto optimum). Symptomatically, the guaranteed basic income (or negative tax) has also been conceived of using neoliberal arguments (Friedman and Friedman, 1980), with the argument that it allows for a reduction of the state bureaucracy, and encourages the freedom to choose (by making the poor consumers).

In more acute contributions it is shown that growth can fail to produce any solution for certain extreme conflicts, and may even promote social conflict. Georgescu-Roegen (1971), in the brief chapter on social conflict of his great work about entropy and economics, argues that the greatest cultural evolution (and the greatest technical progress) of human societies generate more conflict because human beings, (unlike the rest of animals that evolve biologically and are dependent on their own endosomatic instruments), possess exosomatic instruments (the so-called means of production, or capital goods) that greatly facilitate inequality and the asymmetry of power; and perhaps in the most primitive economies and rudimentary stages, a reduction of conflict and social inequality would be possible. In an essay on conflicts as pillars of modern democracies, Hirschman (1998) shows that there are two types of conflicts, those that are divisible or negotiable (related to the distributive differences that tormented Marx) and are engines of inclusion and the expansion of entitlements and income, and the 'all-or-nothing disputes' that are indivisible or non-negotiable and which are related to deep divergences about values and cultural codes (differences rooted in dissimilar visions of the world, different languages and religions). The work of Mann (2005) can be understood as an explanation of the indivisible conflicts inherent in the most modern democracies and the most opulent countries.

The bioeconomics, its derivatives, and some unrealizable agendas

The economist Boulding (1966) argued that only the deranged, and the economists, could suppose a world with unlimited growth, and that (five centuries after Columbus!) they had not discovered the roundness and finitude of the planet. Today, beyond what Boulding proposed, we could find three stages in the evolution of economic thought: the cowboy economy (which assumes a world without limits); illusions of steady states (belief in the possibility of a sustainable economy in a world of fixed borders); the stage of the postponable apocalypse, in a world with increasingly restrictive and contracting limits, a planet Earth subject to an ineluctable entropic process, where it might be possible to postpone that inevitable degradation through attempts to 'degrow' the economy.

For economists who profess belief in unlimited economic growth, planet Earth is an inexhaustible source of resources, a world of expansive boundaries. Economic resources are infinitely available, and perpetual growth is possible provided the border for the extraction and use of natural resources is continually expanded; the world obeys only the first law of thermodynamics, and functions like a motor with perpetual motion. This mechanist approach is found in conventional economic theories: classical political economy (Smith, Ricardo, Marx) offers diverse and dissimilar solutions to the modern social conflict between different social classes (capitalists, rentiers and wage earners) and they seek to expand and perpetuate growth; Keynes, with his formulas of public and private expenditures (and Hitler with monstrous expenditures in war), "successfully" solved the great economic crisis of 1929; liberal diehards like Hayek and Friedman have deified growth and the consumerist society; social choice theorists such as Arrow, Sen and Rawls, have proposed solutions to social conflict and models of social justice, including metrics of human development, without examining the problems of growth.

For economists who propose steady state models of sustainable development, planet Earth is finite and has limited and fixed borders: thus, the economic process resembles a cycle of exchange and reproduction similar to the models of conventional economics. In this perspective, natural resources are finite as is the planet's capacity to absorb waste. Societies are also limited systems, there are social limits to growth as masterfully explained by Hirsch (1977). Those who believe in the steady state assume that there can be a balanced growth, and that it is possible to maintain a constant rhythm in the flows of inputs and outputs of the economy. There are several versions of the steady state: a world of contemplative people with peaceful tastes and values (the opposite of satisfied pigs of vulgar utilitarianism), who are supposedly dedicated to growing intellectually (as in the utopian vision of J. S. Mill); an economy where the impetuous exponential rhythms with which population and capital grow are drastically diminished, and it is possible for offspring and means of labor to grow stabilized (within given limits), as in the formulations of J. M. Keynes allusive to the so-called euthanasia of the rentier, and in the proposals of the prophets of overpopulation (such as R. Malthus, and G. Hardin), and in the prospective models of the quartet who wrote the *Limits of Growth* (Meadow, Meadows, Randers and Behrens 1972); a happy world with effective slogans (sustainable development, green growth, etc.) where it is possible to grow on the condition of stabilizing the population, promoting the use of clean energies (hydroelectric, wind and solar), and techniques that capture carbon and reduce greenhouse gas emissions.

This approach of steady states and "avoidable apocalypses" fits very strongly with the work of authors who have worked on the problem of collective action known as the tragedy of the commons. Both the pessimistic versions (tragedy) of this paradigm (Hardin 1968: Schelling 2006), and the most optimistic (those who, like Ostrom (1991), argue that successful governance of common pool resources is possible) show, basically, the following: if, in a finite environment (a natural niche such as a forest or a lake, or the entire planet) all, or a majority, or at least a significant number of (greedy) individuals intensively do an activity over a period of time, then they can exhaust natural resources by subtraction, deterioration and pollution. Actions such as sexual reproduction, migration to cities, the colonization of virgin lands and agricultural expansion, as well as livestock herding and fishing, can end in tragedies, when selfishness and myopia predominate among collectivities. With a monumental fieldwork, Ostrom and her followers have shown, at least in local areas, that communities (of peasants and indigenous people) have managed to agree on rules for the preservation of common resources, and they have had success in terms of environmental preservation.

For the realistic apocalyptists, the Earth is a semi-closed system, an unstable environment subject to entropy: that is to say, we live in an entropic world, governed by the second law of thermodynamics, where matter and energy (including the resources on which we rely) pass from states of low entropy (order and availability) to states of high entropy (disorder, dispersion and non-availability), in an ineluctable tendency. One of the important concepts behind bioeconomics is "entropy". According to Burkett, entropy is "the measure of the total disorder, randomness, or chaos in the system: increased entropy implies greater disorder" (2006, p. 142). The second law of thermodynamics says that the entropy of an isolated system can only increase, never reduce, that is, move from a more ordered state to a less ordered (or more disordered) state.

The planet Earth depends on an exogenous energy source (a gigantic flow of clean energy from the sun) and endogenous and very limited stocks of harmful fossil fuels, and a limited and perishable layer of plant bark and water that are a source of renewable resources. Photosynthesis, the factory of renewable resources of life, has guaranteed the subsistence of all creatures, and of humanity up to now. Today, life's continuation into the future is in question, due to the extraction and combustion of fossil fuels that began with the ceaseless development of the industrial revolution. We cannot reverse the entropy but we could, at least, postpone it. A steady state, at present, is equivalent to the comfortable permanence of the status quo (maintaining the current level of growth and promoting sustainable development), and the advisable thing is an economic reduction, a dismantling of the economic apparatus with negative rates of growth, and with the use of more traditional techniques (and, therefore, more intensive in human effort and endo-somatic energy expenditure). In this radical approach, the bioeconomy and its derivatives are located as ecological economy and political ecology, as sharply affirmed by Georgescu-Roegen:

> This vision of a blissful world in which both population and capital stock remain constant, once expounded with his usual skill by John Stuart Mill ... was until recently in oblivion. Because of the spectacular revival of this myth of ecological salvation, it is well to point out its various logical and factual snags. The crucial error consists in not seeing that not only

growth, but also a zero-growths state, nay, even a declining state which does not converge toward annihilation, cannot exist forever in a finite environment.

(Georgescu-Roegen 1975, p. 367)

Heat is an essential part of the theory of thermodynamics, and is central to the concept of entropy, because heat can only dissipate. If an object or area is isolated, the heat it contains will never go from a cold to a hot state. The most meaningful example is perhaps the one of an ice cube in a glass, where the ice represents a state of water with a low entropy, and when energy (heat) is applied to the water, it goes into a state with more entropy, more disorder than the ice cube. The heat that was used to change the state of water did not pass to another object, but it was dissipated. Consequently, the return to a low-entropy state, in this case, the change from liquid to solid, is only possible with the application of more energy. The impossibility of accumulating energy within a system that would make it possible to return to the previous state of entropy is one of the strongest arguments for the irreversibility of the natural state of the resources used on a large scale in the capitalist productive system.

The firsts to observe the entropy from an economic point of view were Nicholas Georgescu-Roegen (the main pioneer of bioeconomics) and this concept is explained by (Daly and Farley 2011, pp. 61–76). Georgescou-Roegen and Daly argued that if the economic process does not produce or consume matter-energy, but only absorbs and discards, then the economic process is a process of transforming low-entropy matter-energy into a state of high entropy (Georgescu-Roegen, 1971: Daly 1974).

The combined productive use of human labor and low entropy matter and energy aims at producing goods and services useful to society, but generates high costs through a single-direction entropy conversion. It converts low-entropy matter and energy to high-entropy matter and energy, that is, it transforms matter and energy from a more ordered to a less ordered state (Burkett, 2006). Man cannot infinitely transform matter and energy from a low-entropy matter and energy into high-entropy matter and energy without bringing about ecosystem catastrophes (Daly and Farley, 2011). The central point of these findings is that infinite growth on a finite planet is impossible.

In the perspective of Bonaiuti (2011) there are the following natural limitations to economic growth:

1 The economic process has an entropic nature: there is an irreversible degradation of matter and energy.
2 There are positive and negative feedback relationships: positive ones due to self-increase and exponential returns (for example, the growth of the human population and the returns on compound interest); the negatives are characterized by self-correction (the preservation of plant and animal species is an example). Economic growth, through what conventional economists, from Adam Smith, would call a virtuous feedback between

supply (sharpening of the division of labor and technical innovation) and demand (market expansion and insatiable and expansive desires of consumers), exerts pressure on natural systems and accelerates the degradation of nature.

3   The right size is relevant in nature: the large or small scale of a process is relevant, as is the size of an organism or an organization. A variation in size requires a transformation in the structure of the organism or organization. For neoclassical economists, exponents of methodological individualism, the variation in the size of groups, companies and organizations is insignificant and does not alter the structure in decision-making or in collective action.

4   Natural systems are diverse and allow the development of multiple species: the wise virtue of nature is that the biological system does not maximize variables and, therefore, avoids the excesses and discomforts of unbridled growth.

5   Biological systems have multiple purposes, unlike systems such as the modern economy (centered on utility).

6   Biological systems present a combination of competitive and cooperative behaviors. A competitive evolution as explained by Charles Darwin occurs in natural (and social) environments of relative abundance in rich niches such as the Galapagos Island, and a tough economic competition as happens in areas such as cosmopolitan London and was theorized by Adam Smith. The context is relevant: there are expansive and colonizing systems, where competition and the success of the strongest prevail; and there are other non-expansive systems where the important thing is cooperation and some equilibrium. The conventional economy of growth, development and imperialism is clearly colonizing.

7   Direct learning, life or death: natural organisms face directly and by themselves the uncertainty and the processes of trial and error inherent in learning, for example, if a tiny amoeba misses then it dies.(Bonaiuti 2011, pp. 171–195)

Boniauti's seven insights can also be considered the first step towards a program of degrowth. In clear opposition to the concept of economic growth, Serge Latouche presents the idea of degrowth. In his words:

> The watchword of degrowth especially has an aim to strongly signal the abandonment of the target of growth for the sake of growth, a foolish objective whose engine is precisely the unrestrained search for profit by the holders of capital, and whose consequences are disastrous for the environment. Rigorously, it would be best to speak about 'agrowth', as one speaks about atheism. It actually means quite precisely, the abandonment of a religion: the religion of the economy, growth, progress and development.
>
> (Latouche 2006, pp. 13–14)

For the Research and Degrowth Association this concept can be understood as:

> a downscaling of production and consumption that increases human well-being and enhances ecological conditions and equity on the planet. It calls for a future where societies live within their ecological means, with open, localized economies and resources more equally distributed through new forms of democratic institutions. Such societies will no longer have to 'grow or die.' Material accumulation will no longer hold a prime position in the population's cultural imaginary. The primacy of efficiency will be substituted by a focus on sufficiency, and innovation will no longer focus on technology for technology's sake but will concentrate on new social and technical arrangements that will enable us to live convivially and frugally. Degrowth does not only challenge the centrality of GDP as an overarching policy objective but proposes a framework for transformation to a lower and sustainable level of production and consumption, a shrinking of the economic system to leave more space for human cooperation and ecosystems.
>
> (Degrowth and Research, 2018)

Other authors have come similar approaches. In relation to capitalist expansion. David Harvey (2007) explains that conflicts generated by capital movement in its own exploitation dynamics on work and land is central to Marxist tradition. From that point of view, it is unlikely that capitalism will ever present the capacity to be a nonviolent system, at least where the exploitation of nature is concerned. The incompatibility between growth and preservation of nature is, in fact, accentuated in capitalism: "capitalism is environmentally unsustainable and the hope of making it sustainable is the most misleading illusion of contemporary political, social and economic thinking" (Marques 2016, p. 529)

How can such an illusion be dealt with? From Hirschman's classic text about exit, voice and loyalty, it is possible to affirm that the societies with greater economic surplus located in the centers of power (like the United States, Europe, and part of Asia), and the inhabitants of the cities, have large and substantial surpluses that keeps them in an illusion of normality (their alert mechanisms are dormant), and only the inhabitants of the countryside and of the marginal zones, and the animals of the jungles, can directly observe situations of scarcity and anomaly in the availability and quality of natural resources (Hirschman 1970, p. 6). This may allow us to perceive some relevant research agendas, and also some stormy hybridizations. Some of these are outlined below.

Daly, for example, in an attempt to reconcile economic and ecological growth, a "founding member of the journal Ecological Economics", the professor (H. Daly 1974) proposes a definition of sustainable development anchored the assumption that a steady state is feasible. He follows the static state approach of J. S. Mill, with its stable and static economy and population and with a constant stock of capital, which in turn allows a low rate of growth so as not to overwhelm the regeneration and assimilation capacities of the natural ecosystem. However, as Bonaiuti (2011) explained, although growth and development are different concepts, they are closely linked, because whatever the bias towards which development is aimed (whether it is measured in indicators of opulence, estimated in indicators of human development and happiness, or valued in terms of some institutional progress and democratization, etc.), development always refers to a set of institutional structures and organizations that always, also, implies some growth.

Sustainable development, as it has been conceived and implemented, is reduced to a set of strictly technical solutions (reduction in the use of fossil fuels, adoption of clean and renewable energies, reduction of greenhouse gas emissions, etc.) that keeps the institutional structures intact (including transnational corporations and global markets), and does not transform the collective imagination (the consumer society and the insatiable desire for profit). This means that the various technical and "green" solutions of sustainable development will perpetuate the Jevons Paradox: any energy savings and reductions of pollution that those solutions generate would be canceled by the market all the same, because consumers will buy and use such innovations in even greater, and more damaging, amounts than before. Thus, the eco-efficient technical advances will bring with them more entropy and pollution (Boniauti 2011, pp. 44–48).

It is impossible to reconcile bioeconomy with capitalism, and there is an unrealizable marriage between capitalist development and ecological economy. According to (Foster 2002), the environmental degradation resulting from capitalist dynamics for production is as basic as its profit-seeking nature. The diverse traditions in Political Economy do not converge, at least not where the effects of capitalism on the environment are concerned. Thus, there has been, so far, no such a thing as Political Economy of the environment, which opens up challenging interdisciplinary possibilities. According to Netto and Brazz (2006), Political Economy addresses issues directly related to the material interests of determined economic and social classes or groups. In other words, the study of Political Economy deals with the materiality necessary for social interaction, that is, the production, realization and accumulation of material wealth. From this point of view, the various theories on economics all deal, directly or indirectly, with the environment and with capitalist production, since contemporary society will always demand natural resources to maintain and reproduce humanity's household.

The Marxian and Marxist traditions have, potentially, some interesting synergy with Ecological Economics. There have already been some attempts to reconcile Marx and Engels with Ecological Economics, and the most fruitful of these arose at the end of the twentieth century and in the early twenty-first, when environmental studies started to point out that the degradation of nature was a consequence of human capitalist actions – thus bringing the Marxist tradition to the environmental debate. Burkett's *Marxism and Ecological Economics: Toward a Red and Green Political Economy* from 2006 and the O'Connor studies from the 1990s are two major contributions to this convergence between capitalist critics and those dealing with Ecological Economic problems. These in turn build on critiques about capitalist dynamics from the Marxian perspective and environmental protection that date back to the 19th century with and Marx and Engels' debate with Podolinsky (Martinez-Alier and Schlupman 1987), in which the latter tried to connect the socialist theory to the laws of thermodynamics elements and nature's exploitation by man. Thus, Burkett's work fulfills the opportunity to lead a rapprochement of two streams that converge in criticizing capitalism and its harmful dynamics that impact on labor, class, and nature.

Marx targets the exploitation in the capitalistic relationship between value and labor, represented by his labor theory of value, derived from Smith and Ricardo's classical theory. Besides, even for Marx in nineteenth century, it was already clear the conflicts coming up from the capital, labor and land combination in terms of human exploitation and nature resources conditions towards value generation on capitalism, as the following passage shows:

> Moreover, all progress in capitalistic agriculture is a progress in the art, not only of robbing the laborer, but of robbing the soil; all progress in increasing the fertility of the soil for a given time, is a progress towards ruining the lasting sources of that fertility. The more a country starts its development on the foundation of modern industry, like the United States, for example, the more rapid is this process of destruction. Capitalist production, therefore, develops technology, and the combining together of various processes into a social whole, only by sapping the original sources of all wealth — the soil and the laborer.
>
> (Marx 1970, p. 555)

Marx's words "the original sources of all wealth" means something much more aligned to the problems of twenty-first century than those of the nineteenth century. In this sense, although his emphasis on labor seems to be stronger, Marx tries to balance the importance of labor and soil for capitalism.

As for the perspective of environmentalist Keynesianism, there is a recent and original work about degrowth produced by Jackson (2017) that collects important contributions from Keynes and Amartya Sen, and which proposes a "Green New Deal" that includes the generation of employment in the protection of nature and in the care of others, instead of occupying people in producing more prejudicial material prosperity. In the path suggested by Sen, he suggests working for a flourishing of human capabilities within the ecological limits of a finite planet.

Finally, there is still not a conventional political economy directly handling contemporary environmental problems. Not only does no Green Political Economy exist (although there is a political ecology), there is not a single theory where environmental problems are internalized within economic theory. From the point of view of production, the environment as well as labor, is a tool to exploit and generate more value, so an NPE dedicated to environment protection should reinvent the value generation in contemporary human society – something which would be revolutionary. Therefore,

Ecological Economics has an important role to play in reconsidering and adapting Political Economy to twenty-first-century challenges, especially those regarding entropy, degrowth and bioeconomics.

Moral and ethical economy of civil disobedience

In his classic article on moral economy, the great British historian E. P. Thompson, showed that "the food riot in eighteenth-century England was a highly-complex form of direct popular action," which implied that the rebel masses were not mere economic subjects (homo oeconomicus) moved by incentives of their stomachs, but were people with values and moral principles clearly opposed to the logic of the market (Thompson 1971, 79).

Thompson was emphatic that:

> [T]hese grievances operated within a popular consensus as to what were legitimate and what were illegitimate practices in marketing, milling, baking, etc. This in its turn was grounded upon a traditional view of social norms and standards, of the proper economic functions of several parties within the community, which, taken together, can be said to constitute the moral economy of the poor. An outrage to these moral assumptions, remove as much as current deprivation, was the usual occasion for direct action.
>
> (Thompson 1971, p. 71)

In recent approaches to moral economy, work emerges that explains the various forms of insubordination (conscientious objection, civil disobedience, and non-economic cooperation) engaged in by people who refuse to participate or collaborate with unjust and violent transactions. The works of Scott (2009; 2012), in particular, present both theories and empirical cases of collectivities that evade the payment of taxes and the participation in commercial transactions via the radical method of fleeing towards some niche of independence and geographical isolation. In a more conventional perspective, there is some work in experimental games theory (Camerer 2003) that shows how certain individuals (from different geographic and cultural backgrounds), exhibit a diversity of social preferences, may reject unfair transactions, and can have a process of social learning in the area of justice. In the perspective of political philosophy there is a strong research about the moral limits to the market, in the work made by (Sandel 2012).

Investigations of the moral economy of subsistence are interesting in that they are contrary to those privileged and parasitic social sectors (which have large surpluses and have means of work), which through finance play with information, resources and the lives of other people and a morality based on putting 'skin in the game' (Scott 1976; Taleb 2014)

The political economy of love (and other non-egoistic motivations)

Boulding has suggested that there are three types of power: threatening power (based on issuing credible threats, making strategic use of potential violence); economic power (based on the ability to buy wills through incentives, in the strategic management of bribes), and integrative power (that through donations and ideals of vital social and political projects) allows communities to be built (Boulding 1989). Using Boulding's typology, we can affirm that the conventional economy is based on systems of incentives and repression that result from threatening power and commercial power. An economy of nonviolence would be much more intensive in powers of integration, in loving voluntary actions of people, and in pedagogy to foster cooperation.

In an earlier work (Boulding, *The Economy of Love and Fear* 1973), Boulding demonstrated that the dominant economic systems and theories are based on two types of transactions: mandatory unidirectional transactions, such as taxes (which, just as in an extortion or robbery, is paid out of fear), and bidirectional transactions (of exchange, of giving and receiving) that, in the market society, are biased by obtaining more than what is received (in competitive markets individuals are interested, in search of profit) and correspond to malevolent preferences. Love (understood as a donation, gift, grant), is a one-way transaction (of giving without receiving, or waiting for the recipient to be generous in a future with others), and a free and voluntary act, who loves doing it voluntarily.

> Love for Christians is embodied in the sermon on the mountain of Jesus, like this: You have heard that it was said, 'An eye for an eye and a tooth for a tooth.' But I tell you not to oppose an evil person. If someone slaps you on your right cheek, turn your other cheek to him as well. If someone wants to sue you in order to take your shirt, let him have your coat too. If someone forces you to go one mile, go two miles with him. Give to everyone who asks you for something. Don't turn anyone away who wants to borrow something from you.... You have heard that it was said, 'Love your neighbor, and hate your enemy.' But I tell you this: Love your enemies, and pray for those who persecute you. In this way you show that you are children of your Father in heaven. He makes his sun rise on people whether they are good or evil. He lets rain fall on them whether they are just or unjust. If you love those who love you, do you deserve a reward? Even the tax collectors do that! Are you doing anything remarkable if you welcome only your friends? Everyone does that! That is why you must be perfect as your Father in heaven is perfect.
>
> (Holy Bible, 1995)

In a more mundane, and less ideal, context reciprocity is still anchored in the logic of exchange and insurance, and there is a social or obligation to ensure reciprocity (Mauss, 1990: Gintis, Bowles, Ferh, and Boyd, 2004). However, the competition for favors, and for the opportunity to give more than one has received, as shown in Mauss's text, would be placed in the field of benevolent preferences. Magnanimity or altruism correspond more to unconditional love, and are fundamental to the cementing of cooperative processes that would be impossible without unconditional co-operators (Schelling, 2006). In relation to altruism there are findings in biology, specifically about cooperation in societies of humble and elemental amoeba (Strassmann, Zhu and Queller 2000).

Love is an act of volition aimed at caring for what is loved, and also an emotional force based on empathy, and was theorized by Adam Smith in his *Theory of Moral Sentiments* (2011). Empathy is a kind of moral feeling that allows us to put ourselves in the place of the other (to emotionally imagine what another being can experience), and which is an economic resource subject to scarcity: we feel greater empathy for the closest beings (and indifference for the most distant in geography and time). There is, thus, an economy of love. When learning to love there is a trajectory of increasing returns (similar to that of a knowledge economy), but if too much love is asked there is a kind of fatigue and you enter a path of diminishing returns (Hirschman, 2002). The empathy (or sympathy) theorized by Adam Smith in his theory of moral feelings is a fundamental basis for building love, which is an essential emotion to promote justice (Nussbaum 2015).

Nature and humanity, particularly when there is some common resource, or a community is threatened by a common enemy, has motivations such as mutual aid, cooperation, and a kind of spontaneous communism (Graeber, 2011), and, moreover, mutualism has allowed evolution (Kropotkin 2014).

Extended perspectives of choice

According to Sen (1977), in economic theory it has been assumed that the economic subject is little less than a rational rat, which responds to garrote and cheese incentives. Thanks to the contributions of authors such as (Frankfurt 1971; Hirschman 2002; Sen 2009), and literary inspirations such as (Dostoevsky 1984), it is possible propose some theoretical models that do not mutilate the human being in that fashion. An expanded perspective of choice is characterized by three basic insights:

i   the human being is not a wanton or senseless entity, or a passive subject that responds to propensities and allows itself to be influenced, like a pet, by selective incentives;

ii while rational subjects, with strict preferences, can hardly formulate first-order judgments (hierarchize baskets of goods), people have the capacity to formulate second-order judgments, to question their daily preferences (questioning the sense of their existence), and

iii to devise meta-preferences or alternative values (give a meaning to their life, through a long-term political and life project).

Conventional economics is anchored in tastes, whims, and propensities, while an approach to the economy of nonviolence emphasizes values and ideologies. Sedlacek (2013), in his pleasant and suggestive book, argues that the gross error of conventional economists has been their exclusive focus on utility, and that the most important decision is to rescue ethics, value judgments, and normative economics and refocus the meaning of economics around fundamental questions such as those relating to good and evil. Models based on the chimerical invisible hand of Hume, Smith and Mandeville see the human being as a vicious hedonist (and sometimes as a sadist or masochist) who maximizes pleasure and minimizes pain. More constructive perspectives can emerge when we see that people incur great risks and sacrifices to fulfil their duties and to do good works, as in the philosophical remarks of the Stoics, Kant, and Christianity. However, as Sen (2009) shows, there is no universal and definitive vision of the good and the just, and it is then pertinent to combine philosophical and normative approaches with the empirical evidence about the different scenarios and social states to see if they are good and just. In conventional theories (and in the field of practical life, shaped by policies and strategies emanating from such theories), the subjects do not choose, they simply have a script of action to respond to, with pre-ordered and normal reactions, in reaction to stimuli (incentives) to predictable situations (in a list of future problems). The weight of institutions, with some cultural and religious codes, and sets of inherited ancestral habits and customs, subjects the human being to a few rules that are difficult to break, and to the opinion of some ecclesiastical or cultural authority. Rational choice becomes a booklet of maximization and minimization, and of coherent codes of conduct, in which pre-ordered choices are framed in areas of control (situations of certainty and risk). Only when the choice is open, when it comes to creating something new and original in the face of a radically unknown future, when it is necessary to adapt to the unknown and deal with highly improbable events (black swans), then there is an uncertainty that favors a libertarian choice (Schalke 1979; Shackle 1991; Taleb 2008). Free will, understood as a genuine original and creative choice, one not determined or prefigured by the past, is not exclusive of human beings and has the most insignificant particular of life, and without it life and nature could not change the history (Conway and Kochen 2009).

Bibliography

Arrow, John Kenneth. 1963. *Social Choice and Individual Valules*. Connecticut: Yale University Press.

Baker, Stephen. 2008. *The Numerati*. Boston: Houghton Mifflin Company.

Beckett, Samuel. 1982. *Waiting for Godot: A Tragicomedy in Two Acts*. New York: Grove Press.

Benjamin, Walter. 2009. *On the Concept of History*. New York: Classic House Books.

Bonaiuti, Mauro. 2011. *From Bioeconomics to Degrowth: Georgescu-Roegen's "New Economics" in Eight Essays*. New York: Routledge.

Boulding, Kenneth. 1966. The Economics of the Coming Spaceship Earth. In *Environmental Quality in a Growing Economy*, H. Jarret, 3–14. Baltimore: Johns Hopkins University Press.

Boulding, Kenneth. 1973. *The Economy of Love and Fear*. New York: Wadsworth Publishing Company.

Boulding, Kenneth. 1989. *Three Faces of Power*. London: Sage.

Buchanan, James. 1965. An Economic Theory of Clubs. *Economica* 1–14.

Buchanan, James and Tullock, Gordon. 1972. *The Calculus of Consent: Logic Foundations of a Constitutional Democracy*. Ann Arbor: University of Michigan Press.

Burkett, Paul. 2006. *Marxism and Ecological Economics: Toward a Red and Green Political Economy*. Boston: Brill Leiden.

Camerer, Colin. 2003. *Behavioral Game Theory Experiments in Strategic Interaction*. New Jersey: Princeton University Press.

Cante, Fredy. 2015. *Handbook of Research on Transitional Justice and Peace Building in Turbulent Regions*. Hershey: Igi Global.

Carson, Rachel. 1962. *Silent Spring*. Boston: Houghton Mifflin.

Conway, John, and Simon Kochen. 2009. The Strong Free Will Theorem. *Notices from the AMS* 226–232.

Credit-Suisse. 2016. *Credit Suisse*. 28 December. Available online at www.credit-suisse.com/corporate/en/articles/news-and-expertise/the-global-wealth-pyram id-2016-201612.html

Dahrendorf, Ralf. 2007. *The Modern Social Conflict: The Politics of Liberty*. New York: Routledge.

Daly, Hermann. 1974. The Economics of the Steady State. *American Economic Review* 15–21.

Daly, Herman. 1999. How long can neoclassical eonomist ignore the contributions of Georgescu-Roegen? In *Bioeconomics and Sustainability. Essays in Honor of Nicholas Georgescu-Roegen*, Kozo Mayumi, 20. Northampton: Edward Elgar.

Daly, Hermann, and J. Farley. 2011. *Ecological Economics: Principles and Applications*. Washington: Island Press.

Degrowth and Research. 2018. *degrowth org*. 17 February. Available online at https://degrowth.org/definition-2/

Dostoevsky, Fyodor. 1984. *Notes from Underground*. Boston: Vintage.

Downs, Anthony. 1957. *An Economic Theory of Democracy*. New York: Harper.

Ehrlich, Paul. 1968. *The Population Bomb*. New York: Ballantine Books.

Forbes. 2018. *Forbes*. 6 March. Available online at www.forbes.com/sites/luisakroll/2018/03/06/forbes-billionaires-2018-meet-the-richest-people-on-the-planet/#23329edd6523

Foster, John. 2002. *Monthly Review an Independent Socialist Magazine*. 2 September. Available online at https://monthlyreview.org/2002/09/01/capitalism-and-ecology/

Frankfurt, Harry. 1971. Freedom of the Will and the Concept of a Person. *Journal of Philosophy* 5–20.

Friedman, Milton, and Rose Friedman. 1980. *Free to Choose*. New York: Harcourt.

FSIN. 2017. *Food Security Information Network*. 8 March. Available online at http://www.ipcinfo.org/fileadmin/user_upload/ipcinfo/docs/Global_Report_FoodCrisis_2017_Summary.pdf

Georgescu-Roegen, Nicholas. 1975. Energy and Economic Myths. *Southern Economic Journal* 347–381.

Georgescu-Roegen, Nicolas. 1971. *The Entropy Law and the Economic Process*. Boston: Harvard University Press.

Gintis, Herbert, Samuel Bowles, Ernst Ferh, and Robert Boyd. 2004. *Moral Sentiments and Material Interests the Foundations of Cooperation in Economic Life*. Boston: MIT Press.

Graeber, David. 2011. *Debt: The First 5000 Years*. New York: Melville House.

Hagemann, Harald, Vadim Kufenko, and Danila Raskov. 2016. Game theory modeling for the Cold War on both sides of the Iron Curtain. *History of Human Sciences* 99–124.

Hardin, Garret. 1968. The Tragedy of Commons. *Science* 1243–1248.

Harvey, David. 2007. *The Limits to Capital*. Boston: Verso.

Hayek, Friedrich. 1966. The Principles of a Liberal Social Order. *Il Politico* 101–118.

Hayek, Friedrich. 1988. *The Fatal Conceit: The Errors of Socialism*. Chicago: Chicago University Press.

Hirsch, Fred. 1977. *Social Limits to Growth*. London: Routledge and Kegan Paul Ltd.

Hirschman, Albert. 1970. *Exit, Voice, and Loyalty: responses to decline in firms, organizations and states*. Cambridge, MA: Harvard University Press.

Hirschman, Albert. 1998. *A Propensity to Self-subversion*. Boston: Harvard University Pres.

Hirschman, Albert. 2002. *Shifting Involvements: Private Interest and Public Action*. New Jersey: Princeton University Press.

Holy Bible. 1995. *Biblegateway*. 1 January. Available online at https://www.biblegatewa y.com/passage/?search=Matthew+5&version=GW

Huxley, Aldous. 1932. *Brave New World*. New York: Harper & Brothers.

Jackson, Tim. 2017. *Prosperity without Growth Foundations for the Economy of Tomorrow*. London: Routledge.

Kalecki, Michal. 1971. Class Struggle and the Distribution of National Income. *Kyklos* 1–9.

Keynes, John Maynard. 1990. *The General Theory of Employment, Interest and Money*. Chicago: Encyclopedia Britannica.

Klein, Naomi. 2008. *The Shock Doctrine: The Rise of Disaster Capitalism*. New York: Picador.

Klein, Naomi. 2014. *This Changes Everything*. New York: Simon & Schuster.

Kropotkin, Peter. 2014. *Mutual Aid: A Factor in Evolution*. New York: Dancing Unicorn Books.

La-Boétie, Etienne. 2012. *On Voluntary Servitude*. Indianapolis: Hackett and Publishing.

Latouche, Serge. 2006. *O desafio do decrescimento*. Lisboa: Ipiaget.

MacPherson, C. B. 2011. *The Political Theory of Possessive Individualism: From Hobbes to Locke*. London: Oxford University Press.

Mann, Michael. 2005. *The Dark Side of Democracy: Explaining Ethnic Cleansing*. Cambridge: Cambridge University Press.

Marques, Luiz. 2016. *Capitalismo e Colapso Ambiental*. Campinas: Unicamp.

Martinez-Alier, Joan, and Klaus Schlupman. 1987. *Ecological Economics: Energy, Environment and Society*. Oxford: Basil Blackwell.

Marx, Karl. 1970. Capital: A Critique of Political Economy. In *The Capitalist Process of Production*, Karl Marx, 550–580. New York: Cossimo Classics.

Marx, Karl. 2010. *The Capital: A Critique of Political Economy*. Boston: Pacific Publishing Studio.

Marx, Carlos and Engels, Federico. 1998. *Manifiesto Comunista*. Barcelona: Crítica.

Mauss, Marcel. 1990. *The Gift: Forms and Functions of Exchange in Archaic Societies*. London: Routledge.

Mayumi, Kozo. 2001. *The Origins of Ecological Economics: The Bioeconomics of Georgescu-Roegen*. London: Routledge.

Meadows, Donella, Dennis Meadows, Jørgen Randers, and William Behrens. 1972. *The Limits to Growth*. New York: Universe Books.

Milgram, Stanley. 1974. *Obediency to Authority*. New York: Harper and Row.

Mill, J. S. 1885. *Principles of Political Economy*. New York: Appleton and Company.

Mishan, James. 1993. *The Cost of Economic Growth*. London: Praeger.

Netto, J., and P. Braz. 2006. *Economia Política: uma introdução crítica*. Sao Paulo: Cortez.
New Internationalist. 2008. *The New Internationalist*. 2 June. Available online at https://newint.org/features/2008/06/01/nuclear-weapons-facts
Nozick, Robert. 1974. *Anarchy, State and Utopia*. New York: Basic Books.
Nussbaum, Martha. 2015. *Political Emotions: Why Love Matters for Justice*. Boston: Harvard University Press.
Nygardshaug, Gert. 2014. *Le zoo de Mengele*. Paris: Editions 84.
Orwell, George. 1949. *Nineteen Eighty-Four*. London: Secker & Warburg.
Ostrom, Elinor. 1991. *Governing the Commons: The Evolutions of Institutions for Collective Action*. Cambridge: Cambridge University Press.
Parijs, Philippe. 1997. *Real Freedom for All: What (if Anything) Can Justify Capitalism?* Oxford: Oxford University Press.
Patel, Raj. 2012. *Stuffed and Starved: The Hidden Battle for the World Food System - Revised and Updated*. New York: Melville House Printing.
Polanyi, Karl. 2001. *The Great Transformation: The Economic and Political Origins of our Time*. Boston: Beacon Press.
Pope Francis. 2015. *Laudato Si – On Care for Our Common Home*. Vatican: Editrice Vatican Libreria.
Rawls, John. 1971. *A Theory of Justice*. Boston: Harvard University Press.
Ricardo, David. 1817. *On the Principles of Political Economy and Taxation*. London: John Murray.
Sandel, Michael. 2012. *What Money Can't Buy: The Moral Limits of Markets*. New York: Farrar, Strauss and Giroux.
Schalke, George. 1979. *Imagination and the Nature of Choice*. Edinburgh: Edinburgh University Press.
Schelling, Thomas. 2005. *Nobelprize*. 16 December. Available online at www.nobelprize.org/nobel_prizes/economic-sciences/laureates/2005/schelling-lecture.html
Schelling, Thomas. 2006. *Micromotives and Macrobehavior*. London: W.W. Norton and Company.
Schumacher, Ernst. 1973. *All the Small is Beautiful*. New York: Harper & Collins.
Schumpeter, Joseph. 1942. *Capitalism, Socialism and Democracy*. New York: Harper & Collins.
Scott, James. 1976. *The Moral Economy of the Peasant: Rebellion and Subsistence in Southeast Asia*. London: Yale University Press.
Scott, James. 2009. *The Art of Not Being Governed: An Anarchist History of Upland Southeast Asia*. Connecticut: Yale University Press.
Scott, James. 2012. *Two Cheers for Anarchism: Six Easy Pieces on Autonomy, Dignity, and Meaningful Work and Play*. New York: Princeton University Press.
Sedlacek, Tomas. 2013. *Economics of Good and Evil: The Quest for Economic Meaning from Gilgamesh to Wall Street*. Oxford: Oxford University Press.
Sen, Amartya. 1977. Rational Fools: A Critique of the Behavioral Foundations of Economic Theory. *Philosophy & Public Affairs* 317–344.
Sen, Amartya. 2009. *The Idea of Justice*. Boston: Harvard University Press.
Sen, Amartya. 2017. *Collective Choice and Social Welfare: an expanded edition*. Boston: Harvard University Press.
Shackle, George. 1991. *Epistemics and Economics: A Critique of Economic Doctrines*. London: Routledge.
Smith, Adam. 1776. *An Inquiry into the Nature and Causes of the Wealth of Nations*. London: W. Strahan and T. Cadell.

Smith, Adam. 2011. *Theory of Moral Sentiments.* London: Gutenberg Publishers.

Sraffa, Piero. 1960. *Production of Commodities by means Commodities.* London: Cambridge University Press.

Steinbeck, John. 2002. *Grapes of Wrath.* New York: Penguin Books.

Strassmann, Joan, Yong Zhu, and David Queller. 2000. Altruism and social cheating in the social amoeba Dictyostelium discoideum. *Nature* 965–970.

Taleb, Nassim. 2008. *The Black Swan: The Impact of the Highly Improbable.* New York: Penguin.

Taleb, Nassim. 2014. *Antifragile: Things That Gain from Disorder.* New York: Random House.

Thompson, Edward P. 1971. The Moral Economy of the English Crowd in the Eighteenth Century. *Past & Present* 76–136.

Tiebout, Charles. 1956. A Pure Theory of Local Expenditures. *Journal of Political Economy* 416–424.

Zimbardo, Philipe. 2008. *The Lucifer Effect.* New York: Random House.

Part I
A critique of conventional and violent economy

1 Money, credit and interest in light of unconventional perspective

Kozo Torasan Mayumi

Introduction

Monetary management is the most important item for a nation-state whenever the state requires money for financing war or for combatting inflation after war. In fact, the establishment of modern national banks is fundamentally related to financing war or combatting inflation. I present here two cases: England and Japan.

As H. Meulen described:

> In 1694 the Bank of England was founded and set up in the midst of the goldsmith–banker system. The circumstances of its establishment arc note-worthy. William III was in urgent need of money for the prosecution of continental wars. The conspiracies of the Stuart faction, however, rendered his throne unstable, and merchants were unwilling to risk their gold in loans to him. At length a body of London merchants and others were induced to make a loan to him at a certain interest on condition that he permitted them to issue notes to the amount of the loan.
>
> (Meulen 1917: 69)

The Government of Meiji Japan authorized 153 national banks between 1876 and 1879. The Government and these national banks issued an enormous amount of inconvertible bank notes to finance the Seinan Civil War of 1877. Thus, the Government of Meiji Japan had to establish the Bank of Japan in 1882 to manage rampant inflation that continued during and after the Seinan Civil War (Shizume 2017).

Both the England and Japan cases indicate the inherent relation between war and money. Therefore, the selection of my topic, Money, Credit and Interest, would be vindicated and suitable for the leitmotiv of this book, *Nonviolent Political Economy*.

In 2003, R, Lucas Jr. bravely declared in his presidential address to the American Economic Association that the 'central problem of depression-prevention has been solved, for all practical purposes, and has in fact been solved for many decades' (Lucas 2003: 1). Given that the Lehman Shock happened only a few years later in

2009, it should be worthwhile to reconsider various problems associated with money, interest and credit and worth considering an alternative perspective that has not attracted sufficient attention from conventional economists.

The second section of this chapter, 'Reconsidering the myth of barter, money and credit', assesses the widely accepted view that there is progressive development from barter to money to credit. It points out: (i) barter in its purest form does not require written record because barter entails final settlement involving *equal exchange* of wants only in terms of goods and services; (ii) anthropological studies suggest that barter is much rarer than commonly believed, involving only strangers or even enemies; (iii) the two cases of nails in Scotland and dried cod in Newfoundland that Adam Smith saw as transition from commodity currency to metallic money actually show a credit system; (iv) credit system started in the ancient Babylonian times, the inevitable result of *unequal exchange* that requires records of credit and debt arrangement and (v) the banking activity occurred as early as around 350BC in the Roman Republic.

The section on 'The origin of money interest' discusses the origin of money interest and the distinction between structural decay and functional decay. This section shows: (i) the entropy law can be applied to material decay by using Clausius' idea of disgregation; (ii) distinguishing functional decay from material decay offers clues to the emergence of money interest; (iii) despite the inevitable material decay, the functional aspect of money is legally and institutionally guaranteed; (iv) scholarly views of money and capital interest held by S. Gesell, von Böhm-Bawerk and I. Fisher deserve critical examination; (v) if, as Soddy suggests, the principal of loan money is allowed to decrease, the total money interest to be paid never exceeds the principal. Soddy's idea may also apply to redemption of national bonds and (vi) the phenomenon of the intentional functional decay is linked to the tendency toward increased unsustainable consumption in modern socioeconomic systems.

The section on 'Debt creation and control' places particular focus on problems associated with debt created directly or indirectly by the banking system. This section demonstrates that: (i) any form of promise to pay is an abstract right or property of demanding future payment from the debtor. This abstract right, termed *general liquidity*, includes items such as coins, bank notes, credit cards, derivatives and national bonds. While general liquidity has a hierarchical structure related to the degree of difficulty in exchanging for goods and services, there is *no essential difference* between items of general liquidity because all such items can be *ultimately* exchanged into goods and services in the market; (ii) general liquidity has a dual nature that is regarded as *a debt communally*, and regarded as *a form of wealth individually* that causes progressive expansion of debt, mainly through the financial system; (iii) credit expansion through the financial system is not controlled by the elected representatives; (iv) taxation can eliminate excessive debt, so general liquidity must be combined properly with tax imposition under the control of the elected representatives; (v) the deposit associated with the credit creation mechanism dates back to the idea of Mutuum in the Roman law and (vi) proper use of a credit system is exemplified by cash credit in eighteenth century Scotland that was based on the idea of *accommodation paper* in the language of the present financial system.

The chapter conclusion touches upon several other important issues not discussed in earlier sections.

Reconsidering the myth of barter, money and credit

It is generally accepted by economists that barter comes first, followed by money and then by credit, in particular through the banking system development. Adam Smith may be primarily responsible for such an idea due to statements like 'when barter ceases, and money has become the common instrument of commerce' (Smith 1976: 36).

In a similar way, Samuelson and Nordhous in a well-known textbook state: '[as] economies develop, people no longer barter one good for another. Instead, they sell goods for money and then use money to buy other goods' (2010: 458); and '[the] financial system is one of the most important and innovative sectors of a modern economy' (2010: 453). Here, Samuelson and Nordhous's definition on money is the means of payment in the form of currency and checks (2010:33).

First of all, let us discuss the true nature of barter. Barter is a method of exchange that must reach the final settlement and is supposed to achieve the equal exchange among people involved only in terms of goods and services. Successful barter always requires a perfect matching in which each party in a transaction must offer something in the required amount to the other person. Therefore, barter always requires the double coincidence of wants (Graeber 2011), often very difficult to achieve actually.

The accumulated anthropological study shows that barter was conducted mainly between strangers who might otherwise be enemies. For example, Graeber presented crucial case studies, in particular the Nambikwara of Brazil and the Gunwinggu people in Australia. Graeber states: what 'all such cases of trade through barter have in common is that they are meetings with strangers who will, likely as not, never meet again, and with whom one certainly will not enter into any ongoing relations. This is why a direct one-on-one exchange is appropriate: each side makes their trade and walks away' (2011: 32).

Before describing the historical development of the credit theory of money, it is useful to investigate whether or not there was a transitional period from commodity currency to metallic money. According to Adam Smith, there was a transitional period from commodity currency such as nails in Scotland or dried cod at Newfoundland, to the metallic money (A. Smith 1995: 37). However, Adam Smith's reasoning was placed in doubt as early as in William Playfair's edition of the *Wealth of Nations* in 1805 and in greater detail in Thomas Smith's *An Essay on Currency and Banking* in 1832 (Innes 1913). It is worthwhile to directly investigate in detail these two important works here.

First of all, Thomas Smith states that

the only value attached to these articles [dried cod at Newfoundland and nails in Scotland] is the cost of the labour hours in catching or making them, and whenever that cannot be got they will neither be caught nor made. The real fact however, is that neither of these articles ever was used or could be used as money.

(Smith 1832: 15)

Concerning the dried cod in Newfoundland, both the fisherman and traders from the ports of France braved harsh environmental conditions. Fishermen who had codfish fit for trade could obtain in return *any articles* that the fisher-man might need in a credit system based on mutual trust. Final settlement of negotiation between fishermen and traders was achieved either by livre or the pound depending on where negotiation occurred according to the agreed upon exchange rate. For example, fishermen negotiating in an area under English jurisdiction

> sold their catch to the traders at the market price in pounds, shillings and pence, and *obtained in return a credit on their books*, with which they paid for their supplies. Balances due by the traders were paid for by drafts on England or France.
>
> (Innes 1913: 378, italics added)

Concerning nails in Scotland, because of the difficulty in making nails by steam machinery, nails were made by hand. Several villages around Falkirk near the great iron works at Carron, were inhabited by a hardy group of people whose sole occupation, men, women and children, was the making nails (Smith 1832). These people worked hard but gained little, so they lacked a good access to the circulating medium of the country and their only way to obtain necessities was to sell nails to Falkirk storekeepers.

Playfair shows these people using nails as part of a credit system, not using nails as commodity currency: brokers

> furnish the poor nailers with iron nail rods, or small slit bars, to work up into nails; and during the time they are working, give them a credit for bread, cheese, and chandlery goods, which they pay for in nails when the iron is worked up. Nails have indeed two properties that are essential to money. Their value is known from their size and number, or weight; and they are divisible into all possible quantities: and though they may therefore be paid away by the indigent maker with more ease than other produce of his hands, yet one transfer or two of property does not intitle to be called money.
>
> (Smith 1995: 37 footnote)

Actually, the credit system was well established long before Adam Smith tried unsuccessfully to use cod from Newfoundland or nails from Scotland as examples of transition from barter to money. In fact, the credit system is as old as money itself. However, difficulty in making standardized coinage due to poor technology made it impossible to have a large-scale coin making for a wide spread of circulation. To overcome the double coincidence of want required for barter and the shortage of coins, a credit and debt record system emerged in ancient Babylonia using *shubai* (contract) tablets. The oldest of these tablets used 2000–3000BC are dried clay having the shape and size of a cake of hand soap. Most *shubai* record simple transactions as '*she*', which is thought to be an assumed point of comparison related to a unit of measure for grain of some sort (Innes 1913). *Shubai* were kept in sealed containers that provided protection against fraudulent tampering. Such protection suggests that *shubai* were obviously not merely intended as records to remain in the possession of the debtor. Instead, *shubai* were signed and sealed documents issued to the creditor, and could be passed from creditor to creditor until the debt was paid and the tablet was broken (Innes 1913).

Another early example of credit system was the tally stick used in medieval times to account for credit or debt. Like the *shubai* system, the tally system resulted from unequal exchange that demanded a record of unsettled credit or debt. The tally stick was intended to be tamper-proof device using a series of notches in a time when there was constantly a shortage of coins and people were mostly illiterate. The split tally was commonly used to record bilateral exchange of credits and debts with each party receiving a half of the stick as proof of the transaction. When both parts of the split tally were rejoined, there was a completely identifiable unit (The "Kick Them All Out" Projects 2017).

Much commerce in Medieval Europe was recorded entirely with tally sticks that were used to control purchases of goods, loans of money and settlement of debts there. The great periodical fairs served as clearing houses where merchants gathered with their tally sticks to settle their credits and debts (Innes 1913)

It has long been recognized that the need for credit or money stems directly from unequal transactions: 'Credit is anything which is of no direct use in itself: but which is taken in exchange for something else, solely in the Belief or Confidence that we have the Right to exchange it away again for something else we do require' (Macleod 1883: 36). As such, credit or money is something *of no direct use in itself*. Rather, credit or money is the abstract right or property of demanding something to be paid or done by somebody in the future.

Regarding the origin of banking Samuelson and Nordhous state that 'Commercial banking began in England with the goldsmiths, who developed the practice of storing people's gold and valuables for safekeeping' (2010: 463). Titus Livius already referred to the existence of banking businesses around 350BC in his *Ab Urbe Condita Libri*, now available in English as *History of Rome*. Therefore, Samuelson and Nordhous' explanation is not exact at all. In fact, Macleod (1883: 161–162) shows that banking was first practiced by the Romans in Europe when Rome began to take control of neighbouring towns. Foreigners brought local coins with them and the Roman government created private agencies called Argentarii to exchange foreign money for Roman money. In time the Argentarii expanded their business, so that private persons could deposit money with them for the purpose of security. In such a case the Argentarii acquired no property, instead they simply took care of money. Gradually the Argentarii developed new business which in modern language would be termed banking. The Argentarii received money in the form of personal loan to themselves and paid interest for that money, in such a way money became the property of Argentarii and they could trade with it as they pleased much as modern bankers do.

The origin of money interest in light of structural and functional decay

The second law of thermodynamics (the entropy law) scientifically interprets the universal tendency of heat to disperse from a high localization and spread out unless heat is constrained. It is common knowledge that like heat, all material objects tend to disperse or decay.

In 1862, Clausius tried to quantify material dispersion within a thermo-dynamic system before his final formulation of the entropy law. Clausius (1862) defined a new variable called the *disgregation* that quantifies the degree of the molecular dispersion in a thermodynamic system. In so doing, Clausius seems to have recognized that change in disgregation corresponds to change in posi-tion of molecules in the system and that disregation is more fundamental than entropy because disgregation can be used to interpret the true nature of entropy (Klein 1961). Before introducing the disgregation concept, his analysis was confined only to the cyclic process that is supposed to be returned to the initial state after transformation, therefore there must be *no change within the system between the initial state and the final state*. It seems that Clausius became more concerned with the general transformation, not restricted to the cyclic process, so that changes within the system after any type of transformation, not restricted to cyclic processes, can be investigated. Furthermore, as Gibbs cor-rectly indicated in 1889 in his obituary dedicated to Clausius, the disgregation does not depend on the velocities of particles within the system (Gibbs 1994). Therefore, the disgregation differs from the entropy concept that is generally believed to refer only to the dissipation of energy based on the distribution of the particle velocities.

Entropy S can be related with thermal content of a system and disgregation by equating entropy equals heat dispersion (d'H/T) plus material dispersion (d'Z):

$$dS = d'H/T + d'Z \quad (1)$$

where T is the absolute temperature, H is the thermal content of the system and Z is disgregation. It must be emphasized that entropy S is a state function, thus dS is a total differential, while neither d'H/T nor d'Z is a total differential.

Relation (1) confirms that the concept of entropy can be safely applied not only to energy, but also to matter! In fact, in the case of the diffusion of two perfect gases, the diffusion phenomenon must be interpreted as dissipation of matter. Planck supports this interpretation (1945: 104 footnote, italics added):

the case of diffusion of two perfect gases 'would be more to the point to *speak of a dissipation of matter than of a dissipation of energy.*' Thus, the dissipation matter, namely, disgregation, is of vital importance for interpreting the meaning of entropy.

Georgescu-Roegen similarly tried to formulate the material dissipation or matter in bulk dissipation, in particular the dissipation of mineral resources in the economics process, as the fourth law of thermodynamics (Georgescu-Roegen 1977). The fourth law implies that flows of dissipated matter in bulk increase with the scale of the economic production and consumption activities and that there is great difficulty in maintaining the large-scale material structures in modern industrial society.

Now it is clear to the readers of this chapter, the entropy concept can be safely applied to both energy and matter.

However, perhaps the readers will be astonished if I tell that the diffusion of material structure based on disgregation could be used to explain the clue to the origin of money interest. Every material object has material structure. i.e., *structural element* and particular purpose for use, i.e., *functional element*. As a structural element decays due to entropy law, its functional element jointly decays and the material object may no longer be used for the particular purpose for which it was originally intended.

Hard currencies such as coins and bank notes, for example, cannot avoid the entropy law, so they suffer material decay as time goes on, 'losing' the material structure. However, the functional element does not decay even money suffers material decay. This functional aspect of money, despite the inevitable material decay, is legally and institutionally guaranteed. Therefore, legal and institutional arrangement gives money, in fact, any form of money including coins and bank notes, the far superior position compared with the goods or wares when making economic exchanges. This superiority guarantees the ability of money to able to postpone, if desired, the timing of transactions, because of the special ability to keep the functional element intact despite the inevitable material decay due to the entropy law.

To use examples from Japan and the USA, the functional element of Bank of Japan notes is legally guaranteed since: 'The Bank of Japan shall exchange, without fees, Bank of Japan notes rendered unfit for further circulation due to defacement, mutilation, or other causes, pursuant to an Ordinance of the Ministry of Finance' (Article 48). US law also stipulates that

> Lawfully held mutilated paper currency of the United States may be submitted for examination in accord with the provisions in this subpart. Such currency may be redeemed at face amount if sufficient remnants of any relevant security feature and clearly more than one-half of the original note remains.
>
> (Legal Information Institute 2017)

To repeat, money interest derives from the special characteristic of money, that is the possibility to postpone the timing of transaction. The ability to control the timing of transactions with money is legally and institutionally arranged in socioeconomic systems. The emergence of other types of interests associated with capital and financial assets can be deduced as a corollary from the emergence of money.

Here it is useful to introduce Gesell's free money theory. Gesell's free-money theory regards money as a medium of exchange that should depreciate over time at a certain rate. By this theory, monetary devaluation corresponds to commodity depreciation through stamping currency to indicate devaluation. In this way, money is supposed to serve only as a means of exchange for commodities and is prevented from being unnecessarily withheld from the market.

As already emphasized, the emergence of money interest has nothing to do with the material of money. However, Gesell did not pay due attention to the fact that material of money does not matter at all. It is the legal and institutional arrangement that really matters. Gesell missed the crucial distinction between the material decay and the functional decay that is legally and institutionally authorized as money, not coming from the nature of material structure of money. To wit, Gesell states

> *The physical properties of the traditional form of money* (metal money and paper-money) allow it to be withdrawn indefinitely from the market without material cost of storage, The merchant can therefore force the possessors of wares to make him a special payment in return for the fact that he refrains from arbitrarily postponing, delaying, or, if necessary, preventing the exchange of wares by holding back his money. This special payment, sharply to be distinguished from commercial profit, cannot of course be exacted by the ordinary purchaser, Only the merchant approaching the market as owner of money can exact this tribute.
>
> (2013: 171, italics added)

Gesell calls this special payment within the economic system as *basic interest*.

It is well known that von Böhm-Bawerk proposed a theory of capital interest in *The Positive Theory of Interest*, based on the marginal utility analysis. The alleged rationale of his theory is that '[p]resent goods are, as a rule, worth more than future goods of like kind and number' (2007: 237). However, there is the fundamental fallacy of his alleged theory. He claims (2007: 250) that '[m]ost goods, and among them, particularly, money, which represents all kinds of goods indifferently, are durable, and can, therefore, be reserved for the service for the future'. On this point, Wicksell made a strong point (Wicksell 1970: 108): 'This is certainly a great exaggeration'. Wicksell properly indicated that Böhm-Bawerk's examples such as ice or fruit cannot be regarded as exceptions and that all food-staffs are perishable goods without exception. The crucial flaw in Böhm-Bawerk's theory appears to be paying insufficient attention to structural decay related to the entropy law, so all goods are seen to be durable.

Thus, Böhm-Bawerk's theory is not applicable to capital interest in general but only applicable to money loan in which the money has *immediate* need for goods or investment activity. In such a way, the money borrower regards present goods as being more valuable than future goods.

Following the similar reasoning along with Böhm-Bawerk, Fisher (2012) showed that the rate of interest in terms of a given good cannot become negative if the good can be stocked without significant expense, a condition that is met by money. Furthermore, Fisher states 'as long as our monetary standard is gold or other imperishable commodity, so that there is always the opportunity to hoard some of it, no rate of interest expressed therein is likely to fall to zero, much less to fall below zero' (Fisher 2012: 41). Here Fisher also does not understand the true nature of money, not the coins made of gold or silver. The materials of money do not matter, as already mentioned. Fisher, along with Gesell and Böhm-Bawerk, did not notice the distinction between the material decay and the functional decay that explains the true origin of the emergence of money interest.

Soddy raised an interesting question concerning how to pay loan interest of money, following implicitly Gesell's free money idea (Soddy 2003). Though it can be agreed to pay in one year's time, say, US$ 5 for the use of US$ 100 loan lent now, this is not the same as agreeing to pay another US$ 5 at the end of the second year. Rather the value of the US$ 100 at the first year has to be discounted to its present value US$ 95, so that the second year's interest ought to be five per cent of US$ 95 and so on. Under these circumstances *the total interest accruing becomes nearer and nearer to the principal and can never exceed the principal, regardless of loan duration.* To illustrate:

A: the principal
f: the fraction of the principal accruing as interest
t: the time in years
i: the rate of interest per cent per annum

Between the period $(t, t + dt)$, the interest accruing is
$A(f+df)-Af=(A-Af)\times i/100\times dt$ (2).
Therefore, we obtain
$df/((1-f))= i/100 \ dt$ (3).
Integrating the above expression, we can get
$-\ln(1-f)=it/100$ (4).
The final form we obtain is $f=1-e^{\wedge}((-it)/100)$ (5).

Since f is the fraction of A already paid as interest, as time approaches infinity, f approaches 1. Therefore, the accumulated interest in this scheme cannot exceed the principal A as long as the interest rate i is positive. So, inequality $f<1$ always holds true, while sup $[\![f=1]\!]$.

A similar scheme can be applied to the national bond redemption by taxation. Suppose the taxation rate is p, the following relation can be easily obtained:

$$f = 1 - e^{\wedge}((-ipt)/100) \qquad (6).$$

The relation (6) clearly shows that capital gain tax effectively reduces the interest rate from i to ip since $p < 1$. If $i = 5$ and $p = 0.2$, then for f to reach one half, it will take almost 70 years. Of course, the interest paid in terms of tax must be set aside without defraying the public expenditure, in order not to increase the general liquidity.

At this moment it is instructive to discuss the recent phenomenon of intentional and progressive decay of the functional element by a succession of version-up of the IT and many other industries. For example, the first version of Word for Windows was released in 1990. However, this version was not very popular as Windows users belonged to a minority of the word processor market. Up until now Microsoft has released many new versions, the most recent version in 2017 is Word 2016. In the modern world, where new products are produced according to the strategies adopted by many producers based on the ingenious innovative marketing activities, *intentional functional decay and intentional obsolescence strategies* are often adopted, to try to effectively replace the old functional aspects of commodities by the new ones. In particular the game software or the computer software is the typical items under this ingenious but often environmentally destructive strategies that promote uncritical expansion of consumption. Relatively recent experiences such as Windows XP and Android 4.3 are the typical examples of intentional obsolescence. In particular more than 900 million Android users were troubled when the service support of the product was terminated in 2015. Consumers of IT products must pay unnecessary attention to the period and the content of the free service support or of the timing of new up-graded version issues. They have no other choices but to use the products without free service support or to buy a new version.

Debt creation and control: miscellaneous problems

In essence, the general liquidity including money is the right to demand equivalent services in the future for services already provided. That is to say, money represents debts which are due to people who have done services to other people but have not yet received equivalent services in return. Money's special function is to measure, record and preserve these rights for future use (Macleod 1883). Therefore, the owner of money is *individually* the creditor and the issuer of money *as a whole community* is the debtor. Money has a *dual nature* that implies two completely opposite perspectives. Namely, money can be seen *as a form of wealth from an individual person's perspective* but can be seen *as a debt from a communal perspective*. Under the current socioeconomic systems, the issuer of money is usually a nation state that is a combination of a cultural entity defined in terms of ethnicity with a set of institutions through which public authority is exercised within a particular territorial boundary (Holton 2011). So, a nation state as the issuer of money is a debtor, while money is regarded as a form of wealth by the owner of money individually. Many people seem to forget the dual nature of money. Money is a debt to a nation state and can accumulate progressively with a positive interest rate under the present legal and institutional setting. So, it is important for the democratically elected representatives of a nation state to be in charge of a full control of the total quantity of money (general liquidity) to be issued and of how this total quantity of money is distributed. As K. Popper aptly remarks, '[t]he future depends on ourselves, and we do not depend on any historical necessity' (Popper 1995: xix). Thus, there must be a rule of law that enables people to be able to replace the representatives if circumstances dictate. Therefore, I strongly oppose to the people who endorse the private issue of money Such a representative endorsing the private issue of money was Hayek (1990).

However, there is another crucial role of a nation state, the tax imposition that must be linked to the money creation. We are so accustomed to regard the issue of money as a blessing and taxation as a heavy burden (Innes 1914). This view is based on the individual perspective that money is wealth and that tax is a burden. At the present time, for almost all countries, all tax is *automatically* spent as the public expenditure, so that the important role of tax that could extinguish money debt *if set aside* is completely forgotten. So, both money issue and taxation must be under the control of the elected representatives of a nation state, not under the control of the bureaucratic administration headed by the leading political party.

Let us examine the case of Japan to see whether or not there is an effective coordination between money issue and tax imposition under the control of the elected representatives of a nation state.

The monetary control in Japan is conducted *autonomously by the central bank under the strong influence of the prime minister and the bureaucratic administration.* So, the Bank of Japan is independent from the influence of the Diet, the elected representatives of Japan. In fact, the *Bank of Japan Act* stipulates that 'The Bank of Japan's autonomy regarding currency and monetary control shall be respected' (Article 3 (1)). In addition, any change in the articles of Bank of Japan Act can be made without the consent of the Diet. To wit: 'Any amendments to the articles of incorporation shall not come into effect unless authorized by the Minister of Finance and the Prime Minister' (Article 11 (2)).

Banking license and capital requirement are also authorized without any consent of the Diet. The *Bank Act* in Japan stipulates on banking licenses: 'A person who has not obtained a license from the Prime Minister shall not engage in Banking' (Article 4 (1)); 'The amount of the stated capital of a Bank shall be equal to or more than the amount specified by Cabinet Order' (Article 5 (1)).

It is clear now that all banking activity is not controlled by the elected representatives in Japan. But the situation is similar to the cases of the USA and many other countries.

In Japan the tax law is controlled by the Diet, the elected representatives of the nation. In fact, there are three articles in *The Constitution of Japan* referring to taxation and national finance *under the control of the Diet*: 'The people shall be liable to taxation as provided by law' (Article 30); 'The power to administer national finances shall be exercised as the Diet shall determine' (Article 83); 'No new taxes shall be imposed or existing ones modified except by law or under such conditions as law may prescribe' (Article 84). Fortunately, tax imposition is effectively under the control of the Diet in Japan. However, there must be an effective coordination between money issue and tax imposition under the control of the elected representatives of a nation state.

Before investigating credit creation through the banking system, what does physics tell us about the possibility of creating energy out of nothing? Physics, of course, tells us that before and after the reaction process, including nuclear reaction, the total energy is preserved. In a chemical reaction, the law of conservation of mass is held true, but in a nuclear reaction, the law of con-servation of mass does not hold true because the binding energy of nucleons (proton and neutron) is transformed into heat during the nuclear reaction. But the total energy must be preserved. Thus, in the physical world, we cannot create energy or extinguish energy by human will.

On the other hand, we can create a credit in the banking system out of nothing and extinguish into nothing by human will (Macleod 1889). This credit system is a very innovative discovery in the human history. On the system of bank ledger or accounting books, we can create a credit or extinguish this credit into nothing.

Therefore, within the banking system it is possible to have a situation where one person has certain amount of money and another person also can have the same amount of money. Ruskin strongly opposed to the abuse of this sort of magic in our economic life in his *Unto this Last* originally published in 1862. Ruskin (1985: 227) states 'care in nowise to make more of money, but care to make much of it; remembering always the great, palpable, inevitable fact—the rule and root of all economy—that what one person has, another cannot have'. Schumpeter describes this credit creation: while 'I cannot ride on a claim to a horse, I can, under certain conditions, do exactly the same with claims to money as with money itself' (1951: 97 note).

Why the credit creation system is legally and institutionally possible

In Roman law of mercantilism there were two types of lending, one called *Commodatum* and the other *Mutuum* (Macleod 1883). In the case of commo-datum, if a person lends his book or horse to another person, the borrower can enjoy their use without acquiring the absolute property right. On the other hand, in the case of Mutuum, if a person lends bread or wine to another person, the borrower cannot enjoy their use without destroying or consuming them. Surprisingly or strangely, under Roman law, if a person lends money to another person, money can be another person's property! It seems that money was treated as if money could be consumed! Therefore, the property in such things (bread or wine or money!) in such a loan must be transferred to the borrower. If a person makes a deposit into a bank account, that money is regarded as the absolute property of the banker. This type of loan is also called Mutuum in Roman law. When a banker obtains money as deposit in a book account, the banker necessarily acquires the property in that money. In all cases of the loan of such things as wine, oil, bread, meat, and also of money or postal stamps, the lender cedes the property in the thing lent to the borrower. So, a new property is called into existence and a new contract is supposed to be created between the lender and the borrower.

Many people seem to misunderstand the true nature of bank deposit. Suppose a banker's customers pay certain amount of money to their own accounts. Then the money becomes the banker's absolute property as a form of Mutuum. In fact, the banker buys the money from his customers and exchange for it, he gives them a credit in his bank books. This right of action, credit or debt, in banking language, is termed as a deposit, so that after this operation, the banker has this amount of deposits as liabilities and the same amount as asset. There is no liability until the customer tries to withdraw that money. Macleod boldly states that banks 'are nothing but Debt Shops, and the Royal Exchange is the great Debt Market in Europe' (1883: 158). However, Macleod properly emphasized the excessive use of credit and its serious consequences: it is 'chiefly by the excessive use of Credit that *over production* is brought about, which causes those terrible catastrophes called Commercial Crises' (1883: 285).

The banking system's debt creation is one of the most treacherous items from the point of view of the national control of money. It must be remembered that there were heated discussions of how to control the checking account in the USA shortly after the stock market clash in 1929 (Phillips 1995). In fact, those discussions led to the Chicago plan for banking reforms that was signed by F. Knight and other distinguished economists of the University of Chicago. At around the same time, Fisher (1945), wrote a seminar book *100% Money*, as a practical guide for controlling the checking account. This Chicago plan was never implemented,

On the other hand, there is a very interesting historical event concerning a proper use of credit system that happened in Scotland in the 18th century. This credit system was called Cash Credit (Macleod 1883). In fact, the invention of Cash Credit had advanced the wealth of Scotland. They created an enormous mass of exchangeable real property out of nothing by the mere will of the bank and its customers. The banks in Scotland at that time usually limit their advances to a certain moderate amount and they always take several sureties to cover any possible losses that might arise. These *cautioners* as they called in Scotland law, keep a watchful eye on the proceedings of the borrowers and have always the right of inspecting his account with the bank and of stopping it any time if necessary.

These cash credits were extended in the domain of agriculture and public works as well. The principle of the limits of credit is the present value of the estimated future product. Thus, in these cases credit was used as productive capital exactly in the same way that money is. All these marvellous results, which raised Scotland from the lowest depths of barbarism up to her proud position in the space of 170 years or so are the children of cash credit.

To realize the true nature of cash credit system in Scotland we must pay due attention to the distinction between *commercial paper* and *accommodation paper*. Commercial paper is an unsecured, short-term debt instrument issued by a corporation, typically for the financing of accounts receivable, inventories and meeting short-term liabilities. Maturities on commercial paper rarely range any longer than nine months. Commercial paper is usually issued at a discount rate from face value and reflects prevailing market interest rates. On the other hand, the marvellous results Scotland people have produced are due to accommodation paper. Accommodation paper is a negotiable instrument that provides a third-party promise of payment if the original borrower defaults. Accommodation papers are usually used to support one party's creditworthiness through endorsement by a second party with a better credit rating. The party with a better credit rate in Scotland was called cautioners, already mentioned above.

Conclusion

Both the money issue in the broadest sense of the term, i.e. general liquidity, and *taxation as well* must be under the strict control of the elected representatives of a nation state. So, the Euro system is a very dangerous creation by EU that must assume a superstructure beyond each nation state within EU (Sandbu 2015).

Unfortunately, there are several other important channels through which the large scale of 'money' creation is going on worldwide, beyond the control of any individual nation state: (i) the debt creation by issuing bonds, debentures and derivatives that spreads out into the world market in an accelerated pace where investment banks and investment managers companies play a crucial role; (ii) the open market purchase or sale of national bonds by a particular nation that is supposed to expand or contract the monetary base of the country; (iii) tax evasion (within a list of countries called tax havens) *legally* made but vitiating the national budget system by internationally active industries or individual people (Palan et al. 2010).

One annoying and crucial item is concerned with the existence of a positive interest on money and assets (see Section 3). If one central bank of the major economies such as USA, EU or UK or Japan adopts a new level of interest rate that is used for discounting the bills of exchange, this internal change directly influences, through the world financial market, on the effective exchange rates among concerned countries. Then internal change in the effective exchange rate indirectly triggers the stock market response, the monetary base and many other monetary and real changes. The problem associated with the existence of money interest and its eternal volatility among various countries is always with us under the present legal and institutional arrangement.

What is 'the value of money'? The value of money for exchange of goods and services is equal to the inverse of the general price level that is a weighted average of all goods and services prices. However, there are certain items that also have sales prices such as shares or derivatives. These items are not usually linked to the general price level arguments in economics. The possible link between ordinary goods and services and share or derivative prices is not sufficiently investigated in conventional analysis of the price stability. An increase in stock price is usually regarded as good, whereas an increase in the price of ordinary goods and services is regarded as bad. While we can understand the way conventional economists deal separately with goods and services included in GDP and with assets not included in GDP, what are missing in conventional economics are considerations of the general price index (GPI) that contains not only ordinary goods and services but also share and other financial commodities, it is imperative to study the complicated link between these distinct class of 'commodities'. On the other hand, what is the value of money for exchange of loan money or credits or assets? The price of credit, for example, is the interest rate that can produce a profit (discount) for the owner of credit. The interest rate here, termed the general interest index (GII), is a sort of weighting average of all the interests (returns) associated with various assets. In any way the distinction of the two values of money is important when considering the influence of money and of general credit expansion or contraction on both GPI and GII.

Thus far, the real productive capital, such as buildings or machinery, has been excluded from the category of general liquidity. However, the real productive capital can also be evaluated in terms of money. So, the real productive capital must be included in the general liquidity from purely economic consideration. On the other hand, there must be a distinction between the real productive capital and the monetary assets. The real productive capital is already produced. Therefore, biophysically speaking, if exhaustible energy and materials had been used in producing the real productive capital, then the already exhaustible part of eternal loss would never be recovered. The biophysically irreversible debt can never be recouped through using money. In fact, it is in most cases impossible to directly transform the real productive capital into the consumable goods and services. Furthermore, since the things that can be capitalized in the financial market are regarded as wealth from the individual person's perspective, the real productive capital can also be *easily* transformed into money by the people trying to make income looking for the higher profit in terms of interest or other profit opportunities. Thus, a nation state should make a proper balance among the scale of the real capital production, of financial assets as general liquidity and of goods and services production.

General liquidity is a totality of the virtual liquidity that will be demanded for exchange of consumable goods and services in the future. And this virtual liquidity of promise to pay on a community is going to expand indefinitely as long as the positive interest or other financial returns is supposed to be guaranteed. Thus, we are forced to create further increase of real wealth in terms of goods and services. Furthermore, more production of goods and services inevitably increases unnecessary competition, resulting in the deterioration of the environment that is indispensable for maintaining the biological life on the planet. Inevitably people in the capitalist systems are very busy, that is the reality of such economic systems. We should call this system of debt world as *running solvency* world as described long ago by Mark (1934). It must be remembered that the most important principle of commerce is that a person or nation is only solvent if there are immediately available credits at least equal to the amount of his debts immediately due and presented for payments. If, therefore, the sum of the immediate debts exceeds the sum of the immediate credits, the real value of these debts to creditors will fall to an amount which will make them equal to the amounts of credits (Innes 1913).

Acknowledgement

Prof. Fredy Cante kindly invited me to participate at an early stage in this important book project while I was writing a manuscript for a book tentatively entitled *Reconsidering Global Energy Sources, Monetary Systems and Daunting Bioeconomic Predicaments of Japan*. This chapter is an abbreviated version of Chapter 4 of that manuscript. I would like to thank Prof. Mario Giampietro for his continuous moral support and encouragement towards my new research direction. Certain parts of this chapter result from our extended discussions in Barcelona. Prof. Minoru Sasaki kindly provided information on IT product support systems and other problems associated with software upgrades. I thank Prof. Don Sturge of Tokushima University for help in improving the structure and the language in the first version of this chapter. Prof. John M. Polimeni and Prof. Jesus Ramos-Martin kindly provided me with financial data materials. Prof. Polimeni gave me great help with improving the final version. This work is partially supported by JSPS Grant-In-Aid for Scientific Research (C), No. 16K00673. However, I emphasize that I accept all responsibility for the way in which I have taken advice and criticism into consideration. Any errors in this writing are mine alone.

Bibliography

Böhm-Bawerk, Eugen von, (2007) *The Positive Theory of Capital*, Alabama: Ludwig von Mises Institute.
Clausius, R. (1862) 'On the application of the theorem of the equivalence of transformations to interior work', in T. A. Hirst (ed.) *The Mechanical Theory of Heat with its Applications to the Steam-Engine and to the Physical Properties of Bodies*, London: John van Voorst, 215–250.
Fisher, I. (2012) *The Theory of Interest*, Mansfied Centre, CT: Maritino Publishing.
Fisher, I. (1945) *100% Money*, 3rd edn, New Haven: The City Printing Company.
Georgescu-Roegen, N. (1977) 'The steady state and ecological salvation: a thermodynamic analysis', *BioScience* 27, 4: 266–270.
Gesell, S. (2013) *The Natural Economic Order*, translated by P. Pye, New Delhi: Isha Books.

Gibbs, J. W. (1994) 'Rudorf Julius Emanuel Clausius', in H. A. Bumstead and R. G. van Name (eds) *The Scientific Papers of J. Willard Gibbs* Volume 2, Woodbridge: Ox Bow Press, 261–267.

Graeber, D. (2011) *Debt: The First 5,000 Years*, New York: Melville House Publishing.

Hayek, F. A. (1990) *Denationalisation of Money*, 3rd edn, London: The Institute of Economic Affairs.

Holton, R. J. (2011) *Globalization and the Nation State*, 2nd edn, New York: Palgrave Macmillan.

Innes, A. M. (1913) 'What is money?', *The Banking Law Journal* 30, 5: 377–408.

Innes, A. M. (1914) 'The credit theory of money', *The Banking Law Journal* 31, 1: 151–168.

Bank of Japan Act (2017) Available online at www.japaneselawtranslation.go.jp/law/detail/?id=92&vm=&re=02

Banking Act (2017) Available online at www.japaneselawtranslation.go.jp/law/detail/?id=1967&lvm=01

Klein, M. J. (1961) 'Gibbs on Clausius', *Historical Studies in the Physical Sciences* 1: 127–149.

Legal Information Institute (2017) *The Code of Federal Regulations*.

Lucas, Jr. R. E. (2003) 'Macroeconomic Priorities', *American Economic Review* 93(1): 1–14.

Macleod, H. D. (1883) *The Theory and Practice of Banking* Volume 1, 4th edn, London: Forgotten Books.

Macleod, H. D. (1889) *The Theory of Credit* Volume 1, London: Longmans, Green and Co.

Macleod, H. D. (1894) *The Theory of Credit* Volume 2, London: Longmans, Green and Co.

Mark, J. (1934) *The Modern Idolatry being an Analysis of Usury and the Pathology of Debt*, London: Chatto & Windus.

Meulen, H. (1917) *Industrial Justice through Banking Reform: An Outline of a Policy of Individualism*, London: Richard J. James.

Palan, R., Murphy, R. and Chavagneux, C. (2010) *Tax Havens: How Globalization Really Works*, Ithaca: Cornell University Press.

Phillips, R. J. (1995) *The Chicago Plan and New Deal Banking Reform*, New York: M.E. Sharpe.

Planck, M. (1945) *Treatise on Thermodynamics*, 7th edn, New York: Dover.

Popper, K. (1995) *The Open Society and Its Enemies Volume One: The Spell of Plato*, London: Routledge.

Ruskin, J. (1985) *Unto This Last and Other Writings*, C. Wilmer (ed.), London: Penguin Books.

Samuelson, P. A. and Nordhous, W. D. (2010) *Economics*, 19th edn, New York: Mac-Graw-Hill.

Sandbu, M. (2015) *Europe's Orphan: The Future of the Euro and the Politics of Debt*, Princeton: Princeton University Press.

Schumpeter, J. A. (1951) *The Theory of Economic Development*, Cambridge, MA: Harvard University Press.

Shizume, M. (2017) 'A History of the Bank of Japan, 1882–2016' WINPEC Working Paper Series No. E1719.

Smith, A. (1995) *An Inquiry into the Nature and Causes of the Wealth of Nations*, Volume 1, W. Playfair (ed.), London: William Pickering.

Smith, A. (1976) *An Inquiry into the Nature and Causes of the Wealth of Nations*, E. Cannan (ed.), Chicago: The University of Chicago Press.

Smith, T. (1832) *An Essay on Currency and Banking*, Philadelphia: Jesper Harding.

Soddy, F. (2003) *The Role of Money*, London: George Routledge and Sons, Ltd.

The "Kick Them All Out" Projects (2017) 'Tally Sticks', available online at www.kick themallout.info/article.php/Story-Tally_Sticks

Wikipedia (2017, June 11) 'History of Microsoft Word', available online at https://en. wikipedia.org/wiki/History_of_Microsoft_Word

Wicksell, K. (1970) *Value, Capital and Rent*. New York: Augustus M. Kelley Publisher.

2 The economic nature of man disputed

Anthropology and the 'homo oeconomicus'

Magnus Treiber

The study of economic life and interaction has been a major focus of the anthropological discipline since its beginning. Economic anthropologists study economic conditions and contexts, and thus human economic praxis and thought, and they usually, though not exclusively, base their work on intensive ethnographic fieldwork. The origins of their subdiscipline, however, are far older than modern academic anthropology itself, and date back to the Enlightenment. The history of economic anthropology is thus not only one of empirical research on economic aspects of life, but also the on-going story of a pugnacious discourse, one rooted in the provocations of, amongst others, John Locke (1632-1704), one of the early enlightenment's liberal philosophers. Acts of conquest and expansion by Europe's seafaring nations led to their subsequent contact to indigenous people around the world, and the decisive political and social change this entailed meant also a need for explanations. Protestant morality, elitist though, and asymmetrical political relations all fed into an assumption of national intellectual supremacy. This attitude positioned England at the forefront of human development as such and meant the global dissemination of certain beliefs about individualism, human rights, rationality, progress, and civilisation. Anthropology's ability to look beyond one's own point of view may therefore make an essential contribution to conceiving and discussing ideas of non-violent political economy.

John Locke's provocation

Locke's *Second Treatise of Government* (1690) was more than a visionary call for a modern constitutional state. It also commented on actual social changes and developments, of the kind which economic historian Karl Polanyi would later call, in the title of his work of 1944, *The Great Transformation*. Like other theorists of the social contract, Locke saw state of nature as preceding human history. In that state, all human beings possessed equal rights and enjoyed equal opportunities, but there was no one to guarantee either freedom or protection from others' misbehaviour and abuse. Consequently, a state was needed, even if its creation would lead to social inequality. But why should the emergence of the state lead to social inequality? In answering this question, Locke resorted to a moral idea of work and property:

> God gave the world to men in common; but since he gave it them for their benefit, and the greatest conveniences of life they were capable to draw from it, it cannot be supposed he meant it should always remain common and uncultivated. He gave it to the use of the industrious and rational, (and labour was to be his title to it;) not to the fancy or covetousness of the quarrelsome and contentious.
>
> (Locke, 1690, sect. 34)

Locke's liberal state is also a protective state, one that guarantees legitimate profits, and which disguises a particular morality as a universal rationality. As the 'industrious and rational' need land, economic development starts with the fencing off of individually claimed estates.[1] To prevent illegitimate land-grabbing by a few, Locke suggests that the size of a plot should be no larger than the area its new owner could actually cultivate. According to Bertrand Russell this dictum, if put into reality, would have inevitably led to bloody revolutions all over Europe (1950 [1945], 643). Colonisation of the Americas, however, seemed to offer space for expansion without conflict, at least in Locke's thought. In the process of arriving at this conclusion, Native Americans became Locke's cultural other. Native Americans were used to illustrate a rather abstract idea of a state of nature. They neither sowed nor ploughed, but lived (so it appeared to Locke) entirely from their natural surroundings. And they did so collectively, without fencing off individual land property. To Locke this was an irrational act, an obstacle towards economic growth and rational development:

> The earth, and all that is therein, is given to men for the support and comfort of their being. And tho' all the fruits it naturally produces, and beasts it feeds, belong to mankind in common, as they are produced by the spontaneous hand of nature; and no body has originally a private dominion, exclusive of the rest of mankind, in any of them, as they are thus in their natural state: yet being given for the use of men, there must of necessity be a means to appropriate them some way or other, before they can be of any use, or at all beneficial to any particular man. The fruit, or venison, which nourishes the wild Indian, who knows no enclosure, and is still a tenant in common, must be his, and so his, i.e. a part of him, that another can no longer have any right to it, before it can do him any good for the support of his life.
>
> (Locke, 1690, sect. 26)

In Locke's view, the exclusion of some from the land, and its exploitation by others is necessary and legitimate; social transformation, economic expansion and emerging colonialism became, in his eyes, inevitable, even essential developments of his time, the late seventeenth and eighteenth centuries. The historians Rediker and Linebaugh offer a different account of that period (2000). In their history of the common people of Locke's era, they perceive labour as a 'curse' for most of Locke's contemporaries, not, as he saw it, a moral duty and a source of human progress:

We argue that the many expropriations of the day – of commons by enclosure and conquest, of time by the puritanical abolition of holidays, of the body by child stealing and the burning of women, and of knowledge by the destruction of guilds and assaults on paganism – gave rise to new kinds of workers in a new kind of slavery, enforced directly by terror (Rediker and Linebaugh, 2000, 40).

The enclosure of land had certain direct effects: the expulsion of the rural poor, their migration to the cities, and, finally, their entry into the ranks of a new class of urban poor. Crime blossomed in the newly enlarged urban centres of the poor, provoking, on the part of the elite, a policy of rigid discipline and law enforcement. Karl Polanyi concurs with this picture, describing the "effects on the lives of the people" as "awful beyond description" (1944, 79). It is indeed remarkable that working people, once forcefully relocated to the new American colonies (then a common disciplinary measure for prisoners, beggars, 'fallen women' and orphans) often defected to the communities of the 'wild and uncivilised' Indians, in order to escape hunger and forced labour (Rediker and Linebaugh, 2000, 32–35, 56–59).

Towards a rational world: evolutionism

Yet, the intellectual path towards a particular view of human development was set: all such development would henceforth be seen as rooted in the alleged fact that man was a rational and profit-making 'homo oeconomicus'. This model of human nature would become an ineradicable dogma of philosophers and economists, with consequences for anthropology. While he did not use this term himself, Scottish moral philosopher and economist Adam Smith laid the fundaments for *laissez-faire* economics. His book *The Wealth of Nations* (1776) received enormous attention in intellectual and political circles – attention that was selective, for Smith was critical of the effects the division of labour had on public education and private life (2012 [1776], 777–778). Descendants of this selective interpretation of Smith's model included, in the nineteenth century, Herbert Spencer, who misinterpreted Darwin's biological concept of 'natural selection' (2006 [1859], 51–82) or 'descent with modifications' (Raum, 1992, 296) as 'survival of the fittest' (1864, 444–445). While Darwin's *Origin of Species* (1859) had revolutionised biological thought without introducing any teleological assumptions, Spencer understood and categorised humanity's economic and cultural history as following exactly that sort of teleology. Evolution towards modern society had to, inevitably and without deviation, follow a single track to its ultimate end - the British model of social organization.

Nineteenth century anthropologists, also, held to the teleologies of their age. Their most important representative was Lewis Henry Morgan (1818-1881), a

New York lawyer and senator. He represented the Iroquois in their lawsuit against the Ogden Land Company, and thus was adopted by the Seneca, an Iroquoian people (cf. Petermann, 2004, 480-482). In his book *Ancient Society* (1877) he offered a comprehensive theory of human progress as a process of tripartite evolution that took humanity "from Savagery through Barbarism, to Civilization". His own empirical interest in the life-world of Native Americans saved him from a merely speculative approach. Instead he explained different stages of human evolution as a result of different technological skills – such as smelting iron ore, pottery, or the use of a phonetic alphabet – that emerged under different ecological and topographic conditions. To this end, he had to introduce 'lower', 'middle' and 'upper' substages, which made his theory more detailed, but also more vulnerable to critique. At this time, Morgan had already become known as a founder of the anthropology of kinship, and *Ancient Society* was largely dedicated to the study of the kinship organisations of ancient Romans, Germans and contemporary Native Americans. From this, he built up his model of the universal rules of social transition. For the German socialists Karl Marx and Friedrich Engels this model became an eye-opener, one that confirmed their own interest in, and model of, economic transformation throughout human history. Not only did ethnographic data seem to expose images of the eternally selfish nature of man as mere political ideology (see Marx, 2000 [1857/58]), but Marx and Engels theory of man-made social change and its potential seemed to have been supported by an independent party and his empirical research. Engels was, in fact, so impressed by Morgan's ideas that he dedicated his own work, *Origin of the Family, Private Property and the State* to him (1991 [1884]). Though not a typical evolutionist, Engels incorporated much of that discourse in his own work.

Political anthropology has since vividly attacked the idea of the state as an inevitable evolutionary stage of human development and stressed the continuing existence of anarchic anti-state societies.[2] It is nevertheless remarkable how comparative ethnographic data helped Marx and Engels to sketch capitalism as a specific historical phenomenon and materially conveyed social relationship. Ethnographic and historic findings backed their conviction that contemporary industrialisation with its disastrous social consequences would not be human development's final stage (cf. Krader, 1979). Half a century later in her fragmentary *Einführung in die Nationalökonomie* (usually translated as 'Introduction to Political Economy'), Rosa Luxemburg was already able to refer to much more anthropological literature – studying Australia, the Americas or Africa – in order to formulate substantive arguments against simplistic economics, but she still discussed *Ancient Society* at length (1990 [1925]). Images of what a future world without exploitation might look like could indeed be drawn from historic past as well as from contemporary ethnographic research. Luxemburg's search for an original communist society was continued by 20th century anthropologists.

Ethnographic economy: organised wilderness and the culture of social bonding

After 1918, academic anthropology became more ethnographic in its focus and more professional in its self-perception. In Britain, Bronislaw Malinowski and Alfred Radcliffe-Brown founded a new era of research-based social anthropology, while in the United States German émigré Franz Boas became the father of American cultural anthropology. All three based their reputations on thorough field work. Malinowski's ethnography of the Trobriand Islands (off the coast of New Guinea) and that archipelago's interethnic exchange of prestigious necklaces and bracelets (the famous Kula-trade), and Boas' extensive research work on the Kwakiutl and their lavish potlatch-festivals in British Columbia, both inspired *Essai sur le Don* (or 'the Gift', 1925) the seminal work of the French social scientist and religious studies' scholar, Marcel Mauss. From his uncle Émile Durkheim Mauss had already learned to integrate anthropological research with more abstract examples of sociological theory, blurring the boundaries and working areas of both disciplines. Again, the comparison of ethnographic detail from different areas of the world backed a universal argument against the fundamental assumptions of 'homo oeconomicus'. Mauss held that the mutual obligations of giving, taking and returning gifts – obligations which could not easily be evaded in well-integrated non-industrial societies – enmeshed people in social bonding, shared cultural forms and moral perceptions. It was the gift, in other words, that made society. This in turn implied that credit was not a technical innovation of the Italian economies of the Renaissance era, but rather, a fundamental trait of human interaction: "Men had learnt how to pledge their honour and their name long before they knew how to sign the latter" (Mauss, 2008, 48).

Credit creates a social bond between gift-giver and gift-receiver – one based on the time between the act of giving and its reciprocal return. David Graeber, whose alternative economic history *Debt: The First 5,000 Years* broadly supports Mauss' views, still points out a possible flaw in the concept of reciprocity - the assumption that it must inherently involve an idea of credit redemption and make-up pay. For him it is not gifts that create social bonds, but debts. Only when debts become non-reimbursable do they become the basis for political hierarchies (Graeber, 2011, 109-113).[3] With Mauss the debate shifted from the classical Marxist focus on production towards circulation and the consumption of goods. Like Karl Polanyi, but unlike Marx and Engels, he did not put production first. According to Polanyi, there has always been trade, but the important fact is that trade has always taken a socially embedded form. Thus, neither local markets nor long-distance trade had the potential to initiate capitalism's fundamental economic transformation. That transformation needed, Polanyi held, the vital intervention of the emerging mercantilist European state, with its forced creation of a national market and economy against the conservative resistance of guilds and cities. In time, the political construction of one national economy led to the construction of others and opened the way to capitalism and industrialisation through commodification of "labor, land, and money". Polanyi called this triad "fictitious commodities" (2001 [1994], 71), as they lacked essential characteristics of goods and could not 'really' be exchanged. This was the crucial point where the market system emancipated itself from social limits and control, and became a self-regulating system, subduing society and human life.

> We recall our parallel between the ravages of the enclosures in English history and the social catastrophe which followed the Industrial Revolution. Improvements, we said, are as a rule, bought at the price of social dislocation. If the rate of dislocation is too great, the community must succumb in the process.
>
> (Polanyi, 2001 [1994], 79)

Polanyi wrote his text at the height of the Second World War. Clearly, he was all too well aware of the consequences of that 'social catastrophe'. Despite his dissenting focus on circulation, he did not only share Marx's and Luxemburg's interest in anthropology and history, but also their assumption of specific social forms that preceded industrialisation but were eventually overturned due to their limited potential for economic innovation. Nevertheless, he was optimistic that critical voices could raise awareness, 'protect society' and steer against the stream of market liberalism. In that sense Polanyi has not only been an important advocate of better working conditions and labour law during difficult times, but also an early protagonist of ecological thought and activism (2001 [1994], 76).

Although Polanyi – again like Marx, Engels and Luxemburg – was not an anthropologist himself, he argued on the base of ethnographic research, anthropological findings and historical knowledge. In contrast to classical economists – so-called 'formalists' – he coined an empirically based 'substantivist' approach, which made its way back into anthropological discipline and theory. In their introduction to *Markets in Africa* (1965) Paul Bohannan and Polanyi's student George Dalton separated the 'market system' from actual 'market places' as well as from different spheres of transaction and money use. In their view economic transactions were not necessarily the most important event that could happen in African market places, which were also where marriage partners could be found, news exchanged, or law cases decided. The market day was – and certainly still is – a multifaceted event. This social and cultural embedding also restricted the use of money. While 'marketless' societies only allowed the sale of prestigious goods in cases of emergency, in 'peripheral markets' agricultural surplus could easily be converted into cash. Nevertheless, money could be described as 'special-purpose-money', in order to pay bridewealth or taxes – or to buy specific goods from outside the peasants' subsistence economy, such as a bicycle.

Anthropological substantivism stressed the social and cultural embeddedness of local economies against a superimposed ideal of economic rationality, despite its origins in the vibrant era of decolonisation it did not develop a global perspective, and it did not make an issue of exploitative mechanisms within the cultures and societies it examined.

French Neo-Marxism: back to production, re-production and exploitation

> I disagree with Polanyi's rejection of the theory of value. In fact, Polanyi was a socialist but never accepted the Marxist theory of value of commodities as congealed social labour. He never accepted the view of profit as unpaid labour, or the fact that exploitation entails one group depriving another group of access to the means of production.
>
> (Godelier, 1984, 37)

Unconvinced by both substantivism's culturalist approach and French structuralism's apparent disinterest in economic and political questions, three French anthropologists – Claude Meillassoux, Maurice Godelier, and Emmanuel Terray – attempted to develop a proper Marxist toolkit with which to study and analyse non-industrial societies and economies. All three were strongly influenced by French anthropologist Claude Lévi-Strauss, whose intellectual dominance they nevertheless tried to overcome, and each of them played a role in the Paris student revolts of 1968. Despite their critical stand towards each other, they could agree on a programmatic research question and a common approach: in order to study the origins of economic exploitation one had to analyse the respective local division of labour and identify its smallest units. Only then could the social mechanisms of production and (especially in Meillassoux' case) of reproduction be reconstructed (Terray, 1972, 104). Meillassoux had done extensive fieldwork on the Guro's agricultural economy in Ivory Coast, West Africa, in the 1960s. On this basis he developed his innovative theory of domestic exploitation in agricultural societies, bringing together the previously unrelated fields of economic anthropology and the anthropology of kinship (1975). In his view, the "main features of the domestic agricultural economy" were "delayed production resulting from investment of human energy in the land, accumulation, storage, and organised and managed distribution of the produce" (Meillasoux, 1981 [1975], 40). An established agricultural cycle requires essential preparatory work and generates "an endlessly repeated series of advances and returns" (Meillasoux, 1981 [1975], 41). These pass not only from season to season, but also from generation to generation. To ensure this passage, the agricultural labour of productive young men is continuously needed, and this has direct consequences for social reproduction. If, in this model, agricultural production is the task of young men, then young women have to give birth to the next generation. Young women thus become society's essential asset and are subjected to restriction and control: "nothing can replace a pubescent fertile woman in her reproductive functions except another pubescent fertile woman" (Meillasoux, 1981 [1975], 44). To ensure the continuity of such a society political management is needed and this, finally, is the task of old men. It is they who draw moral authority from previously invested labour, and it is their politics of marriage and patrilineal filiation that regulates the peaceful in- and outflow of fertile women and ensures that the group's supply labour will be secure over long periods of time. In Meillassoux' constellation elders, freed from daily labour and its troubles, are of course eager to keep this influential and privileged position, and to legitimise their life at the expense of women and young men. This legitimation takes place through cultural ideology and ritual performance: thus, being determines consciousness. So, even life in non-industrial agricultural economies is inherently exploitative.

Meillassoux is pragmatic about this result: yes, he says, an original communism cannot be found in agricultural society, but it might still be expected beyond agriculture, among hunter-gatherer societies or, as he calls them, 'bands'. Here occasional voluntary membership substitutes filiation and dependency over generations, "children are adopted by members of the band as a whole" (1981, 16) and mobility is granted to everyone. In fact, the 'band' comes close to the "community of free individuals" that Marx imagined (2000 [1857/58], 113) - but one has to admit, however, that Meillassoux uses the 'band' merely as a foil for comparison, without further empirical research.

Maurice Godelier has certainly been the most productive and creative among the French Neo-Marxists. Among his numerous writings there is an ethnographic article from 1969, published in the journal *L'Homme*, which discusses the role of 'salt money' among the Baruya in New Guinea. There, salt is mainly produced as a commodity for trade and exchange with neighbouring groups. Inside Baruya society – which practises agriculture and pig breeding, is lineage-based and hierarchically organised – salt is limited to the sphere of prestigious goods and cannot be traded; salt production engages the whole group, although in different ways, and the final product is socially distributed according to strict rules. When exchanged to the outside salt becomes special-purpose money with specific exchange-rates; the latter are not imposed by a self-regulating market system, but by external political relations. Salt trade allows the Baruya to buy necessities, they are unable to produce themselves, but it also serves to avoid conflict and war. As salt trade is contained and socially controlled in two ways – internally and externally – social inequality, Godelier argues, does not entail exploitation.

French Neo-Marxism has sometimes been perceived as a technical and dogmatic approach; Sidney Mintz, who brought much of its ideas into the American discourse[4], stresses also the implicit moral motivation that lay behind it:

> The so-called 'natives' [...] are now often cane cutters, rubber tappers, pearl fishermen, storekeepers, or merchant seamen. Feathers and plumes have been replaced by hardhats and sunglasses, fiber skirts by denims and rags, preliteracy by illiteracy, rituals by movies, indigenous drinks by Coca

Cola. But social and cultural change have not ended; the history of such change is if anything, more important to understand now than ever before. The total passing of another world from view, however tragic, must be recorded. For many of us, it must be protested as well.

(Mintz, 1984, 30)

From the global margins towards the capitalist 'heart of darkness'

With Marshall Sahlins' essay "The original affluent society" capitalist discourse was directly addressed. The trigger was the work of John Kenneth Galbraith, an American economist and author of *The Affluent Society*, who hailed consumerism – the American way of life of the 1950s and 60s – as an unseen human achievement in a long-lasting emancipation from poverty and need. Thanks to economic development towards capitalism, he argued, all human needs could finally be satisfied. Sahlins, as much familiar with American Neo-Evolutionism as with French Structuralism and Neo-Marxism, took a different view: "[I]t was not until culture neared the height of its material achievements that it erected a shrine to the Unattainable: Infinite Needs" (1972, 39) – "all these Good Things within a man's reach – but never all within his grasp" (1972, 4). Based on much ethnographic material from Australia, Southern Africa and Tierra del Fuego he rehabilitated hunter-and-gatherer societies and their apparently inefficient 'subsistence economies'. Here, he argued, people did not live in poverty, as they were able to satisfy their needs while working less than peasantry or industrial labour force. Certainly, to live from fruits and game in the immediate surroundings required mobility in order to avoid "diminishing returns" (1972, 33). In other words, the 'good life' as it was defined here, did not allow the taking of more than one could carry. Thus, the lack of further material needs and things do no longer appear as a result of disability and impotence, but instead as the result of a deliberate political decision with all its consequences: their "policy of débarrassement" (1972, 33) also includes practices of infanticide and geronticide, or the killing of the elderly.

Although Sahlins analysis did not remain uncontested, his intellectual attack on Western ideology was well received among the young rebellious minds of the 1970s. According to Kurt Beck, Sahlins' collection of programmatic essays in *Stone Age Economics* (1972) prepared anthropology's cultural turn (Beck, 2001), and indeed anthropologists Igor Kopytoff, Nancy Scheper-Hughes, Jean and John Comaroff and, later, David Graeber would further develop this focus on culture as a means to understand economic phenomena. While Rosa Luxemburg had hoped that capitalism would eventually vanish with nothing left to sell (1990 [1925], 777–778), Igor Kopytoff argued that commodification, though a cultural process, tends to integrate more and more, so far exempted items into the market (1986). In the 1980s he was among the first to discuss the commodification of human ova and organs, a topic that Nancy Scheper-

Hughes and others carried on (2000). Jean and John Comaroff confirmed a global shift towards consumerist ideology. They sought to

> interrogate the experiential contradictions at the core of neo-liberal capit-
> alism, of capitalism in its millennial manifestation: the fact that it appears
> both to include and to marginalize in unanticipated ways; to produce
> desire and expectation on a global scale [...], yet to decrease the certainty
> of work or the security of persons; to magnify class differences but to
> undercut class consciousness; above all, to offer up vast, almost instanta-
> neous riches to those who master its spectral technologies – and, simulta-
> neously, to threaten the very existence of those who do not.
>
> (Comaroff and Comaroff, 2001, 8)

Freed from cold-war restrictions, 1990s neo-liberal capitalism disclosed its ideological character. Flexibility and uncertainty became the two opposing sides of a single coin. Economic anthropologist Keith Hart had described a similar phenomenon for urban Ghana already in the 1970s, when African states and economies were unable to provide formal and safe labour conditions to all the hopeful newcomers from the countryside (1997). Emerging informality did not only provide make-shift ways to survive (Lindell, 2010), but also invited unscrupulousness and, eventually, criminalisation (Bayart, Ellis and Hibou, 1993; Treiber, 2016). Crisis, after all, also includes chance and possibility (Mbembe, 2000). The arrival of economic crisis in the global North encour-aged anthropological fieldwork in the centres of global capitalism itself – yet another ethnographic 'heart of darkness'.

Financial crisis after 2007 resulted in massive redundancies; ironically also jobs in the financial sector became highly insecure. In her *Ethnography of Wall Street* (2009) Karen Ho describes bankers' "culture of liquidity" and "smartness" as ways to survive, but also to perform and to prove oneself. Caitlin Zaloom did her fieldwork at the 'Chicago Board of Trade (CBOT)' and at the 'London Inter-national Financial Futures Exchange' (LIFFE) years before the financial bubble burst. Her findings would also prove most disappointing to anyone who believed that the world's economic system is steered by wise and clear-sighted experts. She explicitly recurs to enlightenment's concept of rational economic man, morally disciplined, uplifted, and cleansed from any residual animal nature (2006, 112). Empirically she is unable to find anything else than the sheer opposite: To allow pure economic competition, traders consider social veneer an obstacle and primal animal-like aggression an essential feature.[5] Thus, Zaloom speaks of maverick individuals, who turn social bonds and values upside down.

> Each deal parades the speaker's masculine potency in front of other men.
> Where fucking is the rule, asociality reigns as a principal of action. Fucking
> and being fucked, both in sexual and financial terms, are shorthand for the
> use of one person for the pleasure or profit of another.
>
> (Zaloom, 2006, 123)

Zaloom considers an excessive Christmas party at which all male members of her trading company eventually strip of their clothes on the dance floor "an integral part of performing the style of economic man" (2006, 118). Traders' permanent showing-off and their self-disciplining submission to the demands of their profession go together. "The market is always right", they say (2006, 138). Whoever shows emotions – because of losses or private chagrin – will be punished by further losses. Trading demands constant presence of mind and separates traders from the space and time outside. Successful trading is not an effect of being well-informed or having a degree in business studies; it is the effect of decisions made immediately without the consideration of any other consequence than profit. Constant subjection to the rules of trade and market are "difficult and painful to maintain" (2006, 140), rendering professionals in the heart of capitalism into damaged and unhappy personalities, as one of her informants admits:

> When you have a profit, normally you'd get out, but because you're down money, you're trying to squeeze it, get more out of it. [You] turn into a loser. Hate yourself. Hate yourself. Consumed with self-hatred. I'd still be down money but instead I tried to squeeze it for another five hundred and now I lost seven hundred. Hate myself, threw my pen. Oftentimes I'll throw my pen. Just hate yourself.
>
> (Zaloom, 2006, 140)

Reaching out

It is no wonder, then, that Enlightenment's idea of man as a rational economic being who rightfully subdues the world and exploits its riches has been broadly challenged, especially since the world's most recent economic crisis. Economic anthropology and its long tradition of opposing a simplistic and speculative vision of human nature has once again become influential beyond disciplinary boundaries (e.g. Graeber, 2011).[6] Today, explanations of the state of the world can no longer be satisfyingly grounded in the alleged profit-maximising character of man. As Marshall Sahlins pugnaciously puts it:

> I am going against the grain of the genetic determinism now so popular in America for its seeming ability to explain all manner of cultural forms by an innate disposition of competitive self-interest. In combination with an analogous Economic Science of autonomous individuals devoted singularly to their own satisfactions by the 'rational choice' of everything, not to mention the common native wisdom of the same ilk, such fashionable disciplines as Evolutionary Psychology or Sociobiology are making an all-purpose social science of the 'selfish gene.'
>
> (Sahlins, 2008, 2)

Anthropology, in contrast to other disciplines, makes no claim to pin down man's nature. It can only show and reflect upon man's cultural variety, respective processes and conditions. There is no way of simply transferring alternative economic and political culture from the past or from the world's margins into modern complex life, says Hermann Amborn, who recently published on anarchist societies in southern Ethiopia (2016, 239–241). However, a century and a half of anthropological debate on local and global economic issues – debate that has exposed uneasy transformations, exploitations, expansions and catastrophes, but also alternative modes of production and circulation – stands also for a common goal: to rope in the unbound market and economy, and find concrete ways to re-establish joint social, cultural, and political control over them, wherever it got lost.

Notes

1 Individualism is the key to both aspects of liberalism, to its blessing of economic profit as well as to its support for individual rights and the prohibition of slavery.
2 Anarchistic societies that did not establish state authority and structures have long been a vividly discussed topic in political anthropology: see, for example, Edward E. Evans-Pritchard and Meyer Fortes (1940), Paul and Laura Bohannan (1968) or Pierre Clastres (2006 [1974]). More recently, James C. Scott (2009), David Graeber (2004) and Hermann Amborn (2016) have published on the topic.
3 Thomas Widlok provides another critique. He stresses that reciprocity may be expected, but is never guaranteed. What looks like a quasi-mechanical system of social solidarity, is a theoretical model after all – while real life may entail insecurity and uncertainty (2017, 1-29).
4 A similar contribution to American and global academic debate was made by Eric Wolf, author of the seminal book *Europe and the People Without History* (1997 [1982]). For the Latin American context see the more recent works of Alejandro Balazote and Hugo Trinchero (both 2007).
5 Characterised by 'pure', masculine , animal-like aggression Zaloom's "pit", the trading floor or dealing room reminds us very much of Clifford Geertz' description of the Balinese cockfight, a classical text of anthropological theory (1972).
6 The success of David Graeber's book *Debt: The First 5,000 Years* (2011) is just one prominent example of this trend. Graeber's book has become an international best-seller and has fuelled intellectual debate over the moral grounds of economic relations. While marketing and business psychology know both, the homo oeconomicus as well as the 'irrational consumer', 2017's Nobel prize winner in economics, Richard H. Thaler, questions pure profit seeking in his behavioural economics – mildly at least (2015).

References

Amborn, H. (2016). *Das Recht als Hort der Anarchie*. Berlin: Matthes & Seitz.
Balazote, A. (2007). *Antropología Económica y Economía Política*. Córdoba: Centro de Estudios Avanzados.
Bayart, J.-F., Ellis, S., and Hibou, B. (1999). *The Criminalization of the State in Africa*. Oxford: James Currey.
Beck, K. (2001). Marshall Sahlins. Stone Age Economics. In Ch. Feest, & K.-H. Kohl (Eds), *Hauptwerke der Ethnologie* (pp. 413–418). Stuttgart: Alfred Kröner Verlag.
Bohannan, P., and Bohannan, L. (1968). *Tiv Economy*. London: Longmans.

Bohannan, P., and Dalton, G. (1965). Introduction. In P. Bohannan, and G. Dalton (Eds), *Markets in Africa. Eight Subsistence Economies in Transition* (pp. 1–32). Garden City, NY: Anchor Books.

Clastres, P. (2006 [1974]). *Society Against the State*. Cambridge, MA: MIT Press.

Comaroff, J. and Comaroff, J. L. (2001). Millennial Capitalism. First Thoughts on a Second Coming. In J. Comaroff and J. L. Comaroff (Eds), *Millennial Capitalism and the Culture of Neoliberalism* (pp. 1–56). Durham: Duke University Press.

Engels, F. (1991 [1884]). Der Ursprung der Familie, des Privateigentums und des Staats. *Marx-Engels-Werke* (Vol. 21, pp. 25–173). Berlin: Dietz-Verlag.

Evans-Pritchard, E., and Fortes, M. (1940). *African Political Systems*. London: Oxford University Press.

Darwin, Ch. (2006 [1859]). *On the Origin of Species by Means of Natural Selection or the Preservation of Favoured Races in the Struggle for Life*. New York: Dover Publications.

Galbraith, J. K. (1958). *The Affluent Society*. New York: Mentor Book.

Geertz, C. (1972). Deep Play: Notes on the Balinese Cockfight. *Daedalus*, 191(1), 1–37.

Godelier, M. (1969). La 'monnaie de sel' des Baruya de Nouvelle-Guinée. *L'Homme*, 9(2), 5–37.

Godelier, M. (1984). To Be a Marxist in Anthropology. In S. Mintz, M. Godelier, and B. Trigger (Eds), *On Marxist Perspectives in Anthropology. Essays in Honor of Harry Hoijer 1981* (pp. 35–58). Malibu: Undena Publications.

Graeber, D. (2011). *Debt: The First 5,000 Years*. Brooklyn, NY: Melville House.

Graeber, D. (2004). *Fragments of an Anarchist Anthropology*. Chicago: Prickly Paradigm Press.

Hart, K. (1997 [1971]). Informal Income Opportunities and Urban Employment in Ghana. In R. Grinker, and C. Steiner (Eds), *Perspectives on Africa. A Reader in Culture, History and Representation* (pp. 142–162). Oxford: Blackwell Publishers.

Ho, K. (2009). *Liquidated. An Ethnography of Wall Street*. Durham: Duke University Press.

Kopytoff, I. (1986). The cultural biography of things. Commoditization as process. In A. Appadurai (Ed.), *The Social Life of Things. Commodities in Cultural Perspective* (pp. 64–92). Cambridge: CUP.

Krader, L. (1979). The Ethnological Notebooks of Karl Marx: A Commentary. In S. Diamond (Ed.), *Toward a Marxist Anthropology. Problems and Perspectives* (pp. 153–171). The Hague, Paris, New York: Mouton Publishers.

Lindell, I. (2010). Introduction. The changing politics of informality – collective organizing, alliances and scales of engagement. In I. Lindell (Ed.), *Africa's Informal Workers. Collective Agency, Alliances and Transnational Organizing in Urban Africa* (pp. 1–32). London, New York: Zed Books.

Locke, J. (1690). *Second Treatise of Government*. Retrieved from EBSCO Publishing eBook collection.

Luxemburg, R. (1990 [1925]). Einführung in die Nationalökonomie. In R. Luxemburg, *Gesammelte Werke* (Vol. 5, pp. 542–778). Berlin: Dietz-Verlag.

Marx, K. (2000 [1857/58]).). *Capital*. Available online at https://ebookcentral-1p roquest-1com- 10083958r1ec1.emedia1.bsb-muenchen.de

Mauss, M. (2008 [1925]). *The Gift. The Form and Reason for Exchange in Archaic Societies* [*Essai sur le Don*]. Abingdon: Routledge.

Mbembe, A. (2000). Everything can be Negotiated. Ambiguities and Challenges in a Time of Uncertainty. In B. Berner, and P. Trulsson (Eds), *Manoeuvring in an Environment of Uncertainty* (pp. 265–276). Aldershot: Ashgate.

Meillassoux, C. (1981 [1975]). *Maidens, Meal and Money. Capitalism and the Domestic Community.* Cambridge: Cambridge University Press.

Mintz, S. (1984). American Anthropology in the Marxist Tradition. In S. Mintz, M. Godelier, and B. Trigger (Eds), *On Marxist Perspectives in Anthropology. Essays in Honor of Harry Hoijer 1981* (pp. 11–34). Malibu: Undena Publications.

Morgan, L. H. (1877). *Ancient Society or Researches in the Lines of Human Progress from Savagery through Barbarism to Civilization.* London: MacMillan & Company.

Petermann, W. (2004). *Die Geschichte der Ethnologie.* Wuppertal: Peter Hammer Verlag.

Polanyi, K. (2001 [1944]). *The Great Transformation. The Political and Economic Origins of Our Time.* Boston: Beacon Press.

Raum, J. W. (1992). Evolutionismus. In H. Fischer (Ed.), *Ethnologie. Einführung und Überblick* (pp. 283–309). Berlin: Reimer.

Russell, B. (1950 [1945]): *Philosophie des Abendlandes. Ihr Zusammenhang mit der politischen und der sozialen Entwicklung.* Hamburg: Europaverlag.

Rediker, M., Linebaugh, P. (2000). *Many-Headed Hydra.* Boston, MA: Beacon Press.

Sahlins, M. (1972). The Original Affluent Society. In M. Sahlins, *Stone Age Economics* (pp. 1–39). Chicago: Aldine/Atherton.

Sahlins, M. (2008). *The Western Illusion of Human Nature.* Chicago: Prickly Paradigm Press.

Scheper-Hughes, N. (2000). The Global Traffic in Human Organs. *Current Anthropology,* 41(2), 191–224.

Scott, J. C. (2009). *The Art of Not Being Governed. An Anarchist History of Upland Southeast Asia.* New Haven: Yale University Press.

Smith, A. (2012 [1776]). *An Inquiry into the Nature and Causes of the Wealth of Nations.* Ware, Hertfordshire: Wordsworth.

Spencer, H. (1864). *The Principles of Biology,* Volume 1. London: Williams and Norgate.

Terray, E. (1972). *Marxism and 'Primitive' Societies. Two Studies.* New York: Monthly Review Press.

Thaler, R.H. (2015). *Misbehaving: The Making of Behavioral Economics.* London: W.W. Norton.

Treiber, M. (2016). Informality and Informalization among Eritrean Refugees: Why migration does not provide a lesson in democracy. In F. Cante and H. Quehl (Eds), *Handbook of Research on Transitional Justice and Peace Building in Turbulent Regions* (pp. 158–180). Hershey, PA: IGI Global.

Trinchero, H., and BalazoteA. (2007). *De la economía política a la antropología.* Buenos Aires: Eudeba.

Widlok, T. (2017). *Anthropology and the Economy of Sharing.* London: Routledge.

Wolf, E. (1997 [1982]). *Europe and the People without History.* Berkeley, Los Angeles: University of California Press.

Zaloom, C. (2006). *Out of the Pits. Trading and Technology from Chicago to London.* Chicago: University of Chicago Press.

Part II
Self-organized collective action and preservation of commons

3 Emergent collective action

Complexifying the world

Carlos Eduardo Maldonado

Introduction

Without going into any hierarchy or juxtaposition, we can safely say that the natural sciences are about what reality is, and what is nature. Physics, chemistry, mathematics and also computational science come along that concern. On the other side, the most basic assumption of the social sciences is about how we live, how we have lived, how we could live. The core of the issue is the balance or imbalance between what each individual considers to be good, right or rational, and the search for common goods, mutual benefit, agreement, alas, cooperation.

Collective action theory belongs to a triad that makes up probably the most important theory within the field of social sciences, namely, rational choice theory, game theory, and collection action theory.

Rational choice theory (RCT) is an understanding ranging from the standpoint of economics at large that studies the way in which human choices, whether individually or socially considered can be assessed as rational. Thus, rational choice theory stands on the theory of rationality, a most important philosophical and scientific theory that triggers, so to speak, all the explanations and understandings of choice in society and vis-à-vis nature. Naturally, the theory of rational choice has suffered a number of criticisms as well as changes and improvements that all have contributed to nurture and develop the theory further on.

Philosophically speaking, economics is not about trade, commerce, banking or expenses and production, for instance. On the contrary, economics is about the relationship between ends and means, thus, for example: is an end sufficient for any means to be set out in order to reach that end? Or else, the consideration about the means is necessary in order to set out a given end and to reach it?

Game theory (GT) is a theory from mathematical interest, closely related to RCT. Game, as it is well known, is the name coined to denote any interaction among human beings. The core of this theory is the distinction between cooperative and non-cooperative games, anchoring however on the issue whether the latter can be transformed, or give rise, to cooperative games. Game theory has enlarged its scope, and has thus made important contributions to numerous fields, such as ecology, landscape biology, or international relations, among others.

Philosophically speaking, mathematics is not about numbers, functions and shapes. Rather, it is about order and disorder, symmetries and asymmetries. If so, the focus lies in studying the relationships that enable or hinder symmetry or asymmetry.

Collective action theory (CAT) originates from politics and political science at large, and focuses on whether agreement is possible in the midst of the existence of free-riders, i.e. those who are not willing to pay their quota, so to speak, in order to attain the desired goal or agreement. The link that leads from game theory to collective action is exactly the possibility or the need to reach cooperative games and the hurdles arisen by free-riders. Surprisingly, the theory argues that any agreement is safely possible would free-riding not hinder the possibility of cooperation or agreement.

Philosophically speaking, politics is not about the state, a government or a given political regime. Instead, politics is about how life is possible within the framework of the polis. In other words, whether or not life is possible and how it is, in the middle of justice and injustice, agreement or disagreement, for instance.

A number of well-known and distinguished authors and research centers are to be mentioned along the lines above. The list, in any case, is well known by those truly concerned with the set of issues, items and problems that gather RCT, GT, and CAT. This is not a review chapter. Instead, I prefer to call the attention towards a different and novel aspect, namely *emergent collective action* (ECA). In order to do so, various arguments are required, thus: firstly, I shall summarize (traditional) CAT. A state-of-the-art about the concepts, concerns, and problems constitutive of CAT will enable to prepare the field for ECA.

The second argument consists in making clear what "emergence" means. This will open up the door, so to speak, to complexity science, which is the domain where emergent properties, emergent behaviors and emergent systems are properly understood. By so doing, hence, a bridge is set out that allows to bring classical CAT and complexity science, i.e. complexity theory. Joining both fields is important both for the understanding as well as for managing real situations in the world.

On this ground, emergent collective action will rightly exposed and discussed. The claim will be put forward arguing that leadership is possible without the existence of leaders, very much as strategy is possible without this entailing the need for a strategy to exist. Such apparent contradiction will be illustrated with examples ranging from ethology to politics, from economics to sociology. Emergent collective action is the type of action that corresponds to the ongoing world "out there", nowadays.

The final section of this chapter will be then devoted to synthesizing what our world actually is, so that science and research can shed new lights on the possibilities of life towards the future. The main challenge for humanity in the coming future consists in making herself possible in the long run. Nothing assures or warranties that such are or will be the case. ECA wants to be a concept and an action that seeks to make mankind possible on Earth. Making real such a possibility however truly means making possible life as-we-know-it very much as life-as-it-could-be.

(Classical) collective action theory: a state-of-the-art

As it is well known, the theory of collective action was originally formulated by Olson in an already classical book (1965). Since then, the theory has known important developments (Hardin, 1982; Sandler, 1992; Schutz and Sandy, 2012). The truth is that collective action (theory) is a vital and ongoing theory that is being enriched and enlarged growingly thanks to contributions from sociology and anthropology, political theory and international relations, economics and psychology, mainly.

The basic ground upon which the triad of RCT, GT, and CAT are bred is the theory of rationality that is articulated in two main domains, thus: a theory of explanation, and a theory of justification. The leading thread consists in the claim that, more often than thought, individual rationality is not sufficient for collective rationality. The crux of the discussion is then the relationship between ontological individualism versus methodological individualism. The bibliography on the subject, ranging from epistemology to the philosophy of science is large and rich. The origins of the discussion go back to the dawn of modernity in general, and to A. Smith in particular and his idea of the invisible hand of the market – a theory that invites us to re-consider his *Theory of Moral Sentiments*, rather than the often quoted and read *An Inquiry into the Nature and Causes of the Wealth of Nations*.

Typically, the Prisoner's Dilemma serves both as ground and motivation for studying issues concerning rational choice, cooperation or defeat, free-riding or collective action. The Prisoner's Dilemma stands on the rationale of Modernity's rationality, namely self-interest, selfishness or egoism. In other words, the issue concerns how individual rationality can lead or afford for collective rationality. The question then is how, if at all, is cooperation possible. Until Axelrod's work (1997) a key to solve the problem was not foreseen. We shall come back to Axelrod's contribution in the last section, below.

Now, the theory of collective action (CAT) focuses on when there will be individual action toward collective action. Therefore, CAT is not simply a theory of organized groups. Buchanan and Tullock's classical study (1965) sheds much better lights on the question about organizations, for example. More exactly, the main concern in CAT is about the provision of collective goods. According to Ostrom (1995), institutions evolve in order for such a provision to be possible or feasible.

Being as it may be, according to one author, the truth is that collective action is unquestionably successful "in predicting negligible voluntary activity in many fields" (Hardin, 1982, p. 11). Individual rationality is usually called as narrow rationality, and collective rationality is named as wide or bounded rationality (Elster, 1995). Straightforwardly said, individual rationality constitutes an obstacle for collective action.

Provided that individual rationality – i.e. preferences and expectations, beliefs and motives – is insufficient for collective rationality a series of considerations arise, thus:

- Is collective action voluntary, or else a government (i.e. institution) may have to provide or facilitate or boost the collective action?
- Can collective action be expected, and if so why and how, when and where?
- Individuals can be organized in different groups; if so, does the size of the group foster or hinder collective action?
- Is liberty, or need, or tragedy a condition for collective action? Why?
- Does the benefit for the group also warranty the benefit for each individual?
- Does symmetry or asymmetry of information play any role in collective action?

These questions have been the subject of study by anthropologists, social workers, politicians, economists, experts in communication systems, private corporate organizations as well as military, not to mention philosophers and managers. Not one single answer has been provided, but an array of different interpretations, replies, and commentaries. The theory of collective has known a number of ups and downs, of criticisms and reviews. Yet, the main problem consists currently in the very collective action that is taking place "out there" in the world, with a variety of forms, structures, justifications and forms of organization that – it appears – largely surpass the classical theory, as formulated by authors such as Olson. Literally, new forms of collective actions emerge that call for new understandings and explanations.

All in all, four main characteristics can be identified when dealing with classical TCA. Firstly, the TCA is centered around an instrumental human action and it points to solving problems pertaining collective action via the design of selective incentives – say, carrot and stick that make of human beings sort of pets. To be sure, this is the other side of the token of A. Smith's invisible hand.

Secondly, there are some interpretations, such as Parfit's (1981) and Sen's (2011) that solve the problem about the lack of cooperation throughout psychological solutions and volunteer changes. Another characteristic is the one that claims that it is important to show that human beings do cooperate in collective action as persons guided by meta-preferences, namely values and morality. In this third sense, Thompson (1971) and Hirschman (2002) strongly help support the debate, notwithstanding the moment when these two last works were originally written and published. Non-violent action arises here at the very core of the considerations.

Finally, Hardin (1982) clearly shows that collective action is not just a question regarding free riders, but it is grounded on the power of coordination. Hardin brings as examples and cases, among others, the experience of Paris Commune in 1848, and the amazing power of cooperation that generates decentralized and spontaneous collective actions in times previous to the information age and the social networks.

After the considerations stated above, we turn now our head to the concept of emergence.

The concept of emergence, revisited

The complexity of collective action arises firstly from the recognition of non-causality. Non-causal behaviors stand at the outset of collective action, in contrast to individual action, in many cases where causality pervades the explanations and understandings of individual agency. A strong contrast arises here from an epistemological point of view, namely, classical TCA stands very much along the same grounds as classical mechanics, or also, classical engineering. Causality reigns and pervades the explanations regarding human cooperation, or defeat.

To be sure, causality does exist but only under two provisos, thus: at the local level, and under controlled circumstances. Regardless of the science or discipline, causality is restricted and, at the same time, fostered by these two conditions. Outside of locality and controlled circumstances, causality ceases to exist. More specifically, at the level meso or macro – in the social world – causality becomes but a mere word – even if terms such as "multi-causality", "multi-varied analysis" or "multi-dimensional studies" are introduced, as it happens.

When non-causality takes place, emergence comes to the fore. Thus, emergent behaviors, emergent structures, and emergent agents have been taking the main roles in the change of the world, recently. Let's stop here for a while.

The world in which classical TCA arose was the world of the cold war - hence, the names of Th. Schelling and Olson, to name but two very conspicuous names. However, in the second decade of the twenty-first century, the world has been tagged differently. A number of appropriate, even though, different names have been coined, thus: the information society, the knowledge society, the network society, a non-zero-sum world, or also, the world of the fourth industrial revolution. Five different names for one and the same phenomenon, namely, a highly dynamic, increasingly unpredictable world, i.e. society – at large.

The concept "emergence" was originally introduced at the end of the nineteenth century by the biologist and the father of ecology, E. Haeckel (1834–1919), when particularly studying morphology. However, a wider and solid use of the concept took place only at the end of the twentieth century thanks to the work by J. Holland. In this sense, emergence is the concept that replaces causality when there is no direct (and causal) relationship between cause(s) and effect(s), and certainly the effect cannot be reduced to the input that causes it. The output is literally larger, ampler and more than what was considered at the input.

Indeed, the story of causality has four main moments, as follows:

- Initially, given a cause, we can find the effect of that cause. However, very soon, the effect was paid little attention, for the focus lied then in the question about the cause of the cause; and hereafter, the cause of the cause of the cause, and so on, until, with Aristotle, the question was about the "first cause" that was not cased herself. Christianity would eventually adopt such an understanding as the question about god – as the ultimate cause.
- A second stance regarding causality was the discovery that one and the same cause can have more than one effect. Historically speaking such a moment occurred around the discovery of America by the end of fifteenth century. However, very soon, again, the attention was displaced from the numerous effects to the question about the cause that originated those effects; and back to moment nr. 1.
- During the nineteenth century, the discovery was made that one effect could me originated by more than one cause. The concept of multi-causality, and multi-varied analysis was hence introduced. This third moment, nonetheless, did not supersede the question about the first un-caused cause.
- Finally, the recognition was made that the cause could be well known, very much as the effect itself could be easily identified – whether in the mode of the above different situations. However, no direct or explicit relation could be established between cause and effect. This is how, briefly said, the concept of emergence arose.

Now, the framework in which the concept of emergence has been adequately incorporated is complexity science, i.e. complexity theory, namely, the study of systems, phenomena and behaviors characterized by instability, fluctuations, perturbations, uncertainty, and non-linearity, among other properties. Thinking in terms of complexity entails henceforth not thinking about causality, any longer.

Much coming from little – that is the accurate and yet short comprehension of emergence (Holland, 1998). "We will not understand life and living organisms until we understand emergence". The concept of emergence allows seeing order where causality seems to be at odds and permits to discover a hidden order in chaotic behaviors.

In times of continuous and many times unpredictable change, human beings behave correspondingly non-linearly; in other words, in unexpected ways, creating new frameworks, or modifying the ones already existing, and establishing always new relations and structures that were previously unforeseen.

Strongly nonlinear interactions among different agents displace normal explanations and understandings based on average behavior, symmetry versus asymmetry configurations, interests versus expectations, and the like. If classical TCA was grounded on both justification theory as well as rational choice theory (Gauthier, 1998; Schweers Cook and Levi, 1990), emergence, i.e. complex theory considers a quite different view on rationality and intelligence, namely swarm intelligence. In order to explain what swarm intelligence consists of vis-à-vis collective action let us shift to the core of this chapter.

What is emergent collective action?

Bounded rationality sets up the entire field for collective action, when viewed from the tradition. This happens just because individual rationality is not enough for sustaining and making possible collective rationality. As a consequence, even though collective action is supposed to be voluntary, it is not the case that it can be (always) expected. The trouble is, hence, about the failure of collective action. It goes without saying that collective action is not precisely about a theory of organized groups – which is a quite different issue that concerns mainly politicians, religious leaders, and businessmen, mainly.

Classically speaking, the problem that gives rise to collective action theory lies in the importance or the role of the free-rider. Without the free-rider, it has been said, collective action is feasible and doable or attainable. This said, things seem to be much more complex, as it happens.

When studied from the standpoint of history, sociology or anthropology, for instance, the truth is that first come riots, parades, social upheaval, and then the organization; not the other way around. Now, upheavals and riots, for instance, are forms of collective action that were not considered as such by the classics (Olson, Ostrom, Hardin). If so, can CAT say something about phenomena such as the Chilean Students movement, the Arab Spring – in its manifold forms – Occupy Wall Street, or the Movement of Anti-Austerity, or also de Dignity Movement – to name but some? One thing seems to be clear in these forms of collective action, namely, strategy is possible without strategists, very much as leadership is possible without leaders – a most magnificent challenge for the theory, indeed. This is exactly what emergent collective action consists of.

Emergent collective action corresponds to what in terms of rationality we find as swarm intelligence. Originally coined by (Bonabeau, Dorigo and Theraulaz, 1999) and (Kennedy and Eberhart, 2001). Over against the tradition, swarm intelligence is a discipline within the sciences of complexity that explicitly assesses from the outset that thinking is social. Thus, the old discussion between ontological individualism versus methodological individualism does not stand here, any more.

Behaviors exhibiting swarm intelligence has been observed and studied among school-fish, flocks of birds, herds (zebras and antelopes), but also in problems of optimization, particle swarms (in the sub-atomic world), among others. Importantly, swarm intelligence does deal with issues regarding human behaviors, i.e. cooperative behavior (see Kennedy and Eberhart, 2001, Chapters

3 and 5). Swarm intelligence is a behavior that crosses nature and sub-atomic particles. Culture and politics and economics all alike, that is not to be identified merely with collective intelligence.

To be sure, swarm intelligence entails a collective behavior in which the individuals as such do not matter at all – in extremis, they do not exist by themselves – but they exist in function of the whole. Yet, the explanations about how such a collective behavior emerges is simple. Swarm intelligence is the outcome of self-organized systems. Thus, self-organization arises as the rationale for emergent collective behaviors.

In other words, there is not a plan, a strategy, a program set out at the beginning, but a series of possibilities, hurdles, troubles, spaces that give rise to swarm intelligence simply because each individual gets a higher or better profit together with the swarms than if he or she would act on its own.

Self-organization is a concept that both crosses chemistry and biology, social systems and physics, biochemistry and even mathematics, that serves to explain that under certain circumstances, a behavior is possible that does not need nor grounds on traditional explanations – such as deliberation, agreements, preferences, choices – whether rational or not -, cognitive assessments, and the like. On the contrary, self-organization happens spontaneously provided a number of basic conditions.

Among those conditions or explanations, we have: Boolean networks, autocatalytic networks, B-Z equations in chemistry and biochemistry, self-organized criticality (SOC) as explained by Bak, or nonlinear interactions among various agents. 'Agent' here is the technical term used to denote human beings, animals, and other systems and organisms. Whereas the classical theory of collective action understands collective action as a sort of strategy (Schelling, 1981), both-self-organization and emergence allow for a complex view in which the usual individual-social interactions are taken as motives for rationally improving the world (Ostrom, 1995): the care for the environment and ecological concerns has been numerously times – not without good reasons – as sound triggering for collective action.

More radically, whereas classical TCA is typically anthropocentric or anthropomorphic, swarm intelligence, and hence ECA can be said bio-centric, eco-centric, or also, matter-and-energy centric. The suffix certainly plays here an odd role, for it could suggest the idea of a centrality, something that clearly does not exist in nature and reality.

Emergence and self-organization arise, then, as two very much intertwined concepts suitable for explaining nonlinearity. In other words, it is about the concern for situations and problems that admit more than one solution, where traditional strategies such as priorization, maximization, optimization, choose of second-best alternatives and others alike – become simple irrelevant if not impossible. Self-organization and emergence are complex concepts that correspond to complex times, behaviors and a complex world.

Emergent collective action (ECA) is, therefore, a form of self-organization that spontaneously happens that radically shapes the very space and time of human actions, and organization. Straightforwardly said, space and time are changed as emergent collective actions takes place. Undoubtedly, the new technologies – mobile phones, social networks, Internet, and more largely the web 2.0 and the web 3.0 – do contribute for the mode and speed of emergent collective action among human beings, even though such a new form of collective action does not entirely depend on the new techs. Gathering, discussing, acting stand as the real factor that fosters or boosts, as well as catalyzes and maintains collective cooperation.

Now, learning – moreover, continuously learning and reflecting on events as they happen – is a condition *sine qua non* for emergent collective action to stay and endure. Permanent communication, continuous networking, and an active personal participation in assemblies, meetings, and reunions are very active practices through which learning does take place. Learning arises thereafter as a condition for adaptation. Emergent collective action are highly adaptive behaviors, indeed.

This point should be highlighted, namely the very recognition that ECA is an adaptive collective behavior – which, furthermore, suits very well the very idea of swarm intelligence – whence sustainable in time. The Achilles tendon of classical CAT is the sustainability of collective action in time. The crux of the issue is and remains always the permanence in time of collective cooperative behaviors. ECA does provide for good solutions and examples that pervade nature, society and animals, for instance. At the lowest levels of life and living organisms, Strassmann, Zhu, and Queller (2000), have studied the importance of collective action and temporality among a specific kind of bacteria.

Even though emergent collective actions arise spontaneously, it becomes a steady adaptive action in time thanks to the correspondingly emergent learnings achieved permanently. Self-organized local movements ranging from Japan to Italy, from Germany to France, from Mexico to the United States, for example, are becoming and have become alternative social movements that regularly meet, discuss, network, and learn from their own experience as well as from other similar social movements around the world. Roughly said, the internet serves as a ground for sharing their memories and learnings as well as keeping collective action alive. Olson's works, to name but one, are pre-internet – whence his worries about the failure of collective action.

When emergent collective action happens, the very experience is that the social system integrates and unifies much more than individuals: the common concern, the common goals and targets, the common assets and experiences are what truly matters; not only at the end of the day but form the very outset of collective action.

Selfishness (over against all the traditional studies around the Prisoner's Dilemma) simply does not take place, so the free-rider is excluded from the very beginning when considering emergent collective action. The ZADs (*Zone à Defendre*) in France; the water movement in Italy; the search for alternative space movements, in Japan; the anti-consumerism movements, in the U.S.; the Zapatist movement, in Mexico – to name but just a few emergent collective movements around some places in the world are clear examples of the reflections that precede and illustrates how and when emergent collective actions happens. Studying each experience would be the subject of a different text (chapter).

An argument for some cases about ECA

There are some good examples all around the world that allow understanding what ECA is and how it takes place. Openly said, ECA are alternative ways of collective action, i.e. non-institutionalist ways of action and organization. More radically said ECA are forms of resistance, if not of rebellion and transgression, over against the past and the prevailing ways of living, of economics, and politics.

Emergent collective action has been observed in a number of places, not just the ones just mentioned (ZAD, etc.). The most recent of these actions takes place in Catalonia in the framework of the fight for its independence. Numerous local organizations – neighbors, peasants, trade-unions, students' organizations, and even some political parties – such is most notably the case of CUP (Popular Unity Candidacy), one of the most radical political parties in Catalonia –, are creating brand new forms of organizations, actions, and initiatives that firmly correspond to ECA. These forms, however, are very rarely reported in the grand mass-media (see: www.elcritic.cat/blogs/sergipicazo/2017/09/26/the-catalan-revolt/ and https://societatcivilcatalana.cat/es/noticias/insurreccion-y-desastre).

In Japan, a growing alternative movement has been emerging since at least 2010 that openly reject militarism and antinuclear demonstrations. This movement has been mainly triggered by young people in an atmosphere of rock and songs that clearly brings out the importance of local leaders (for a thorough view, see: http://apjjf.org/2016/13/Oguma.html).

In Italy, a fantastic feat has been studied, namely the emergence of social movements within organizations (Draege, Chironi, and della Porta, 2016), i.e. parties. Such a phenomenon has taken place also in Turkey. In other words, an institutional stance such as political parties are been "subverted" so to speak in order to allow for more flexible actions and organizations that express new feelings and sentiments of a large amount of population. As mentioned above, riots precede organizations, not the other way around. Either new organizations are locally created, or else also nee movements within organizations are emerging that express new forms of collective action.

In the three cases mentioned self-management is a salient feature that both expresses new complex forms of actions as well as the very complexification of collective actions as it was previously known. In Australia, to mention one case, self-management is a conspicuous form of ECA (cf. www.uow.edu.au/~bmartin/pubs/98tk/tk15.html). However, self-management is not an exclusive experience in Australia, but is has been studied and developed in a number of places.

In Chile, a singular combination is currently taking place, thus: the Chilean student movement joints plans, experiences and programs together with the Mapuche movement, the Feminist movement and the Environmental movement. (As is well known, Chile is one of the countries where violence against women is very high, and the opportunities for education correspond to such violence (Donoso and von Büllow, 2017).) As general trend, these movements can be understood either as left-winged or also as alternative.

Now, it should be noted that all these alternative movements are critical against capitalism, (neo)-liberalism, or the free-market system – as you wish. The cases mentioned are just a very small show of a truly large and growing sample of new actors, new movements and forms of collective action around the world. The common trait that defines them all is that they are local movements, local forms of collective action. Yet, many of those movements are clearly interconnected with each other, they learn continuously from others' experiences, and unceasingly study their own process vey much as the processes of other alternative movements in other countries.

The list of cases that support the argument for ECA is large and growing, indeed. Here I just want to bring some illustrations that help understand the very concept introduced here. It would be the subject of a different paper to focus solely on the cases of ECA. That list does include a number of movements in countries as varied as Brazil (www.brasilwire.com/brazilian-social-m ovements/), Mexico (http://enlacezapatista.ezln.org.mx), or India (www.the betterindia.com/18248/most-powerful-social-citizens-movements-in-india/) among many others.

Without any doubt, in the midst of internet and computer-savvy activists, Anonymous can be said to be a movement (the call themselves a "legion") of non-violent ECA – in a world that calls for a hacker mindset and reckons the importance of information and alternative political actions in a cyber world (see: http://anonhq.com). As they call it, "anonymous is an idea".

Anti-capitalist as they may be, nonetheless, it should be highlighted by all means that the movements mentioned are absolutely non-violent collective action. Yes, resistance does happen, very much as rebellion or even insurrection; yet, non-violence the landmark of ECA.

Humanity's most astounding challenge ever: conceiving and making future possible

As studied by Axelrod in an agent-based modelling, long term interactions "force" us to cooperation (Axelrod, 1977). Time arises hence as the rationale for cooperation, and therefore for collective action. Such radically changes are all considerations about any theory of collective action.

I would like to make explicit here a tacit assessment in classical CAT, thus: the time span of classical collective action theory is a human, period; moreover, an individually human – no more no less. Under such a proviso, collective action is to fail, nearly inevitably. This means, the time span will always be short-sighted, so to speak. Vis-à-vis such a perspective, it should be clear that most if not all recent alternative social movements that exhibit emergent collective action take as emotional, theoretical or practical experience the relationship with nature – either in environmental-like issues and concerns, in ecological reflections and practices, and other similar tenets.

The observation just made entails that classical collective action theory is basically anthropocentric. In contrast, most of alternative emergent collective action are more and more rather bio-centric, or eco-centric – being the suffix a serious linguistics problem here, though. It is nature that teaches us a time span wonderfully much more complex than the mere human time scale. Emergent collective action arises in the framework of a naturalistic – earth-like – and even cosmic consideration of time. Emergent collective action arises at the hinge of true civilizatory change we are currently facing nearly everywhere around the globe. The cornerstone of such a change consists in the shift from a mere human time span to a wider and deeper time scale, nature's – the entire weave of life – life-as-we-know-it, and life-as-it-could-be-possible.[1]

Briefly said, history is what happens when nature allows us to.

Humanity faces actually a most challenging and compelling defy that no previous age had ever known, namely her own survival as a whole, making future possible given the systemic and systematic crises that are ongoing in front and around us all. It is my contention in this text that emergent collective action is possible (to be understood and acted) within the frame of the survival of humanity – if not life as a whole.

As it follows from the above, emergent collective action means a collective action that, nonetheless, is sustainable in time. It is true that emergent collective action arises spontaneously, but it is also true – there is no contradiction here – it is the kind of collective action that learns and adapts – hence, unceasingly – to brand new experiences, brand new interactions, and brand-new learnings.

This said, this text is far away from doomsday arguments or also from Millenarialism claims (Cohn, 1983). According to those worldviews, we would be facing the end of humanity as such, and the disappearance of all known form of life due to what euphemistically has been called as the "Anthropocene" – which is currently producing the sixth massive extinction. We certainly face challenges and threats but not the end. It is just the end of a civilization. Now, given the fact that mankind is nowadays living in a non-zero-sum world, the vanishing of a civilization might imply the end of nearly of cultures and peoples. Evidences, however, must be provided in this direction.

Being as it may be, for the first time in history, the future is not given, and definitely not given beforehand and for sure. Mankind must build it or plant it – two quite different takes, though. (One is centered on the capacities and capabilities of human beings; the other is grounded on planting, waiting, taking care, having patience, loving, and observing the time of nature).

Now, caring for future is a question that concerns many if not all of us. Whence, collective action encounters a real robust rationale. It is exactly because the future is not given beforehand, but is rather uncertain, that collective action is emergent – that means not-planned, not a subject of strategy, not a question of symmetry versus asymmetry of information, for example. The game has changed once the rules have changed completely

A non-conclusive conclusion

The story of concepts – very much as well as that of metaphors – goes hand in hand very much with the very story of behaviors, systems, and phenomena. A realist standpoint would claim that reality always precedes – and surpasses – science, by and large. Science comes, like Hegel's owl, at the end of the day, when the sunset is coming by and the moon sheds her first rays on earth. In contrast, a more organic and vivid view allows grasp that concepts – and metaphors – are basically contemporary. Generally said, each moment in history creates the science it needs and allows, very much as each science both shapes and mirrors the very period it arises in and contributes to create.

Whether we like or not, whether we agree or not, the world has become increasingly complex. Therefore, new concepts, tools, approaches and languages are necessary and start to be coined, here and there. If an analogy is permitted here, very much as thermodynamics knows of two moments, classical thermodynamics and non-equilibrium thermodynamics, in the same tenure, the theory of collective action faces two moments – the classical theory of collective action and the emergent collective action. Strategy, leadership, interactions have completely changed, for good, it appears.

Time is the most crucial issue for life, if not for human life alone. The story of the frog that is boiling in the pot, slowly, without her noticing it, has been told one and thousand times to warn about the global challenges life is facing nowadays. However, for the first time in history, the concern about time is not merely a human affair, but a matter that finds as its target or output, so to speak, the entire weave of life.

New forms of cooperation are demanded and being made possible that defies the classical theories and models about human action – whether individually considered or socially studied. It goes without saying that the input of the action belongs to mankind. But for the first time on earth, the output are not the human beings themselves, but nature as a whole. This is exactly the reason why we call here for emergent collective action because our world has become magnificently complex. A complex world asks for correspondingly complex interpretations, forms of organization and interactions.

Note

1 The distinction, and in fact, the very concepts "life-as-we-know-it", and "life-as-it-could-be-possible" arise originally within the framework of artificial life (AL). The main idea here is the difference between a naturalistic understanding and approach to life, and the one based on modelling and simulation. The biological sciences, f.i. fall within the same scope as the social and human sciences vis-à-vis the first consideration. On the contrary, taking up life in the second tenure entails the study of as many

phase spaces as possible. To be sure, swarm intelligence is a discipline closely inter-twined with complexity science at large and with artificial life in particular.

Acknowledgements

The author of this chapter wish to thank two anonymous reviewers for their critical comments and suggestions that truly helped us understand better our own text and purpose. Their criticisms were just, accurate and sharp, which is an evidence of their good common sense and knowledge.

References

Axelrod, R. (1997). *The complexity of cooperation: agent-based modeling of competition and collaboration*. Princeton, NJ: Princeton University Press.
Bonabeau, E.Dorigo, M.Theraulaz, G. (1999). *Swarm Intelligence. From Natural to Artificial Systems*. New York, Oxford: Oxford University Press.
Buchanan, J.M. and Tullock, G. (1965). *The Calculus of Consent. Logical Foundations of Constitutional Democracy*. Indianapolis: Liberty Fund, Inc.
Cohn, N. (1983). *The Pursuit of the Millennium: Revolutionary Milenarians and Mystical Anarchists of the Middle Ages*. Oxford: Oxford University Press.
Donoso, S.von Büllow, M. (eds.), (2017). *Social Movements in Chile. Organization, Trajectories, and Political Consequences*. Berlin: Springer Verlag.
Draege, J.B.Chironi, D. and della Porta, D. (2016). "Social Movements within Organizations: Ocuupy Parties in Italy and Turkey", *South European Society and Politics*, 22, 2, pp. 139–156.
Elster, J. (1995). *The Cement of Society. A Study of Social Order*. Cambridge: Cambridge University Press.
Gauthier, D. (1998). *Egoísmo, moralidad y sociedad liberal*. Barcelona: Paidós.
Hardin, R. (1982). *Collective Action*. Baltimore and London: The Johns Hopkins University Press.
Hirschman, A.O. (2002). *Shifting Involvements: Private Interest and Public Action*. Princeton, NJ: Princeton University Press.
Holland, J. (1998). *Emergence. From Chaos to Order*. Reading, MA: Helix Books.
Johnson, S. (2001). *Emergence. The Connected Lives of Ants, Brains, Cities, and Software*. New York: Scribner.
Kennedy, J., and Eberhart, R.C. (2001). *Swarm Intelligence*. New York: Morgan Kaufman Publishers.
Klein, N. (2008). *The Shock Doctrine. The Rise of Disaster Capitalism*. New York: Picador.
Klein, N. (2009). *No Logo*. New York: Picador.
Maldonado, C.E. (2000). *Sociedad civil, racionalidad colectiva y acción colectiva*. Bogotá: Ed. Universidad Libre.
Olson, M. (1965). *The Logic of Collective Action*. Cambridge, MA: Harvard University Press.
Ostrom, E. (1995). *Governing the Commons. The Evolution of Institutions for Collective Action*. Cambridge: Cambridge University Press.
Parfit, D. (1981). *Prudence, Morality, and the Prisoner's Dilemma*. Reprinted in Jon Elster (Ed.), *Rational Choice*. New York: NYU Press.
Sandler, T. (1992). *Collective Action. Theory and Applications*. Ann Arbor: The University of Michigan Press.

Schelling, Th. (1981). *The Strategy of Conflict.* London: Wiley & Sons.

Schutz, A. and Sandy, M. (2012). *Collective Action for Social Change: An Introduction to Community Organizing.* London: Palgrave MacMillan.

Schweers Cook, K. and Levi, M. (Eds), (1990). *The Limits of Rationality.* Chicago and London: The University of Chicago Press.

Sen, A. (2011). *The Idea of Justice.* Cambridge, MA: Harvard University Press.

Strassmann, J.E.Zhu, Y. and Queller, D.C. (2000). "Altruism and social cheating in the social amoeba Dictyostelium discoideum", *Nature*, 408, 965–967.

Thompson, E.P. (1971). "The Moral Economy of the English Crowd in the Eighteen Century", *Past and Present*, 50, pp. 76–136.

4 Self-organized collective action in the Floating Island Project

Nathalie Mezza-Garcia

Introduction

Elinor[1,2] Ostrom's (1990) work is widely recognized for having approached governance of the commons. However, Henry & Dietz's (2011) point on how there is still a long way before Ostrom's work on the governance of the commons is taken more broadly and seriously in environmental settings, despite that many environmental problems are, in fact, problems of the commons. That is, where there are limited shared resources, such as water systems, the ecosystem and the environment. This chapter is concerned with the Floating Island Project, a human settlement to be built on the ocean of French Polynesia in 2019, where voluntary forms of governance proposed to organize it, I claim, are collective action solutions for dealing with shared limited resources (Olson 2009; Ostrom, 2010). Before venturing any further, it is worth noting that, for the purposes of this research, the notion of governance is understood as "the attempt to steer society and the economy through collective actions and forms of regulation that link values and objectives to outputs and outcomes" (Torfing, 2012, p. 3). In other words, "governance as the complex art of steering multiple agencies, institutions, and systems that are both operationally autonomous from one another and structurally coupled through various forms of reciprocal interdependence" (Jessop, 1997, p. 1).

Essentially, what I illustrate in what follows is how the form of decentralized governance proposed by Blue Frontiers, the private company in charge of building the Floating Island Project, which emphasizes the importance of bottom-up emergence self-organized dynamics and interactions, is a self-organized form of collective action, despite that the political economy that inspired it, libertarianism, is usually associated with individual endeavors. Approaching the Floating Island Project as a case study attempts at extending existing work on forms of governance that present the properties of complex systems. Due to space reasons, however, specific discussions on complexity are out of consideration. For that Maldonado (2013), Maldonado & Mezza-Garcia (2016), Mainzer (2007), Bar-Yam (2009), Schuster (2004), Mezza-Garcia (2013a, 2013b) and Zia et al. (2014) have elaborated arguments in the direction of complexity and governance in more elegant ways. Yet, from complexity science I take the concepts of self-organization and emergence in relation of the Floating Island. As we shall see, for the case study of the Floating Island, the concepts of self-governance and self-organization and emergence are highly relevant, as they can explain how organization and, therefore, governance, in complex systems emerge properly without any central control by local information processing dynamics that in bottom-up ways give way to nested hierarchies or heterarchies (see: Mezza-Garcia, forthcoming). Self-organized governance, and, in particular, voluntary governance, is a position that defends the existence of mechanisms that increase the degrees of freedom in complex societies.

In what follows, I expand on the political aspects of the Floating Island Project as a case of seasteading and an illustration of complex voluntary governance and self-organized collective action. I start with a chronological account of the project. I then describe the legal regulatory framework for the current stage of the Floating Island Project, emphasizing on its environmental and economic concerns and how they relate to voluntary complex governance and self-organized collective action. In sum, this chapter introduces the case study of the Floating Island Project and the key political strands that run throughout its development, which speak to the broader scope of nonviolent forms of political action. In order to build the argument, in the second section of this chapter I introduce the Floating Island Project and follow with it an account of the chronology and the political economy behind such a state-of-the-art technological and political endeavor in the second section. In the third section I present the environmental and economic evaluations that influence the planning and construction of the Floating Island, followed by a section on decentralized governance. This leads the way to the final section on complex voluntary governance and final concluding remarks.

The Floating Island Project

This section introduces the Floating Island Project. The floating Island Project is an example of "seasteading" – a term coined by Gramlich (1998) to contrast with ´homesteading´, emphasizing the notion of human settlements floating on the ocean (instead of land). Typically, seasteading involves the establishment of permanent, autonomous communities on the sea (Friedman & Taylor, 2012) and the creation of new technologies for floating platforms that serve various ends, such as housing, industry, research, medicine, food production, energy and fresh water management, among others (Friedman & Taylor, 2010; Quirk, 2017a; Simpson, 2016a, 2016b; White, 2012). At this point, seasteading is a theoretical concept, insofar as there are no complete seasteads in existence yet. That said, there are several seasteading projects, which are in their infancy, of which the Floating Island Project is currently the most advanced, even though it is still being planned and construction has not yet started.

The technological vision of the Floating Island project is to build high-tech autonomous floating cities, starting in the Pacific Ocean -in French Polynesia.

The Floating Island Project stems from a 2017 agreement between The Seasteading Institute, a non-profit think tank located in Palo Alto, California, and the French Polynesian government. The project has officially been defined as "an innovative and low environmental impact concept for bringing new technologies, research horizons and economic activities to Polynesia" (NA, 2017, p. 7). The Floating Island will be composed by smaller detachable islands, which will use a range of innovative and green technologies for food production, fresh water refinement, energy and waste management, and floating platform development.

The political long-term vision underpinning the Floating Island is that it is a first step in the creation of micronations in the open ocean (Friedman & Gramlich, 2009). Furthermore, as Quirk (2017a, p. 31) notes, the aim is that it is possible to "disassemble and assemble [the micronations] according to the choices of the citizens", both physically and politically. In other words, it is not only that the Floating Island Project is an example of kind of spaces for human settlements on the oceans, but that these spaces have both political and physical freedom to be reconfigured as desired. The flexible political and physical arrangements enabled by the lack of boundaries in the ocean and the detachable platforms is expected to decrease the possibilities of the monopolies in governance that land-based nations establish in one territory (Friedman & Taylor, 2012; The Seasteading Institute, 2014).

Authors such Bakunin (1970), Friedman (1989) and Rothbard (1978) consider this ad-hoc authority of states over a territory based on submission and the use of force as illegitimate. I agree. From this that the philosophy and the political economy behind future seasteads, including the Floating Island, is that individuals are able to "vote with their feet" (De Soto, 1998; Lynch, 2017); that is, they can move to alternative settlements of their choice in the face of dissatisfaction with the governance where they are. Hopefully, voting with their feet would allow individuals to benefit from one of the key factors driving the creation of seasteads, which is that this give rise to an explosion in diversity of different governance structures.[3] These governance structures can, indeed, vary across the whole spectrum of possible regulations and, as it happens, gives rise to several important concerns. For example, to what extent do seasteads, including the Floating Island, allow for new kinds of non-hierarchical political relations? From a political point of view, it is also relevant to enquire how might new kinds of flexible and decentralized structures lead to the emergence of new forms of bottom-up and complex voluntary governance? And how, as well, might the flexible legislation and regulations that frame seasteads enable new forms of bottom-up and self-organized governance? These questions are the background focus of this chapter.

As will be further discussed below, the interest in a political economy for new types of human settlements based on alternative types of non-hierarchical forms of governance is in line with a number of current debates which argue that hierarchical modes of decision-making do not always provide optimal solutions in complex environments (Bar-Yam, 2009; Gerrits, 2012; Mainzer, 2007; Room, 2016; Schuster, 2004; Wachhaus, 2012, 2014). As such, this research contributes to the work related to non-hierarchical forms of governance in complex environments.

The environmental motivations of building the Floating Island Project are contained in the document Memorandum of Understanding. The Memorandum of Understanding mentions that the Seasteading Institute has the economic feasibility, the technologies and networks to tackle these two aspects. This backs the intention of French Polynesia to obtain them in exchange of the legal protection for the seastead and a place in its territory. A beautiful example of diplomacy and interesting exchange. The first part of the Memorandum of Understanding contains the motivations of both parts. It explains why the French Polynesian government sees in the creation of floating islands a way to comply with the Taputapuatea Declaration on Climate Change, P.A.C.T. –Polynesian Against Climate Threats (Polynesian Leaders Group, 2015), which expresses the concerns of the Polynesian Leaders Group regarding the vulnerability of their territories in the face of global warming due to sea level rise.[4] The P.A.C.T. also mentions how one third of the world´s small islands that are sinking are located in the in the pacific –despite their insignificant contribution to climate change. It emphasizes the threatening implications that would follow rising sea levels on the identities of Polynesian people as a collective that historically has been intimately integrated with the ocean and nature. In fact, due to their millennial maritime heritage Polynesians call themselves *the people of the canoe.*

Similarly, in the Memorandum of Understanding, The Seasteading Institute condenses its motivation for building floating islands. Namely, how the development of floating islands is a way to help countries with problems of water rising levels, poverty and overpopulation. The P.A.C.T. also calls for the respect of the request of Polynesian leaders of Large Oceanic States and Territories for their shared 10 million square kilometers ocean, which Polynesians call Te Moana o Hiva, to be recognized as their Exclusive Economic Zone. The purpose of this is for them to protect its ecologic, human and economic resources and being able to support in a more controlled way Small Island States and territories[5]. Hence the strategic commitment of the Polynesian government expressed in the Memorandum of Understanding to join "every effort to preserve the natural and cultural Polynesian heritage and thus become the world´s showcase for sustainable development" (Polynesian Leaders Group, 2015, p. 5). This is the main reason for locating in French Polynesia the Floating Island Project. In other words, the problems that the Floating Island Project seeks to tackle are problems of the commons. The fact that the Seasteading Institute is libertarian and that Blue Frontiers is a private company reflects how this political economy does not necessarily needs to be linked with critiques that associate it as an extremely individualistic philosophy (see: Steinberg et al., 2012).

Chronology of the Floating Island Project

To date, the development of the Floating Island Project can be divided in three main stages: a) the Floating City Project, from 2008 to 2016; b) the Floating

Island Project, from 2017 to 2020, and c) the Open Ocean Seasteading, with an undetermined date of starting, but beyond 2021 (see Table 4.1 below). Although the three stages are important to speak about the background political economy of the Floating Island Project, this chapter focuses mostly on the second stage. This is partly because the third stage has not yet happened, partly because this is there is a gap that has not been addressed from an academic point of view regarding the second stage, and partly because the current initial stage of the project provides an opportunity in researching new kinds of political spaces as it happens and they develop in real time. There is an additional stage of seasteading driven by the Blue Frontiers Global Contest (2018), held in partnership with the Nuhanse Network, which aims to bring seasteads to several places of the world. The resulting seasteads from the contest, nevertheless, are out of consideration for this piece of research and do not interact directly with the Floating Island Project. Hence, because the focus of my research is essentially on the second stage, most of this chapter is concerned with introducing this part of the case study and how does it speak to complex voluntary forms of governance as self-organized forms of collective action. That said, by

Table 4.1 Chronology of the Floating Island Project

	Stage 1 Floating City Project		Stage 2 Floating Island Project	Stage 3 Seasteading
	Seasteading	**Host Nation**	**Floating Island Project**	**Open Ocean**
Years	2008–2011	2011–2016	2017–2022	Blue Frontiers Global Contest & Open ocean seasteads
Location			French Polynesia	Open ocean and international waters (possibly –or not– swarming with the flag of French Polynesia)
Led by	The Seasteading Institute, online community forum	The Seasteading Institute, online community	The Seasteading Institute, Blue Frontiers, French Polynesian government	Blue Frontiers and others…
Politics	Libertarian	Libertarian	Neutral, Special Economic Zone, polycentric law, autonomous	Heterarchical and anarchic

(Author's own elaboration)

way of context, it worth briefly outlining the first stage as it provides the historical foundations, and is already relatively well documented.

The first stage of the Floating Island Project is referred to as the Floating City Project and started in 2008 with the creation of The Seasteading Institute. Ideologically, The Seasteading Institute was the result and has been influenced by a family of libertarian thinkers. One of its founding members is Patri Friedman, the grandson of Rose and Milton Friedman (1990); Milton Friedman being the winner of the 1976 Nobel Memorial Prize in Economics. Patri Friedman is also the son of David Friedman, author of *The Machinery of Freedom* (1989), a work that has influenced current views on libertarianism[6] (Johnston, 2005; Nozick, 2013; Parijs, 1997; Vallentyne, 2000). According to Rothbard (1978), libertarianism consists on reducing the role of the states to their minimal expression. Friedman´s libertarianism specifically focuses on the individual capacity to self-govern and for non-state actors to be in charge of governance service provision and legal affairs; and therefore, it argues against the monopoly of governance by nation-states. This is why the word anarchism is embedded in the word anarcho-capitalism, which is another way to refer to libertarianism. The advocacy for the emergence of new nodes of laws and arbitration, voluntary governance and political self-organization are the three aspects of Friedman´s (1989) libertarianism that directly influence the Floating Island Project. I claim that voluntary forms of governance can lead to harmonic interactions from a political and governance point of view.

The Seasteading Institute´s was financially boosted in 2010 by a donation of 1.7 million US dollars by Peter Thiel, who made his fortune in Silicon Valley with PayPal and investing in Facebook. The aim of this contribution was to advance in the creation of a seastead in international waters. Later between 2011 and 2014, following studies made by the Institute (Mutabdzija & Borders, 2011; The Seasteading Institute, 2014) which showed the technical and political challenges of this goal a decision was made by the board and Randolph Hencken, back then the Executive Director of the Seasteading Institute, to look for a host nation.

The advantage of having a host nation has two main key benefits. Firstly, economically, being close to a nation tends to facilitate trade, which can lead to lower prices in exportations and importations if being part of the Exclusive Economic Zone of that country, where the territorial waters cannot "exceed beyond 200 nautical miles from the baselines from which the breadth of the territorial sea is measured" (United Nations, 1982, p. 38). Secondly, politically, being attached to a specific nation means having a flag, which, in turn, translates into protection from other nations, not needing an army to depend on, for instance, against pirates, and not undergoing bureaucratic procedures for seeking autonomy or recognition nor sovereignty from other nations or a sit in the United Nations (Mutabdzija & Borders, 2011). As Marty and Borders explain:

> seasteads will have to operate within broader international legal frameworks. Some seasteads may, in fact, integrate themselves into jurisdictions that will, in turn, impose certain constraints on a seasteader's ability to

innovate law. However, seasteaders who locate outside the territorial waters of sovereign states will have broad discretion in designing and implementing rulesets that are the formative bases of new law.

(Marty & Boarders, 2011, p. 11)

Additionally, there are logistical and engineering issues that come with seasteading in the open ocean, generated by environmental concerns such as big waves, wind speeds and water depth and speed (Stopnitzky et al., 2011). During the nation seeking period, although there were communications with existing nations, the project did not advance to its current form until later on. Relations with French Polynesia started in 2016, when Marc Collins, former Minister of Tourism and business man of Tahiti, contacted The Seasteading Institute regarding the possibility of locating the seastead in French Polynesia. After a few months of discussions between The Seasteading Institute and several members of the French Polynesian government, in January 2017, The Seasteading Institute and Edouard Fritsch, President of French Polynesia, sealed their motivations for creating a floating city together with a legal document entitled *Memorandum of Understanding* (NA, 2017). It was at this point, after having secured French Polynesia to be the nation where the seastead would be located, that the Floating City Project officially became the Floating Island Project and that Blue Frontiers took charge of this stage.

Introducing the Floating Island Project in French Polynesia

This second stage of the Floating Island Project can be divided into two parts: the first, previously called Te Fiti Mokulana,[7] is a pilot project that begins construction in 2019 and is expected to be completed around 2021–2022. The Floating Island Project pilot project in French Polynesia will be financed by private investors in an ICO (Initial Coin Offering round) and platform buyers and will run exclusively on solar, wind and wave power. It works as a "concept-proof" prototype for the bigger future seasteads around the world and for preparing for international waters. Initially, The Floating Island Project "involves approximately 7.5 Ha with 12 platforms projected to require about 0.1% (0.75 Ha) of the total space" (Blue Frontiers, 2018, p. 12). Each platform will be between 14 to 50 square meters and an additional 47.7 hectares of land zone in the coast nearby (Hawkins, 2017), with the possibility to extend it to 100 hectares. The platforms will be located in sea area of 785.000 m^2 and will host around 300 people. The uses will range from residential, commercial and research spaces. Although the preliminary designs of the Floating Island Project are not finished yet, platforms are estimated to cost around US$ 1.500 per square foot. Its scale and manageable size will help the evaluation of the economic and environmental impact of floating settlements in French Polynesia and in the open ocean.

The main aims of the Floating Island Project are set out in the *Memorandum of Understanding* (2017), which is the agreement between the government of

French Polynesia and The Seasteading Institute by means of which they formalized their intention of collaborating in the construction of the Floating Island. It was signed on January 14 2017. Part of this Memorandum of understanding involves completing: a) two evaluations, one environmental and one economic; and b) developing the SeaZone Acts, the regulations that will regulate the Floating Island. Both evaluations are to be completed by September, 2017 by The Seasteading Institute. All being well, this will lead to approval by the French Polynesia government to locate the Floating Island Project in the Polynesian. The following two sections introduce two important aspects and evaluations that will be contained in the SeaZone Acts, the environmental and the economic aspect.

Evaluations: environmental and economic

The economic and environmental evaluations needed to get the permission of the French Polynesia government to build the Floating Island were conducted by Blue Frontiers and Blue Frontiers-Blue21 (2017) and EMSI (2017). The environmental evaluation contemplates aspects such as the effects of the seastead in the Tahitian ecosystem, trying to minimize the negative effects as possible. In fact, the environmental report is to have a statement of sustainability where it will declare its intention to be carbon negative, among other sustainability measures. This includes considering, for instance, how much the water temperature is affected with the shadows of the platforms blocking the sunlight, and which is the effect this has on the coral reef and the life underwater (Blue Frontiers-Blue21, 2018). It will also test the technologies that are being developed in terms of food production, waste management and sustainability. As Bouissou (2017) mentions, the Floating Island can bring to French Polynesia knowledge in terms of how to handle waste, generate electricity from the sea, use nanotechnology to create floating platforms, and bring together scientists, industrialist, and individuals with the financial capacity to build a sustainable future in French Polynesia.

With regards to the economic framework, which will be contained in the legal documents SeaZone Acts, it considers projections on the commercial aspect of the Floating Island Project to estimate market, job and exportation projections (Hawkins, 2017). Most of the companies that will be located in the seastead, though, will focus on what Quirk (2017a) has referred to as the "blue economy" – that is, businesses related to the ocean, either underwater or on its surface. For instance, underwater businesses include: aquaculture and vertical farms, underwater drones, sensory networks, energy generation using wave, current and wind power, and marine currents such as Ocean Thermal Energy Conversion, which uses changes in water temperature to produce energy (Germineau, 2017). Similarly, companies using the upper surface of the platforms will probably be focused more on the production of food, biofuels, medicines and nanotechnologies (The Seasteading Institute, ND). Of course, the Floating Island Project will also have the normal facilities an average city has, such as shared common areas, restaurants and bars.

In addition to blue economy-related businesses, there are three other types of companies that are likely to be an important part of this second stage. The first includes internet companies, some of them from Silicon Valley, which have already shown their interest in investing or in opening an office on the Floating Island Project (Delaune 2017; Germineau, 2017). As a report by The Seasteading Institute (2014) shows, most* of the supporters of the Institute´s work have mentioned high speed internet as one of the highest priorities on the list of criteria if they were to move to there. It is important to add that French Polynesia recently connected a cable to the internet going form Tahiti to Hawaii and another one connecting to New Zealand will soon be connected too. According to Lelei Lelaulu (2017), this might turn out to be one of the most crucial aspects of the Floating Island and will bringing good qualified international workforce and new companies to set up at the seastead.

The second key type of company that expected to emerge during this second stage include financial companies, in particular those working with smart contracts and blockchain-based companies. Currently the team of the Floating Island Project is working on developing the crypto-currency of the seastead and it has stated that one of the ways in which it will decentralize governance is by means of the blockchain (Quirk, 2017b). The blockchain aspect of the Floating Island Project, including the details of the token Varyon (VAR) are another aspect of this doctoral research, but are out of the scope of this introductory chapter.

The third key company to play a key role in the second stage involves private and public research centers. Currently in Tahiti and its two neighboring islands, Tetiaroa and Moorea, there are six university and private research centers. These include: *Institut Louis Malardé*, which deals with public affairs in French Polynesia such as getting rid of Dengue-producing mosquitos; *Criobe*, which studies the corals of Polynesian lagoons; and *The Mana o te Moana*, which protects ocean turtles, cetaceans, fish, rays and corals. It is anticipated that these research centers will have a small research center in the Floating Island Project also. A key focus of the presence of these research centers in the Floating Island is to help with the evaluations contained in the Environmental Assessment Framework regarding of the effects of the seastead in the Tahitian ecosystem, in compliance with the sustainability statement of the Floating Island. Together, the Environmental Assessment Framework and the Seastead Executive Summary, Economic [with] Model Projections for the Floating Island Project serve as the basis for The Seasteading Institute with its team of lawyers to draft the Seazone Acts; the group of legislations and regulations that will legally frame the seastead.

The SeaZone Acts

The SeaZone Acts will give the Floating Island the legal character of a Special Economic Zone within French Polynesia. These are currently being drafted by a group of lawyers, headed by Tom W. Bell, authors of the book on private governance called Your Next Government, from the Nation-State to Stateless

Nations (Bell, 2017) and global authority in polycentric laws. Although it is not possible to affirm any regulations contained in the SeaZone Acts until their signature at some point between September 2017 and December 2017, Germineau (2017) shared that it will cover economic aspects, labor rules, governance, custom duties, international relations, flags and registration, entry, resident permits and all other aspects that an autonomous zone conveys. The SeaZone Acts will give the seastead certain degree of autonomy translated into exceptions from existing regulations and laws that apply for the rest of French Polynesia, drawing inspiration from existing 4,000 Especial Economic Zones worldwide.

The SeaZone acts will, indeed, allow the creation of new procedures on the seastead without having to build on top of the ones that apply in Tahiti (Germineau, 2017). For instance, they will allow the existence of polycentric laws on the seastead, which refer to non-statist laws that individuals can create themselves without the approval or backing by a state for private contracts to take place (Bell, 1991; 1999). Polycentric Laws mediated by the character of a Special Economic Zone are part of the long-term libertarian goal of The Seasteading Institute which is inspired on Friedman´s proposal of privatizing courts and state services, taking away what Friedman (1989) calls `the monopoly of governance´ by nation-states. Nevertheless, the autonomy granted by the SeaZone Acts will be limited by some laws that apply already in French Polynesia, which need to go through the Parliament of France for them to be changed. This is because French Polynesia is still a semi-autonomous territory (overseas state) of France. Despite these limitations, some parts of the SeaZone Acts will be able to be signed by the Polynesian government without having to escalate to French Representatives, since it will consist mostly on sets of decrees and acts with a regulatory and implementation nature, which do not have the same legal character of laws. Despite this, the SeaZone Acts are being drafted to guarantee the maximum autonomy possible in terms of governance by the Floating Island.

As Germineau (2017) mentions, it is very likely that in terms of immigration, the seastead will develop a visa process separate from the rest of French Polynesia. In an ideal scenario, it would implement work visas with regulations similar the Cayman Islands, with emphasis on short periods of time for processing. The visas, however, will be granted for permanence on the seastead only and there is no indication that in the foreseeable panorama the visa will allow entry to the rest of French Polynesia. The main reason is that this is responsibility of France´s immigration department, *L'Office Français de l'Immigration et de l'Intégration*. It is expected, though, that the Floating Island might be able to improve France´s immigration procedures, by helping setting up an online process for individuals to apply for their visas in order to live or work in the seastead without having to attend a French Embassy nor leave their passports there. In order to live or work on the seastead, applicants would have to show a clean police certificate and enough funds to pay for repatriation in case they commit crimes.

An interesting aspect of the flexibility that the Floating Island attempts to implement, partly inspired by the libertarian and free market inspiration of the seastead, is that immigration permits and work visas will not limit individuals to work on one same company located at the seastead for the whole duration of their stay. The reason is that it will be the seastead, and not the companies established in it, which will back up an applicant's immigration procedure. This will give workers the flexibility to move in the companies operating in the Floating Island without their residency being affected by changes in their jobs. Similarly, this will allow individuals who have the economic fluency to live on the seastead and do not want to work to freely do so. It is for this that The Seasteading Institute will try to implement in the seastead only one type of visa that allows individuals to either work and live or just live at the seastead, in a very flexible manner (Germineau, 2017).

Due to the remoteness of French Polynesia, currently most goods have to be shipped, which means that living on the seastead will have similar elevated prices of goods and services in the rest of the country, which are higher than, for example, prices in France or the United Kingdom. However, the Seazone Act and the Special Economic Zone character that it will give to the Floating Island Project and the Floating Island will make goods in the seastead slightly lower than in the island of Tahiti because they will not have to pay for customs duties, VAT or taxes (Germineau, 2017).

Because part of the driving force of the Floating Island is the protection of private property, management of the platforms will depend on ownership, either individual or collective: some residences and platforms will be for single use, while others will be for shared uses and ownership -multipurpose, multi-ownership. Therefore, if a platform is owned collectively by several owners of the buildings in it, it will most likely also be managed collectively. If only one individual owns it, rules that apply will be those chosen by her, within the framework of the SeaZone Acts. According to Quirk (2017a), the most plausible form collective ownership will take will be similar to a condo owners association. From a complexity science point of view, we refer to this libertarian form of governance based on voluntary association as complex voluntary governance.

Lastly, stage 3 of the Floating Island consists on the moment when seasteads exists in several parts of the world —and in international waters. However, it is expected that the legal autonomy provided by SeaZones allows taking into practice innovative human and transhuman enhancements in private clinics and medical research centers on the ocean (Friedman & Gramlich, 2009), including treatments that are nowadays forbidden by countries on land, such as steam cell, cloning and eugenics. These, however, will not be part of the Floating Island Project, since they require political autonomy, if not independence, for their development. However, one day, according to Delaune (2017) this will probably be the most visible science fiction aspect of human settlements on the ocean.

Decentralizing governance to manage problems of the commons

The autonomy exemplified by being able to perform transhumanist enhancements in international waters might, indeed, sound close to science fiction. Simpson (2016a, 2016b) mentions the connection between the project of The Seasteading Institute and Ayn Rand's literature, while Steinberg et al. (2012) mention the utopian character of seasteading. Although full autonomy for a privately-born entity might sound as close to science fiction as artificial islands that float, there are no reasons to believe that the purposes of the medium- and long-term goals of seasteading and The Seasteading Institute might not become a reality. After all, the increasing possibility to self-govern and its relation to the proliferation of decentralized structures and infrastructures is typical from the ethos of a set of trends of the twenty-first century that are making projects such as the Floating Island close to reality, and which reflect the increasing popularization of a libertarian ethos that advocates in favor of voluntary and self-organized forms governance. Although libertarianism is usually associated with individual politics, there is no reason for this not to be connected with self-organized forms of collective action, especially when there are commons mediating, such as the oceans and the interest in preserving it while creating oceanic human settlements. This extends, however, for other types of human settlements and infrastructures that extend beyond seasteading and that I group as part of the same trend which made seasteading a reality in the beginning of the twenty first century; startup societies. That is, micro experiments in governance that exists on a small territory (McKinney, 2018).

The set of trends in which the Floating Island emerges encompasses six key aspects. First, technological conditions that allow taking seriously the creation of human settlements in new types of spaces, such as on Mars (Musk, 2017) or on the ocean, as it is the case of the seasteading. Second, the popularization of decentralized mechanisms for interaction to be implemented in these new and online spaces, such as blockchain (Atzori, 2015; Swan, 2015) added to legal frameworks that reaffirm conditions of decentralization and autonomy, such as polycentric laws (Bell, 1991; Bell, 1999; Mendenhall, 2012; Tiberius, 2017); privately run cities (McKenzie, 2011; Porter, 2008) and Special Economic Zones (Bell, 2017; Friedman & Taylor, 2012). Third, decentralized technologies and infrastructure designed for smart cities based on networked information, such as automation (Gershenson, 2008) and the DAO (Jentzsch, 2016). Fourth, the proliferation of online networked forms of human social interactions with political implications such as the revolutions of the Arab Spring (Fuchs, 2012) and the leaks of Edward Snowden (Lyon, 2015). Fifth, the increasing impact of open source and online platforms for political participation, deliberation and decision-making, some of which have managed to be the engine behind a crowdsourced law (Heikka, 2015). And lastly, the increasing emergence of startup societies, micronations, eco villages and intentional communities which is becoming more popular now than ever (Gebel, ND; Startup Societies Foundation, 2017).

These six aspects provide the key external reasons behind why the Floating Island Project is emerging in this particular moment of time. Seen altogether as a nebulosa of trends, these dynamics that push to decentralization have in common that they point towards bottom-up and self-organized interactions that form nonhierarchical political relations, which can be seen as solutions coming from self-organized forms of collective action to solve problems of the commons. Indeed, they all seem to have political and, therefore, governance implications. After all, in the long term, the decentralized physical and political structures of the Floating Island may lead to the emergence of nonhierarchical political relations and bottom-up self-organized governance forms.

The Floating Island Project can, therefore, be described as an example of sociopolitical self-organization, where governance is voluntary and emerges in a bottom-up way. At the same time, these forms of political self-organization can be seen as mechanisms of collective action. This is further illustrated in (Mezza-Garcia, forthcoming) and with the publications of the SeaZone Acts, where the decentralized physical and political structures and the non-hierarchical political relations of the Floating Island Project become evident thanks to the adaptive nature of the environmental, economic and political regulations that will guide it will directly speak to complex voluntary governance in the Floating Island Project. These properties, behaviors, characteristics and descriptions are some of the main key elements that will be looked in governance regarding the Floating Island.

Conclusion: complex voluntary governance

It stands to reason that where physical and political structures are emergent, self-organized and nested, governance can also be emergent, self-organized and nested. Hence, as stated above, governance in the Floating Island will have the following characteristics: a) bottom-up emergence of governance forms, b) in nonhierarchical political relations, which are c) generated by decentralized political and physical structures. That said, this form of governance can be characterized as *voluntary governance*. This is a concept that has not been extensively discussed in the mainstream literature on governance and complexity (Mezza-Garcia, forthcoming), although it has recently begun to emerge in the last decade, albeit, rather scarcely. As interests this case study, the term voluntary governance stems from the notion of voluntary governance and voluntary societies contained in the work of Friedman (1989, p. 76), who claimed that voluntary institutions "should replace governments in its most essential functions". That is, that societies should be organized by means of voluntary arrangements instead of what he calls coercive nation-states, in a, desirably, anarchic global setting. Barclay (1990) also focused on the notion of voluntarism, specifically, voluntary self-organizing networks that cooperate in anarchic settings. Barclay's and Friedman's view is also shared by Wachhaus (2014), who noted that the emergence of spontaneous order, defined by Collin Ward (1973), a classical anarchist author, was the way in which "given a common need, a collection of people will evolve order out of the situation … this order being more durable and more closely related to their needs than any kind of externally imposed authority could provide" (Wachhaus, 2014. p. 579).

Essentially, voluntary governance allows for an alternative way of approaching political entities with self-organized forms of political organization, including the Floating Island. Furthermore, this approach speaks directly to the libertarian political background of The Seasteading Institute and the Floating Island Project. Indeed, voluntary governance is the official term given to the possible future forms of private governance in the Floating Island (Mendenhall, 2012; Taghizadegan, 2017). This is in line with (Mezza-Garcia, forthcoming), where there is an attention on three shared concepts of governance and complexity to explain voluntary governance: bottom-up forms of self-organized governance, decentralized structures and nonhierarchical political relations. At the same time, these three forms of dynamics are nonviolent forms of political interactions that, within libertarianism, turn into collective action solutions for problems where there are shared resources, such as those related with future oceanic settlements.

At its most extreme, a version of voluntary governance in complex self-organizing political settings has many resonances with anarchism. As Maldonado & Mezza-Garcia (2016) stress, there is a form of anarchism that is equivalent to self-governance. This is based on the approaches of anarchism of Guerin (1970) and Bakunin (1970) Kropotkin (2012) and (Proudhon, 1969) have, who see anarchism as synonym of self-government (Barclay, 1996; Wachhaus, 2012) and systems that self-regulate without any external rulers (Woodcock, 1986). Indeed, Maldonado & Mezza-Garcia (2016, p. 1) go as far as saying that "embracing the theory of complexity inevitably leads towards the acceptance of anarchy" and that anarchism is a complexity-based dynamic. According to them, anarchism is simply an undetermined space for politics that goes against the centralization and top-down imposition of order. Furthermore, they argue, the closest relation between complexity and anarchism is in the increasing degrees of freedom. Quoting them:

> anarchy is the condition for a further search for principles and rules and it reveals, moreover, as the *conditio sine qua non* to any possible life and organization to be. In other words, it is the autonomy, the freedom, the independence that allows for higher or better horizons, dynamics and structures. Anarchy, it appears, is the very seed and proper name for freedom, autonomy and cooperation.
>
> (Maldonado & Mezza-Garcia, 2016, p. 9)

Hence, anarchy, the most nonlinear and complex of political systems, is not opposed to organization but to hierarchical and centralized structures (Maldonado & Mezza-Garcia, 2016; Mezza-Garcia, 2013a; 2013b). As we saw with the Floating Island, a human settlement that sympathizes with freedom-seeking forms of governance and in line with mechanisms of collective action and nonviolent political relations does not opposes forms of governance that can tackle and solve problems of the commons, despite the critiques made to the strain of libertarianism mostly mediated by private companies.

Notes

1   This book chapter is part of the ongoing doctoral research funded at the University of Warwick by Fundación CEIBA, Rodolfo Llinás Doctoral Fellowship.
2   In memoriam of Diego Armando Hernandez Barraza, my smart fellow scientist friend.
3   An increase in variety has inspired the name of the cryptocurrency of Blue FrontierS – the Varyon (VAR) – which will be the mechanism of exchange of goods and services in the Floating Island Project.
4   The Polynesian Leaders Group is formed by the Prime Minister of French Polynesia, the Primer of Niue, the Prime Minister of the Cook Islands, the Prime Minister of Samoa, Ulu-o-Tokelau, the Prime Minister of Tonga and the Prime Minister of Tuvalu.
5   In the Pacific, small island states include Vanatu, Tuvalu, Tonga, Timor-leste, Solomon Islands, Samoa, Papua New Guinea, Palau, Northern Mariana Islands, Niue, New Caledonia, Nauru, Marshal Islands, Kiribati, Guam, French Polynesia, Fiji, Federated States of Micronesia, Cook Islands and the American Samoa.
6   The terms "libertarianism", "anarcho-capitalism" "minarchism" and "libertarian anarchy" have small differences among them, although sometimes to be used interchangeably among authors (see Block, 2002 for more details on the fine differences). I will use the term "libertarianism", as this is the one most currently used among the Floating Island community and relates closer to anarcho-capitalism, which is closely related to the existence of polycentric laws, which will have a space in the Floating Island.
7   Mokulana is an old Polynesian word for floating island (English, Pittman and Lelaulu 2017) and Te Fiti was the code name of the undisclosed location where the Floating Island will be built. The name is inspired on the film Moana and it was defined by Blue Frontiers, the for-profit company created by The Seasteading Institute to build the Floating Islands.

Acknowledgements

I gratefully thank Emma Uprichard and Nathaniel Tkacz for carefully commenting during the writing of this chapter.

References

Atzori, M. (2015). Blockchain Technology and Decentralized Governance: Is the State Still Necessary? (December 1, 2015). doi:doi:10.2139/ssrn.2709713
Bakunin, M. A. (1970). *God and the State*. North Chelmsford, MA: Courier Corporation.
Barclay, H. B. (1990). *People without Government: An Anthropology of Anarchy*. London: Kahn & Averill Publishers.
Bar-Yam, Y. (2009). *Dynamics of Complex Systems*. Reading MA: Addison-Wesley.
Bell, T. W. (1991). Polycentric law. *Humane Studies Review*, 7(1), 92.

Bell, T. W. (1999). Polycentric law in a new century. *Policy: A Journal of Public Policy and Ideas*, 15(1), 34.

Bell, T. W. (2017). *Your Next Government?: From the Nation State to Stateless Nations*. Cambridge: Cambridge University Press.

Blue Frontiers. *Legal Report* [Confidential].

Blue Frontiers-Blue21 (2017) *Environmental Assessment Framework for Floating Island Project in French Polynesia. Preliminary Report.* Blue Frontiers.

Blue Frontiers (2018). Blue Frontiers Global Contest: Make your Own Seastead Competition. Available online at www.blue-frontiers.global/

Bouissou, Jean Christophe (2017). What would a floating city bring to French Polynesia?Youtube. Available online at www.youtube.com/watch?v=cimraA16BRw

De Soto, J. H. (1998). A Libertarian Theory of Free Immigration. *Journal of Libertarian Studies*, 13, 187–198.

Delaune, Greg. (2017). Community Engagement for Sustainable Economic Development. First International Conference on Floating Islands. Tahiti, May 15.

EMSI (2017). *EMSI Impact Analysis, The Floating Island Project.*

English, Kalani, Pittman, Tua, & Lelaulu, Lelei. (2017)Seasteading. Available online at www.seasteading.org/conference-videos-j-kalani-english-tua-pittman-lelei-lelaulu/ (accessed April 1, 2019).

Friedman, David. 1989. *The Machinery of Freedom. A Guide to Radical Capitalism.* Chicago, IL: Open Court Publishing Company.

Friedman, M., & Friedman, R. (1990). *Free to Choose: A Personal Statement.* New York: Houghton Mifflin Harcourt.

Friedman, P., & Gramlich, W. (2009). *Seasteading: A Practical Guide to Homesteading the High Seas.* Palo Alto, CA: The Seasteading Institute.

Friedman, P., & Taylor, B. (2010). Seasteading: Institutional Innovation on the Open Ocean. Paper presented at the Australasian Public Choice Society Conference, December 9–10, 2010, University of Canterbury, Christchurch, New Zealand.

Friedman, P., & Taylor, B. (2012). Seasteading: Competitive Governments on the Ocean. *Kyklos* 65(2), 218–235.

Gebel, Titus (ND). Free Private Cities: The Future of Governance is Private [Blog post]. Available online at www.startupsocieties.com/post/free-private-cities-the-future-of-governance-is-private (accessed on June 17 2017).

Germineau, N. (2017) The SeaZone Acts. Personal communication with Nathalie Mezza-Garcia. June 7 2017.

Gerrits, L. M. (2012). *Punching Clouds.* Litchfield Park: Emergent Publications.

Gershenson, Carlos. (2008). Towards self-organizing bureaucracies. *International Journal of Public Information*, 1–24.

Gramlich, Wayne C. (1998). "Gramlich Family Home Page." Available online at http://gramlich.net/projects/oceania/seastead1.html (accessed January 23, 2017).

Guerin, D. (1970). *Anarchism: From Theory to Practice.* New York: NYU Press.

Hawkins, J. (2017). *Seastead Executive Summary. Economic models and projections for the Floating Island Project.* EMCI.

Heikka, T. (2015). The Rise of the mediating citizen: Time, space, and citizenship in the crowdsourcing of Finnish legislation. *Policy & Internet*, 7(3), 268–291.

Henry, A.D. & Dietz, T., (2011). Information, networks, and the complexity of trust in commons governance. *International Journal of the Commons*, 5(2), 88–212. doi: doi:10.18352/ijc.312

Jentzsch, C. (2016). Decentralized Autonomous Organization to Automate Governance. Available online at https://github.com/slockit/DAO/tree/develop/paper (accessed July 21, 2018).

Jessop, B., (1997). The governance of complexity and the complexity of governance: preliminary remarks on some problems and limits of economic guidance. In Amin, A., & Hausner (eds), *Beyond Markets and Hierarchy: Interactive Governance and Social Complexity*. Cheltenham: Edward Elgar, pp. 111–147.

Jessop,B. (2004). Multi-level governance and multi-level metagovernance. *Multi-level Governance*, 1(9), 49–75.

Johnston, L. (2005). *The Rebirth of Private Policing*. Abingdon: Routledge.

Kropotkin, P. (2012). *Mutual Aid: A Factor of Evolution*. North Chelmsford, MA: Courier Corporation.

Lelaulu, L. (2017). *Lelei Lelaulu: Beyond Moana* [Video File]. Available online at www.youtube.com/watch?v=Bb8KDUWj7C8&t=14s (accessed June 21 2017).

Lynch, C. R. (2017). "Vote with your feet": Neoliberalism, the democratic nation-state, and utopian enclave libertarianism. *Political Geography*, 59, 82–91.

Lyon, D. (2015). *Surveillance after Snowden*. New York: John Wiley & Sons.

Mainzer, K. (2007). *Thinking in Complexity: The Computational Dynamics of Matter, Mind, and Mankind*. Berlin: Springer Science & Business Media.

Maldonado, C. E. (2013). Consecuencias políticas de la complejidad. *Iztapalapa, Revista de Ciencias Sociales y Humanidades*, 74, 189–208.

Maldonado, C., & Mezza-Garcia, N. (2016). Anarchy and complexity. *Emergence: Complexity & Organization*, 18(1), 1–13.

Marty, M., & Borders, M. (2011). *Seasteading Business: Context, Opportunity and Challenge*. Palo Alto: The Seasteading Institute.

McKenzie, E. (2011). *Beyond Privatopia: Rethinking Residential Private Government*. Washington, DC: Urban Institute Press.

McKinney, J. (2018). Startup Societies and Experimental Governance: Joseph McKinney - Blue Frontiers Podcast E10. Available online at www.youtube.com/watch?v=Cm5_Ku-ULQY&index=17&list=PLQlyH_Kk03b-5eU68XoHN_xUEzSE C0AMQ&t=4s (accessed July 25, 2018).

Mendenhall, A. (2012). My "Country" Lies Over the Ocean: Seasteading and Polycentric Law. *Studies in Emergent Order*, 5, 137–156. Available online at: https://ssrn.com/abstract=2212897 (accessed May 30, 2018).

Mezza-Garcia, N. (2013a) Bio-inspired political systems: opening a field. In Gilbert, T. (ed.) *Proceedings of the European Conference on Complex Systems 2012*. Bern: Springer, pp. 758–812.

Mezza-Garcia, N. (2013b). Self-Organized Sociopolitical Interactions as the Best Way to Achieve Organized Patterns in Human Social Systems: Going beyond the Top-Down Control of Classical Political Regimes. Unpublished Undergraduate Thesis. Bogotá: Universidad del Rosario.

Mezza-Garcia, N. (forthcoming). *Proceedings of the Conference on Complex Systems*. September 2017, Cancún.

Musk, E. (2017). Making Humans a Multi-Planetary Species. *New Space*, 5(2), 46–61.

Mutabdzija, D., & Borders, M. (2011). *Charting the Course: Toward a Seasteading Legal Strategy*. Palo Alto: The Seasteading Institute.

NA. (2017). Memorandum of Understanding. Available online at http://2oxut21weba 5oivlniw6igeb-wpengine.netdna-ssl.com/wp-content/uploads/2017/01/Memora

ndum-of-Understanding-MOU-French-Polynesia-The-Seasteading-Institute-Ja
n-13-2017.pdf (accessed January 26, 2017).

Nozick, R. (2013). *Anarchy, State, and Utopia.* New York: Basic Books.

Olson, M. (2009). *The Logic of Collective Action.* Cambridge, MA: Harvard University Press.

Ostrom, E. (1990). *Governing the Commons: The Evolution on Institutions of Collective Action.* Cambridge: Cambridge University Press.

Ostrom, E. (2010). Polycentric systems for coping with collective action and global environmental change. *Global Environmental Change,* 20(4), 550–557.

Polynesian Leaders Group (2015). P.A.C.T. Polynesians Against Climate Threats. Tapuatapuatea Declaration on Climate Change. Available online at www.samoagovt. ws/wp-content/uploads/2015/07/The-Polynesian-P.A.C.T.pdf (accessed March 2017).

Parijs, P. V. (1997). *Real Freedom for All: What (if Anything) Can Justify Capitalism?* Oxford: Oxford University Press.

Porter, O. W. (2008). *Public/Private Partnerships for Local Governments.* Bloomington, Indiana: Author House.

Proudhon, P. J. (1969). *Selected Writings of Pierre-Joseph Proudhon.* New York: Anchor Books.

Quirk, J. (2017a). *Seasteading. How Floating Nations Will Restore the Environment, Enrich the Poor, Cure the Sick, and Liberate Humanity from Politicians.* New York: Free Press.

Quirk, J. (2017b). Presentation given at the Startup Societies Summit, August, 2017, San Francisco.

Room, G. (2016). *Agile Actors on Complex Terrains: Transformative Realism and Public Policy.* Abingdon: Routledge.

Rothbard, M. N. (1978). *For a New Liberty: The Libertarian Manifesto.* Auburn, AL: Ludwig von Mises Institute.

Schuster, P. (2004) The Disaster of Central Control. *Complexity,* 9, 13–14.

Simpson, I. (2016a). Operation Atlantis. *Shima,* 10(2).

Simpson, I. (2016b). "If I'm not a ship, I'm a boat that could be": Seasteading and the post-social political imagination. Master's dissertation, Concordia University.

Startup Societies Foundation. (2017). Startup Societies. Available online atwww.startup societies.com/(accessed April 1, 2019).

Steinberg, P. E., Nyman, E. & CaraccioliM. J. (2012). Atlas Swam: Freedom, Capital, and Floating Sovereignties in the Seasteading Vision. *Antipode,* 44(4), 1532–1550.

Stopnitzky, S., Amar, E., Hogan, J., Petrie, G., Mutabdzija, D., & Marty, M. (2011). *Seasteading Location Study: Ship-Based and Large-Scale City Scenarios.* Palo Alto: The Seasteading Institute

Swan, M. (2015). *Blockchain: Blueprint for a New Economy.* Boston: O'Reilly Media, Inc.

Taghizadegan, Rahim, & Marc-Felix, Otto. (2017). The Praxeology of Coercion: A New Theory of Violence Cycles. *Quarterly Journal of Economics,* 330–344.

The_Seasteading_Institute (2014). *The Floating City Project Report.* Available online at www.seasteading.org/wp-content/uploads/2015/12/Floating-City-Project-Rep ort-4_25_2014.pdf (accessed April 23, 2017).

The_Seasteading_Institute. ND. Frequently Asked Questions. Available online at www. seasteading.org/frequently-asked-questions/ (accessed June 10, 2017).

Tiberius, V. (2017). Seasteads: Creating New Small Seasteads: Creating New Small Societies From Scratch. In *Seasteads: Creating New Small Seasteads: Creating New Small Societies.* Zurich: vdf Hochschulverlag an der ETH, pp. 3–63.

Torfing, J. (2012). Governance Networks. In Levi-Faur, D. (ed.), *The Oxford Handbook of Governance*. Oxford: Oxford University Press, pp. 99–112.

United Nations (1982) *United Nations Convention on the Law on the Sea*. Available online at www.un.org/depts/los/convention_agreements/texts/unclos/unclos_e.pdf (accessed 3 June, 2017).

Vallentyne, P. (2000). *Left-Libertarianism: A Primer*. Basingstoke: Palgrave-Macmillan.

Wachhaus, A. (2014). Governance beyond government. *Administration & Society*, 46(5), 573–593.

Wachhaus, T. A. (2012). Anarchy as a model for network governance. *Public Administration Review*, 72(1), 33–42.

Ward, C. (1973). *Anarchy in Action*. London: Allen and Unwin.

White, J. (2012). Floating cities could redefine human existence. *New Scientist*, 215 (2883), 26–27.

Woodcock, G. (1986). *Anarchism: A History of Libertarian Ideas and Movements*. London: Penguin.

Zia, A., Kauffman, S., Koliba, C., Beckage, B., Vattay, G., & Bomblies, A. (2014). From the habit of control to institutional enablement: Re-envisioning the governance of social-ecological systems from the perspective of complexity sciences. *Complexity, Governance & Networks*, 1(1), 79–88.

5 Buds in the capitalist desert

Emerging socio-economic forms that are changing the world

Guillermo Díaz Muñoz

Introduction: capitalist world-system crisis or systemic metamorphosis?

With the world running amok and an ongoing systemic or structural crisis, thousands of new forms of socio-economical expressions and alternative experiences – without being completely new or perfect – have flourished, of varying quality and in various quantities: cooperatives, mutual funds, diverse associations, barter clubs, peasant economic organizations, indigenous organizations with their own economic projects – and their defense of the territory and common goods – fair trade exchange systems, social, local and community currencies, economic collaboration networks, ethical banks and social and popular finances, among many other socio-economic practices out of the mainstream.

These experiences are distinguished from the private economy – or capital economy – and the public economy because, in their enormous diversity they nearly all share a common matrix of the preeminence of the work over capital, freedom of accession and membership, internal democracy and the reinvestment of surpluses, ethical and social finances, fair exchange and responsible local consumption, among other features. Their aim is not capital accumulation as the main objective, or profit as a predominant interest. They call on their members, with all the human contradictions involved, to show solidarity and struggle for a dignified life in communion with nature.

As someone who has had the good fortune to witness some of these experiences first hand at various stages of my life – as a promoter, advisor and social researcher – I shall try to give an account in this chapter of the hope that they represent.

The twenty-first century's uncontrollable inequalities

Thousands of millions of human beings in today's world suffer from poverty and inequality. A large number of studies have recognized the urgency of the situation, and are issuing warnings about the serious inequalities – not only economic ones – that exist in a deeply aggravated form in the world today.

These studies include those developed by international organizations such as the United Nations (UN, 2015), the United Nations Educational, Scientific and Cultural Organization (UNESCO, 2016) and those produced by private non-profit organizations such as Oxfam International (2016) or prestigious researchers such as Thomas Piketty in his famous book *Capital in the Twenty-first Century* (2014).

To give an instance, in the United Nations report "Transforming our World: The 2030 Agenda for Sustainable Development" (UN, 2015: 5–6) it says that billions of people continue to live in poverty and are deprived of a dignified life while inequalities grow, both within countries and between countries, as well as between genders. Climate risks, the depletion of natural resources, and the presence of unemployment and violence, according to the UN, are threatening to undo many of the advances made in development over the last few decades.

For its part, Oxfam (2016), a non-profit international development organization, has spoken out in its most recent annual reports on the serious economic inequalities across the world. The figures obtained are dramatic, as it was argued that the percentage of wealth in the hands of the richest 1% would surpass 50% of all global wealth in 2016. Likewise, in 2015, just 62 people possessed the same amount of wealth as 3,600,000,000 others (the poorest half of humanity) while in 2010 the same proportion of wealth had been in the hands of 388 people.

Another fundamental contribution to our knowledge of inequalities cones from UNESCO (2016, p. 6). In its World Report on Social Sciences, "Tackling the challenge of inequalities and drawing pathways to a fair world", the organization recognizes seven kinds of inequalities in an Integrative analytical framework: Economic inequality, social inequality, cultural inequality, political inequality, territorial inequality, cognitive inequality and inequality of knowledge. The report also recognizes that poverty, inequality and social justice have a close relationship with one another. That is why it makes an urgent call for a substantial change that will make it possible to adopt an interdisciplinary, multiscale and globally inclusive research agenda capable of finding paths that will lead to greater equality.

The developmentalist trend of globalization and current de-globalizations.

The figures above, although dramatic in all their starkness, cannot quite reflect the tragic situation which billions of people find themselves in. In short, we can affirm that the world is going through a planetary crisis, a kind of multiple crisis. In the words of Edgar Morin (2011: 25)

> Today the world is traversed by a whole gamut of multiple interdependent crises – economic, ecological, social-traditional or modern-Western, urban, rural, political, demographic, and religious – that has now become a planetary crisis. And the process that has made this crisis planetary has three facets: globalization, westernization, and development.

But the neoliberal globalization of today is mired in a deep crisis. The departure of Great Britain from the European Union (commonly referred to as "Brexit") and the recent triumph of Donald Trump in the presidential elections of the United States, have challenged the viability of the prevailing globalization that claims to be for the benefit of many precarious and excluded sectors of the economy both in the north and in the global south. Using the protection of employment within the various nations as a pretext for globalization policies, the real reasons for them are to be found in the interests of conservative sectors. No commitment to an alternative and fair globalization as proposed by the global South is reflected in these dynamics.

In this context, Pope Francis (2015) has put his finger on the scourge of the capitalist world-system in his recent, but already classic, social encyclical "Laudato Si" where he says that: "Not only are there winners and losers among the countries, but also within the poor countries, where various responsibilities must be identified" (135). He says that forms of cooperation or community organization can be facilitated to defend the interests of small producers and preserve local ecosystems from further depredation (139).

So, if we start by recognizing the crisis, in the background we must be wondering about the achievements and failures of development, as well as its theories. It must be said that these theories have undergone continual transformations in their desire to make the socio-economic dynamics that really exist easier to understand:

> The notion of development was adopted in the 1940s, in the context of World War II, as a way to measure the economic progress of countries: countries came to be classed as either developed or underdeveloped. In practical terms, the concept of development has remained associated with other notions such as progress and growth, particularly in the economic sphere and in terms of gross domestic product (GDP), limiting its integrative potential in other human and social areas of life and keeping it subject to the dominant economic interests. Hence its proximity to or distance from well-being and happiness (Western notions) and good living (Andean notion of ancestral peoples) and the need to establish critical bridges between them.
>
> (Díaz, 2014: 19)

According to the same author (Diaz, 2014), development theories can be classified into large groups, all of which appeared in the second half of the last century.

On the one hand, from an orthodox perspective, fundamentally based on liberalism, freedom of the markets, drip theory and economic modernization:

- the neoclassical approach, in the forties and fifties of the last century, with the proposals of Arthur Lewis and William Rostow for changing traditional and archaic rural economies and societies into modern, industrialized and urbanized economies;

- the neoliberal orthodoxy, whose immediate ideological-economic origins go back to Friedrich Hayek and Milton Friedman and which was clearly represented at the end of the eighties by the so-called Washington Consensus – a program designed by academics and international financial organizations such as the International Monetary Fund and the World Bank, and John Williamson – in its first and second generation structural reform proposals;

On the other hand, from a heterodox approach to development – with its criticisms of economic liberalism – we find various currents of thought and positions on development:

- the structuralist economy, where the center-periphery theory led by Raúl Prebisch and the theory of dependence by CEPAL (the Economic Commission for Latin America and the Caribbean, ECLAC) with Theotonio dos Santos and Aníbal Quijano, and others, converge. Both theories were critical of asymmetric trade-exchange relationships between developed (central) and underdeveloped (peripheral) nations and a structure hostile to the periphery. But the dependence theorists go a step further, recognizing the existence of national oligarchies in the peripheral countries linked to relations of exploitation by the central economies. Other expressions of Latin American critical thinking, such as Peripheral Autonomy in the seventies and eighties – with Helio Jaguaribe and his studies of the Inter-imperial system and the autonomies of the peripheries, and Peripheral Realism, in the nineties, with Carlos Escudé – also fit in here with their countercultural and citizen-centered notions;
- the French Regulation economists since the eighties (Robert Boyer at the head, besides Michel Aglieta, Benjamin Coriat and Alain Lipietz), who have studied each specific form of historical-geographical functioning of capitalism. Accumulation and regulation are two central concepts of this theoretical current. In this line of thought, we can locate Amartya Sen, who won the Nobel Prize for Economics in 1998, and his Human Development proposal;
- with Pierre Bourdieu and his economic anthropology, also in the eighties – and his notions of capital, fields and habitus, interest and benefit – the critique of the capitalist economy and conventional economic theory is reinforced;
- among heterodox economists are Joseph Stiglitz, in the nineties, with his proposals to remedy unfair globalization through the necessary normalization and democratization of global institutions and the regulation of multinational companies. We also find Ha-Joon Chang and his research into the myths underpinning current capitalism, especially that of the free market, and Dany Rodrick, who demonstrates how various East Asian countries have travelled a path contrary to the principles of the

Washington Consensus to stimulate their growth and become the new emerging powers;

- finally, since the eighties, sustainable development theory – with Olivier Godard, Franck-Dominique Vivien, and Marie-Claude Smouts, among others – has revived the notion of economic growth, but as something necessarily interwoven with social equity and environmental sustainability.

Going even farther than the heterodox currents of development, and following Díaz (2014), there are other theoretical perspectives such as:

- the world-system theory of Immanuel Wallerstein, who recognizes that the capitalist world-system is characterized by profound differences in cultural development, in the accumulation of political and capital power, and predicts that it will end like the world-systems that preceded it;
- decrease theory which, under the banner of Serge Latouche and other anti-utilitarian authors has aimed since the beginning of this century to abandon the goal of "growth for growth's sake", following the path drawn by Herman Daly and his questioning since the 1960s of economic growth without limits;
- post-development theory, bio-development and good living, with Arturo Escobar, Eduardo Gudynas and Leonardo Boff, whose studies affirm that the way out of developmentalism is through "alternatives to growth" and a commitment to "good living", in accordance with the way of thinking and ecological practices of the ancestral peoples;
- with his alternative epistemological contributions and critiques of current development and globalization, Boaventura de Sousa Santos has been warning us since the nineties about the need to think of the world using the epistemologies of the south – the sociology of absences and emergencies –, which are capable of studying and understanding social reality using what modern sociology has ignored thereby making it impossible to see what is new in the social world, namely several society-transforming innovations (of an ethical, economic, social, cultural, political and environmental kind);
- the neo-Marxist currents with David Harvey and his concept of accumulation by dispossession – of all kinds of citizen rights, lands and territories, common goods, etc. – and John Holloway's proposals about changing the world without taking power by cracking capitalism;
- finally, and as we said at the beginning of this section, for decades Edgar Morin has argued from his "complex thought" that the current world is in a planetary crisis caused by three aspects: globalization, westernization and development. To deal with it, Morin proposes a set of highly suggestive measures – a new way for humanity – to save the planet.

From social resistance and the construction of alternatives: the emergence of Social and Solidarity Economies

Emerging socio-economical experiences.

We can say that the socio-economic reality of today's world has two faces: a. that of prevailing capitalism and its increasing abysmal inequalities and b. the appearance of new and old social and solidarity socio-economic practices.

The current diversity of practices in the Social and Solidarity Economy (ECOSOL) is enormous and has historical roots going back for centuries. At the beginning of the nineteenth century, the first experiences of social economy arose through the mutual associations of workers, and by the end of the same century, this type of economy had already promoted and incorporated the cooperative organizations and community services societies of all kinds.

However, it was not until the last decades of the twentieth century, coinciding with the rise of the neoliberal model as predominant in the world and the structural adjustment reforms imposed on the countries of the global South, and more recently with the reforms applied in countries of the global north like Portugal, Ireland, Greece and Spain, pejoratively known as PIGS by the financial powers of the European Union, that we began to see the emergence and propagation of innumerable practices of collaborative solidarity in the field of the economy, among which the following in particular stand out: the renewal of companies managed by their workers, fair trade or trade with justice and solidarity, solidarity organizations for branding and labelling, organic farming, responsible or critical consumption and solidarity consumption, local employment and trading schemes (LETS), local bartering systems and networks (SEL), Community Exchange Systems (SEC), local systems of labor exchange using social currencies, communion economies, micro-credit systems, people's banks and ethical banks, solidarity purchasing groups, boycott movements, distribution of free software programs, and other practices of a solidarity economy. A considerable number of organizations have developed these practices and they cover the various segments of the productive chains (consumption, trade, service, production and credit) and are increasingly integrated into joint actions in a network, while others have already been acting this way for more than three decades.

It is not possible to give a detailed account of each of them. However, it is useful to refer to some quantitative data on a number of these experiences. According to the International Co-operative Alliance (ICA, 2010), it was estimated that there were around 750,000 cooperatives worldwide in the cooperative sector, which gave employment to about 100 million workers and grouped more than 775 million members.

Some significant examples by country may be these: in France, there were 21,000 cooperatives whose production already represented almost 12% of the country's GDP; Argentina had 8,100 cooperatives that grouped more than 9 million members; the United States recorded about 150 million cooperative partners grouped in 27,600 such enterprises; in India more than 183 million people were members of 446,800 cooperatives; China also has about 160 million cooperative partners and Japan has jobs for more than 380,000 workers in the country's 5,700 cooperatives that associate more than 64 million people.

The mutual insurance companies, for their part, had more than 40 million mutual partners in France, while the Netherlands and Belgium have more than 5 million each. Other examples are Algeria, in Africa, with more than 12 million partners, and Israel with 5 million.

Associations constitute another important segment of the social and solidarity economy. It is estimated that in Western Europe this sector represents 7% of non-agricultural employment (with 28% of all employment in education, 27% of social employment, 22% of employment in health and 10% of employment in culture).

Other important figures are given in a research project by the Americas International Co-operative Alliance into 300 cooperative and mutual enterprises of a global nature. Using the 2004 data, research shows that, together, these businesses have combined sales of nearly US$ 1,000 billion, which is greater than the Canadian gross domestic product for that year (ICA, 2011).

Beyond these social enterprises, the diversity of experiences of social and solidarity economies is enormous. For example, in accordance with the call by the International Colloquium on Social and Complementary Currencies, held in February 2011 in Lyon, France, it was estimated that there were 4,000 to 5,000 schemes of this type in the world, located in more than 50 countries and with a growing variety of models.

In general the diversity of alternative socioeconomic experiences and solidarity is very great (Díaz, 2015: 22–23). These practices can be classified according to:

- the spheres of the economy in which they are inserted: production of goods and services, exchange, consumption, or other forms of economic activity;
- the values, principles, meanings, norms and traditions that drive them: decent and stable work (with the primacy of work and people over capital), self-management or co-management, social security (pensions, health, the care of people), ethical solidarity financing, trade with justice, responsible consumption, natural resources conservation and harmony with the environment, struggle for identity, autonomy, solidarity, empowerment, participatory democracy, equity, inclusion, cooperative social responsibility (CSR), or resistance to domination;
- by the type of practices, which are translated into concrete strategies such as people and groups meeting their needs and proposing concrete ways to address their problems such as through self-consumption, organic-ecological agriculture, agro-industries, industries and crafts, savings and solidarity credit, housing, social, popular and ethical banking, microfinance, formal and informal training, technological research, advice and technical

assistance, recreation, care of people and care for the environment, social and community currencies, fair trade, barter, time banks, solidarity colla-boration networks, open market, solidarity markets, meetings to share experiences, systematization, reflection; communal supply and consump-tion, popular dining, recycling, cultural and identity groups, internal and deliberative democracy in public spheres, lobbying and advocacy in public policies;

- by the type of project they are promoting, depending on their scope and limitations and, finally, through the various territorial scales where their actions as subjects are applied as in the creation of direct or immediate socioeconomic benefits, the construction of networks and organic articu-lations by sector or according to territory (unions, federations, confedera-tions), the promotion of citizen movements for rights, and the promotion of antisystem or non-capitalist movements.
- finally, according to their territorial presence: whether local (community, municipal), subnational regional, national, subcontinental regional, global (south/south, north/south, north/north).

From this characterization, taken as a whole, we can draw some preliminary reflections:

a   the enormous diversity or plurality of the Social and Solidarity Econ-omy, expressed in each one of the variables or analytical views (from the production of goods and services to the learning and sharing of experiences);

b   its integrality or amplitude, seen in the fact that the Social and Solidarity Economy is not restricted to the field of the economy, but tries to cover the diverse aspects of reality in all its complexity for it to be transformed (economy, society, culture, politics) in a meaning horizon, both with regard to its values (of solidarity, giving, justice, equity, responsibility, etc.) and to its incidence in politics or its sub-political participation;

c   its ability to innovate on the basis of tradition, given that it incorporates diverse needs and confronts them through creative, original strategies;

d   its inclusive character, particularly of the marginalized, discriminated against or excluded sectors (women, indigenous people, African Amer-icans, workers, the unemployed or underemployed, among others) and

e   its local-global articulation, in so far as the solidarity economy maintains a foot in the particular strategies of the location and another one in global dynamics.

Another way to recover these experiences is using the figure proposed by Lewis and Conaty (cited in Emily Kawano, 2013: 4). The authors differentiate three types or systems of economy: the private (which includes the dark or criminal economy), the public and the social. They also identify various economic expressions on four scales where these systems are located: at the micro-community level, the small district-regional level, the large national-regional level, and the multinational level of global-social enterprises. It can also be seen from the previous scheme that the social system involves four sectors: social enterprises, volunteering, organizations and the family economy.

Theoretical-conceptual approximations to the Social and Solidarity Economy (ECOSOL)

In the face of this great mosaic of expressions from alternative economies, there are distinct positions on the practices and concepts of the Social and Solidarity Economy in relation to the capitalist system, that have to do with the market, the state and society. Unlike the European approach, which believes that the solidarity economy is compatible with the market and the state, the pre-dominant Latin American perspective is focused on the development of this concept as a global alternative to capitalism.

The theory of a Social and Solidarity Economy is still under construction, so that for many reasons the conventional canon of the economy – in its orthodox and heterodox expressions – remains dominant. As it is not possible in this text to cover all of the currents of thought around the concept, we will try to briefly synthesize and outline as much as possible.

The concept of "solidarity economy" was developed in France and in some Latin American countries during the last quarter of the twentieth century, while the concept of "social economy" had been more used in the rest of the countries of the global North. We can say, in short, that the social or solidarity economy consists of a set of practices which have their origin in various factors: Marxist and utopian socialist ideas from the nineteenth century (with their impact on cooperatives, mutual societies and trade union organizations for salaried workers); from the religious side, the social doctrine of the Catholic church from the nineteenth and twentieth centuries (to which can now be added the encyclical "Laudato Si" of this century) and the Liberation Theology in Latin America from the 1960s; the popular education proposals promoted by Paulo Freire and other education specialists, also in Latin America; the ethnic anthropology of Marcel Mauss and his concept of reciprocity, together with the current idea of anti-utilitarianism; the consequences of recent neo-liberal policies, such as the growth of poverty, inequalities, migrations and precarious employment – combined with unemployment and underemployment – and the dismantling of productive chains and communities. But, finally also, in minorities of all types (ethnic, gender, rural, urban-popular, salaried workers, and others), where the ECOSOL is lived as a form of living well, of identity and meaning, of social sense creation and communitarian cohesion.

Different theoretical and conceptual currents coexist around this concept. In Table 5.1 we try to recover some of them in reference to the various schools of theory, their most representative authors, predominant values and their central characteristics.

Some of the main associated concepts are (Gonzáles, 2009: 4–8):

- Popular Solidarity Economy: not all of the popular economy is a solidarity economy, nor does the economy of solidarity as a whole form a part of the popular economy;
- Labor-focused Social Economy: focused on labor and not on capital, given that the (alternative) economy is seen as a system of production, distribution and consumption with relations oriented by needs satisfaction such as a broader reproduction of human life;
- Economy for Life: which refers to the material conditions (biophysical and socio-institutional) that make life possible and sustainable on the basis of necessities satisfaction;
- Feminist economy: this proposes to break away from the capitalist cultural and material basis of the economy, that is, from a patriarchy that ensures the continuity of a hierarchical and unequal society, both in the symbolic and the material areas;
- Ecological Economy: includes ethical principles such as intergenerational equity, social justice and sustainable management, as well as methodological multidisciplinarity, methodological pluralism and historical openness.

Other closely related concepts whose inclusion seems fundamental are the following:

- Social Economy: Based on historical cooperativism, it is structured around three large families of organizations: cooperatives, mutual societies and associations, with the recent incorporation of Foundations (Monzón and Chaves, n/d: 13).
- Substantive Economy: in his book "The Great Transformation", Polanyi (2001), emphasizes the distinction between two differentiated concepts in economics: the formalist and the substantivist. Polanyi proposes three forms of social integration that are different from each other: reciprocity, which presupposes equality between the parties, the redistribution of resources – through appropriation towards the center and then outwards – and exchange in the market, as in the capitalist economy. It is on the reciprocity side of Substantivism that the thinking of the Solidarity Economy gets its refreshment.
- Marcel Mauss's Economic Anthropology Reciprocity: with a strong influence on the ECOSOL. As an anthropologist, Mauss studied the social significance of the gift in tribal societies and demonstrates that the gift is reciprocal because when a non-commercial link is created (in unpaid exchanges or barter), a social bond is formed, forcing the recipient to receive, and the receiver is then obliged to make a return by means of a counter-gift. For Mauss, the gift is essential in human society. His thinking is deepened by the Anti-Utilitarian Movement in Social Sciences (MAUSS), which makes a radical critique of the individual and selfish

interest that is regarded in classical economic theory as a principle and the driving force for attainment of the general interest (Caillé, 2003).

- Common Property Theory: the Nobel laureate in economics, Elinor Ostrom (2012), demonstrated in her numerous research projects, based on fieldwork, game theory and agent models, that individuals can act collectively to manage shared natural resources in a sustainable manner. From this it can be learned that the conditions for individuals to cooperate, participate and interact in sustainable collective actions are having a common knowledge base, communication, and trust in each other allowing them to work together and share the information available to them.
- Altruism of biology: Martin A. Nowak (2012), as a biologist and mathematician and using his game theory applications, argues in his famous book *SuperCooperators: Altruism, Evolution, and Why We Need Each Other to Succeed*, that creatures of any kind and at level of complexity necessarily cooperate to live, and that human society is immersed in cooperation. We are, says Novak, when we work together, the supreme cooperators, the greatest in the known universe.
- Love in biology: Humberto Maturana and Francisco Varela, Chilean biologists, have made great contributions to biology. Maturana (2009) is the first scientist to explain love in the language of his discipline. In his proposal, love is not a quality or a gift, but rather, is a phenomenon of biological relations. It consists of behavior or the kind of behavior – cooperation, altruism, sacrifice, surrender – through which the other, or any other, emerges as a legitimate other in the vicinity where coexistence is possible, in circumstances in which the other, or any other, can be itself.
- Cooperation and altruism from the post-Marxist economy: two economists whose contributions to the ideas of cooperation, altruism, evolution, game theory and strong reciprocity are channels for these ideas – who have collaborated at various times in different projects – are Herbert Gintis and Samuel Bowles. Bowles is close to neo-Marxist or post-Marxist thinking and has conducted studies on inequalities and income in various countries, discovering that investments in the nutrition, health and education of poor children have not only produced greater economic opportunities but also a better performance of the economy. For this reason, East Asian countries with a relatively even distribution of income levels have considerably outperformed Latin American countries with less equitable income distributions (Bowls, Boyd, Fehr and Gintis, 2005).

In Latin American thought, with its critical contributions to the construction of the concept, we find a good contingent of definitions of ECOSOL.

José Luis Coraggio, an Argentine researcher and one of the major Latin American references in studies of the social-solidarity economy, insists on the value of the human and the self-management of associations in this social economy, as well as its non–lucrative character with its sustainability maintained through ties with the family, the community and nature:

The social and solidarity economy is, then, a practice of economics, in which the production, distribution, circulation and consumption of goods and services are organized in an associated and cooperative manner not based on private profit motive, but for the resolution of necessities, seeking high quality living conditions for all those involved, their families and communities, in collaboration with other communities aiming to solve material needs while establishing social ties of fraternity and solidarity, assuming responsibility for the management of natural resources and having respect for future generations, consolidating harmonious and lasting social ties between communities, without exploitation of the work of others.

(Coraggio, 2009: 28)

Pablo Guerra (2014), a Uruguayan professor at the University of the Republic (Montevideo, Uruguay), is emphatic that work is at the center of socio-economical solidarity practices and that what he calls the C Factor should prevail (cooperate, share, live together, collaborate, etc.):

Socio-economic solidarity practices are characterized by making fundamental use of work and the C Factor in productive processes; distribution based on relationships of reciprocity and altruism; consumption in a critical spirit and based on the recognition of plural human needs, and accumulation with a sense of community, all within the framework of projects that tend towards self-management, cooperation and processes of association. In all cases, whether or not benefits are received is not a criterion of importance (with this we distance ourselves from the North American school of the third sector). Neither is the presence or absence of money in the processes of circulation (with this we distance ourselves from the French currents), or the presence or absence of payment for the factors of production (distancing ourselves, finally, from the most established criteria in the field of social economy).

(Guerra, 2014: 53)

In the same sense, and relating economy and life, for the Mexican economist María Arcelia Gonzáles Butrón, economy for life supposes a recovery of the subject:

In the context of neoliberal globalization, living bodies are being excluded – discarded – as never before in history. Today, as a science for life, economics must recover concrete corporeality in the midst of abstractions, data, figures and models; it has to enter into a dialogue with other sciences and kinds of knowledge to recover its orientation and its ultimate objectives. In this regard, we believe that ethical views of economics and economic practice based on human rights, are fundamental today for the discipline to reaffirm the Subject, Humanity and Life.

(Butrón 2012: 13)

Another prominent Latin American thinker, Luis Razeto, a Chilean researcher of long standing in the study of the ECOSOL, emphasizing solidarity and work, holds that ECOSOL consists of:

> A theoretical and practical search for alternative forms of economy based on solidarity and work. Its principle or foundation is that the introduction of increased and qualitatively higher levels of solidarity in activities, organizations and economic institutions, both at the level of companies in markets, and that of public policies, increases micro and macroeconomic efficiency, as well as generating a set of social and cultural benefits that favor society.

(Razeto, 2010: 47)

For Euclides Mance, a Brazilian liberation philosopher and thinker on solidarity economies, the creation of Collaborative Solidarity Networks is a challenge that needs to be taken up to promote the necessary strengthening of these socioeconomic alternatives. Mance states that:

> The basic objective of these networks is to articulate in a supportive and ecological way the productive chains: a) producing in the networks all that they still consume from the capitalist market: final products, supplies, services, etc.; b) correcting flows of values, in order to avoid refeeding capitalist production, which occurs when solidarity enterprises buy goods and services from capitalist companies; c) generating new jobs and distributing income, through the organization of new economic ventures to meet the demands of the networks themselves; d) guaranteeing the economic conditions for the ethical exercise of public and private liberties. Collective reinvestment of surpluses makes the progressive reduction of everyone's workday possible, with an increase of free time for living well and improved consumption patterns for each person.

(2002: 2)

Aníbal Quijano, a Peruvian and one of the most significant writers on dependency theory and de-colonial studies, proposes that reciprocity can be understood – in the context of Latin American and colonial/modern power – as an organization linked to the community in an integral way, of equality within diversity, with horizontal relationships between various identities, that assumes a shared responsibility for our relationship to the world and the universe. It is:

> a reciprocity that reemerges and expands: a) in the organization of production, exchange or distribution, and reproduction; (b) in being

associated with the community as a collective authority structure; (c) made up of individuals with social equality within diversity and a heterogeneity of individual and collective identities; (d) run by horizontal relationships between individuals of all identities, beginning with differences between sexes and sexualities; (e) using and reproducing relationships with other living beings and f) encouraging a culture of stewardship as inhabitants of the universe.

(2008: 15)

On the other hand, from the religious sphere, the ECOSOL is also being promoted by the Society of Jesus. The Secretariat for Social Justice and Ecology of the General Curia of the Society of Jesus has defined the social and solidarity economy as: "an economic alternative that departs from the common and responds to the common. It is formed from critical analysis of the political, social and cultural; it dignifies the value of work and puts people, communities and environment in harmony at the center of its Praxis" (SJSE, 2016: 24).

We have made a short journey through Latin American thinking on economic solidarity in order to get closer to some precise definitions. The various definitions lead us to think that it is, apparently, what we might call a "bio-economy", a life economy that integrates various dimensions of social life, an alternative economy in producing, exchanging and reproducing; where life, expanded reciprocity and solidarity prevail. It implies a recovery of the subject and of society by means of an expanded reproduction of human life for all, both in social institutions and in cultural constructions through respect for and inclusion of diverse identities, on the basis of social equity and harmony with nature. Not for nothing, as Humberto Maturana (2009: 18) argues in biological terms that the intimate nature of the human social phenomenon derives from its ethical foundation: "Acceptance of and respect for the other, which is at the heart of love as the biological foundation of the social".

In Table 5.1 we have seen some of the main scientific schools and theories that have contributed to the values of altruism, cooperation and reciprocity in socio-economic relations. Now it is convenient to locate the original sources that the concept of Social and Solidarity Economy drinks from. In Table 5.2. it is possible to observe the various theories on the basis of which the concept of the Solidarity Economy is used, such as the Other Economy, that is, an Alter-Economy (alternative economy) or Solidarity Bioeconomy. Depending on the various theoretical and disciplinary traditions such as Marxism, the social doctrine of the Catholic Church, utopian socialism and the ethnic anthropology of Marcel Mauss (2009), in addition to their various socio-economic hybridizations, new conceptual proposals tend to merge concepts around the Solidarity Economy to generate "hybrid conceptual linkages": such as: the Social and Solidarity Economy, Popular Solidarity Economy, Social Solidarity and Ecological Economy, Solidarity Collaboration Networks, and others.

Table 5.1 Alternative economies schools of thought and theoretical currents

School	Authors	Predominant values	Characteristics
French	M. Mauss	Reciprocity	Economic anthropology
			Gift – Counter-gift
	A. Caillé-MAUSS (Social Sciences Anti-utilitarian Movement)	Anti-utilitarianism	Sociology
			Against instrumental rationality and economism
	J.L. Laville	Solidarity Reciprocity	Sociology
			Multiple democratization: internal democracy, solidarity, of the economy and institutionalization
American	E. Ostrom	Cooperation	Socioeconomics
			Based on trust, communication, information
	A. Etzioni	Responsible communitarianism	Socioeconomics
			Multidimensionality of the economy interwoven with politics, culture, society, the environment
	H. Gintis, S. Bowles	Cooperation, altruism, evolution	Post-Marxist Economy
Spanish	J.L. Monzón	Service to people as active citizens	Socioeconomics
			Internal democracy, service and profit or not
Latin American	J.L. Coraggio	Life	Socioeconomics
			Extended Reproduction
	L. Razeto	Solidarity	Socioeconomics
			Cooperation, trust, self-management and association forming
	M. Arruda	Love	Socioeconomics
			Integral humanization
	F. Hinkelammert Quijano	Life	Bio economy

School	Authors	Predominant values	Characteristics
Other			
Frankfurt School	K. Polanyi	Reciprocity	Substantivist economy
Complex thought	E. Morin	Life	Complex thinking and Sociology
			Distributive justice
			Proximity
			Sustainability
	H. Maturana y F. Varela	Love, Life	Biology of love
			Aptitude and adaptation
			Cooperation and competition
	M.A. Nowak	Altruism	Altruism in human behavior
	E. Mance	Collaboration	Socioeconomics
			Collaborative networks in Solidarity
	G. Díaz	Life	Complex thought and socioeconomics
			Inter dimensionality and socio-economic complexity

Source: Own elaboration

ECOSOL as an Emerging Social Movement: metamorphosis of the alternative solidarity economies

For Alberto Melucci (1999), a disciple of Alain Touraine and social movements researcher, there is no social movement as such, as a unity, as something homogeneous and integrated, but only as a plurality of social processes, actors and forms of action, full of internal differences and even conflicts at various times. A social movement is a unit of actors identifying themselves as having a common enemy – in this case the prevailing neoliberal capitalism – who are in possession of an objective, alternative project to transform the predominating reality into another economy or, here, into an alternative economy – with a diversity of actors and an identity that emerges from this objective – an inward-looking identity, as in self-recognition, and outward looking, as in recognition by others.

Hence, we can distinguish a diversified set of actors who are part of the social and solidarity economy movement at the global level. These include the international Network for the Promotion of Social and Solidarity Economy (RIPESS), constituted as a space of promotion of the ECOSOL; the various fair trade networks on national

Table 5.2 Solidarity economy conceptual map as an alternative economy or bio economy

		Liberation theology		
		(L. Boff)	Economy of love	
			(M. Arruda,	
		Popular education	F. Hinkelamert)	
Classical economics	Marxism,	(P. Freire)		**Alter- or**
(A. Smith)	political economy and value theory	Labor economics		**Solidarity**
	(K. Marx)	(L. Gaiger, J.L. Coraggio)		**Bioeconomy**
		Popular economy	Popular Solidarity Economy	
		(J.L. Coraggio,	(J.L. Coraggio,	
		L. Razeto)	L. Razeto)	
Utopian socialism	Cooperativism	Cooperative economy		
(Ch. Fournier)	(Rochdale)	(P. Singer)		
	Ecology	Ecological economy	Ecological social and solidarity economy	
Economic anthropology of reciprocity	(E. Haeckel)	(J. Martínez Alier)	(D. Barkin)	
(M. Mauss)				
	Anti-utilitarianism			
	(A. Caillé)			
Christian social doctrine	Solidarity economy			
	(L. Razeto)			
	Substantive economy	SASE	Social and solidarity economy	
	(K. Polanyi)	(A. Etzioni)	(CIRIEC)	
Socioeconomics	Complex thinking		Solidarity collaborative networks	
	(E. Morin)		(E. Mance)	
	Common goods			

	Liberation theology
(E. Ostrom)	
Biology: Love (H. Maturana) and Altruism (M.A. Nowak)	
Post-Marxian Economy: Cooperation (S. Bowles and H. Gillis)	

Source: own elaboration based on Díaz (2015)

and global scales such as International Fairtrade Labelling Organizations (FLO); the International Co-operative Alliance with about one million cooperative members and its chapter in the Americas (ACI); the International Association of Investors in the Social Economy (INAISE) as a global network of approximately forty financial institutions as its members; the World Social Forum and its several ECOSOL expressions; the Via Campesina, a global organization with 200 million peasants from more than 140 countries; the Network of Latin American Researchers into Social and Solidarity Economy (RILESS); the Mont Blanc Meetings, held annually in France, aiming to give the Social and Solidarity Economy increasingly greater visibility and international incidence, endeavoring to constitute itself in the long run as a kind of counterweight to Davos and a showcase for the social and solidarity economy of the world with actions of transnational relevance; the *Centre International de Recherches et d'Information sur l'Economie Publique, Sociale et Coopérative* (CIRIEC) with chapters in different countries; the Anti-Utilitarian Movement in Social Sciences – MAUSS – based in France, and the Society for the Advancement of the Socio-Economy (SASE), among others.

As social movements researchers have pointed out, it is common for the practices among them to be diverse, including different interests and ideological-political programs. In this sense, and from the values emphasized in complex thought, we can say that there are several tendencies in the economic-solidarity movement (Diaz, 2015: 301–302):

- Radical or antisystem (anticapitalistic, against the liberal state and the market);
- Transitional (non-capitalist, in dialogue with a transformed state and markets);
- Complementary or human face (in dialogue with the State and the market and as a capitalist system complement).
- Bureaucratic statist (State capitalism with a single or dominant party and regulated markets).

In Table 5.3 we give an account of these trends. According to Pablo González Casanova (González, 2004), complex systems can be divided into:

a   autonomous/adaptive/self-regulated/dominant systems and
b   autonomous/adaptive/self-regulated/emergent-alternative systems:

Table 5.3 Typology and analytical synthesis of ECOSOL tendencies in Latin America (with porous borders)

Spheres/ Dimensions	Economy (Market)	Policy (State)	Society (Society and Culture)	Nature (Ecosystems)	Glocalization (Global/local)	Value orientation
Logic-Rationality Complex systems	Exchange	Power	Relationships and Meanings	Sustainability	Spatiality	Value
ECOSOL Type	**Predominant relationship**					
Radical utopian emerging	Anti-capitalist and post-capitalist	Sub-politics	Inclusive non-citizenship with interculturality	Harmonic	Contra-Hegemonic and Alternative	Reciprocity
Utopian emerging transitional	Non-capitalist and post-neo-liberal	Demo-Diversity (representative, participatory and community democracy) Active state, democratic and regulator	Inclusive citizenship with interculturality	Harmonic	Contra-Hegemonic and Alternative	Reciprocity
Adaptive dominant complementary	Capitalist with human face and post-neoliberal	Demo-diversity (representative, participatory and community democracy) Active and democratic State	Inclusive citizenship with interculturality	Harmonic	Nuanced hegemonic International organizations democratization	Equity
Emerging utopian state or bureaucratic	Anti-capitalist, Post-capitalist or State capitalism	Single or dominant party democracy Governing state and owner	Corporate semi-inclusive citizen with interculturality	Harmonic	Contra-Hegemonic and alternative	Social justice

Source: Own elaboration based on (Diaz, 2015)

However, it is possible to notice the emerging-transforming footprint of all of them in other possible economies and worlds.

Final reflections: other economies are possible, or changing the world from the small

In the face of a world that is rapidly destroying itself on a path of selfish individualism and with predatory capitalism in its current state of savagery, we have made a small journey through the emerging economies that are changing the world. These experiences, and the thinkers commenting on them, are raising their bets on the new economies that put human life and the planet at the center of existence. We have tried to recognize the contributions and tendencies of each in various efforts to systematize the experiences and practices, on the one hand, and the conceptual currents that sustain them, on the other.

In this enormous diversity there are complementary interdependent values that make it possible to recognize the meaning given to them by those who put them into practice: resilience, distributive justice and retribution with equity, decent work, anti-utilitarianism, reciprocity, trustful cooperation, democracy in several orders (representative, socially participative and communitarian), love and humanization and, increasingly, life itself. Like everything in life, the new Social and Solidarity Economies are not exempt from limitations, errors and contradictions. However, it seems undeniable that they offer us tentative answers to the systemic inability of capitalism to conserve life on the planet in a more humanizing and a fuller, fairer and more equitable way; in short, one that is more sustainable and has a sense of fraternity and harmony. A simple representation of these values is found in Figure 5.1.

If for Immanuel Wallerstein (2005) capitalism is in its terminal phase and what will follow is uncertainty – towards a new, fairer, egalitarian and democratic world-system, or, in the worst case, towards greater global authoritarianism – we can close this text by opening the door to hope. According to the proposals formulated in his book *The Way: for the Future of Mankind*, starting with a principle of antagonism and complementarity in dialogue (so it is not dichotomous), Morin (2011: 36) invites us to reflect on the following:

> The orientation of growth/decrease means that services for people, green energies, public transport, the plural economy including the social and solidarity economy, the humanizing urbanism of megalopolises, traditional and biological agriculture and stockbreeding, must grow. But it also means a lessening of consumer fever, of the production of industrialized food and non-repairable single use objects, of the predominance of intermediaries in production and consumption, of the traffic of private cars and the transport of goods by road (instead of the railway).

We are called, in a nutshell, to take care of life and its enlarged reproduction. Social and Solidarity Economies have already put up their hands to take part in

Figure 5.1 Values present in the solidarity economies
Source: Own elaboration

social transformation. And even if the outbreaks of alternatives in the wilderness of today's savage capitalism are relatively few in number, these small but significant changes and emergencies can transform the world, in the hope of a metamorphosis of the system.

Bibliography

Boff, L. (2010). *La Madre Tierra como sujeto de Dignidad y de Derechos*. Available online at https://systemicalternatives.org/2014/02/13/la-madre-tierra-como-sujeto-de-dignidad-y-de-derechos/ (accessed June 15, 2018).

Bowls, S., Boyd, R., Fehr, E. and Gintis, H. (2005). *Moral Sentiments and Material Interests: The Foundations of Cooperation in Economic Life*. Cambridge, MA: MIT Press.

Caillé, A. (2003). *"Sur les Concepts en general et solidaire en particulier"*. Paris: L'alter-économie. Available online at www.cairn.info/revue-du-mauss-2003-1-page-215.htm (accessed May 20, 2018).

Coraggio, J.L. (2009). *El rol de la economía social y solidaria en la estrategia de inclusión social*. México: Decisio. Available online at http://decisio.crefal.edu.mx (accessed February 15, 2018).

Díaz, J.G. (2015). *Economías Solidarias en América Latina*. Guadalajara: ITESO.

Díaz, J.G. (2014). ¿Desarrollo Alternativo o Alternativas al desarrollo? Repensando el concepto desde el Sur Global. In *Las alternativas ciudadanas para otros mundos posibles: pensamiento y experiencias*, Enrique Luengo González (coord.). Guadalajara: Complexus Iteso, pp. 19–42.

Gonzáles, M.A. (2012). *Ética de la economía, sujeto y derechos humanos*. México: Polis. Available online at http://polis.revues.org/8509 (accessed January 11, 2018).

Gonzáles, M.A. (2009). *Economía social para la vida: desafíos para la educación*. México: Decisio. Available online at http://decisio.crefal.edu.mx (accessed February 3, 2018).

González, P. (2004). *Las Nuevas Ciencias y las Humanidades. De la Academia a la Política.* Barcelona: Antropos.

Guerra, P. (2014). *Socioeconomía de la solidaridad Una teoría para dar cuenta de las experiencias sociales y económicas alternativas* (2nd ed.). Bogotá: Ediciones de la Universidad Cooperativa de Colombia.

ICA (2010). Statistical information on the co-operative movement. Available online at http://ica.coop/coop/statistics.html (accessed February 2, 2018).

ICA (2011). The 300 global cooperatives. Available online at https://ica.coop/sites/defa ult/files/basic-page-attachments/global300-report-2011-1757377405.pdf   (accessed February 2, 2018).

Mance, E. (2002). *Redes de Colaboración Solidaria.* Curitiba: IFIL.

Kawano, E. (2013). *Social Solidarity Economy: Toward Convergence Across Continental Divides.* United Nations Research Institute for Social Development (UNRISD), 26 Feb 2013. Available online at www.unrisd.org/unrisd/website/newsview.nsf/(http News)/F1E9214CF8EA21A8C1257B1E003B4F65 (accessed January 15, 2018).

Mauss, M. (2009). *Ensayo sobre el don. Forma y función del intercambio en sociedades arcaicas.* Buenos Aires: Katz Editores.

Maturana, H. (2009). *La realidad: ¿objetiva o construida? Fundamentos biológicos de la Realidad (segunda edición).* México: Anthropos.

Melucci, A. (1999). *Acción colectiva, vida cotidiana y democracia.* México: Colegio de México.

Monzón, J.L. and Chaves, R. (n/d). *The Social Economy in the European Union.* Report prepared for the European Economic and Social Committee by the International Centre for Research and Information on the Public, Social and Cooperative Economy (CIRIEC). Available   online   at   www.eesc.europa.eu/resources/docs/ qe-30-12-790-en-c.pdf (accessed February 20, 2018).

Morin, E. (2011). *La Vía: Para el futuro de la humanidad.* Barcelona, Buenos Aires, México: Paidós.

Nowak, M. and Highfield, R. (2012). *SuperCooperators: Altruism, Evolution, and Why We Need Each Other to Succeed.* New York: Free Press.

Ostrom, E. and Walker, J. (2003). *Trust and Reciprocity and Gains from Association: Interdisciplinary Lessons for Experimental Research.* New York: Russell Sage Foundation.

OXFAM. (2016). *Una economía al servicio del 1%. Acabar con los privilegios y la concentración de poder para frenar la desigualdad extrema.* Thematic Report of OXFAM, January 2016. Available online at www.oxfam.org/sites/www.oxfam.org/files/file_attachments/bp 210-economy-one-percent-tax-havens-180116-es_0.pdf (accessed February 1, 2018).

Pope Francis (2015). *Carta Encíclica "Laudato Si" del Santo Padre Francisco sobre El Cuidado de la Casa Común.* Available online at www.aciprensa.com/Docum/LaudatoSi.pdf (accessed March 4, 2018).

Piketty, T. (2014). *El capital en el Siglo XXI.* Madrid: Fondo de Cultura Económica.

Polanyi, K. (2001). *The Great Transformation: The Political and Economic Origins of Our Time.* Boston: Beacon Press.

Polanyi, K. (1976). *El sistema económico como proceso institucionalizado.* In M. Godelier, *Antropología y Economía.* Barcelona: Anagrama, pp. 157–178.

Quijano, A. (2008). *Solidaridad y capitalismo colonial/moderno.* Brasil: Otra Economía. Available online at www.economiasolidaria.org/files/Revista_RILESS_2.pdf (accessed November 4, 2017).

Razeto, L. (2010). *¿Qué es la economía solidaria?* España: FUHEM Ecosocial. Available online at http://base.socioeco.org/docs/que_es_la_economia_solidaria_l.razeto.pdf (accessed October 5, 2017).

SJSE (2016). *Por una economía global justa. Construir sociedades sostenibles e inclusivas.* Secretariado para la Justicia Social y la Ecología. Informe Especial del Grupo de Trabajo sobre Economía del Secretariado para la Justicia Social y la Ecología de la Curia General de la Compañía de Jesús.

UN (United Nations) (2015). *Transforming Our World: The 2030 Agenda for Sustainable Development.* Resolution adopted by the General Assembly on 25 September 2015. Available online at www.un.org/ga/search/view_doc.asp?symbol=A/RES/70/1&Lang=E (accessed March 4, 2018).

UNESCO (2016). *Afrontar el reto de las desigualdades y trazar vías hacia un mundo justo. Informe Mundial sobre Ciencias Sociales.* UNESCO, Instituto de Estudios del Desarrollo y Consejo Internacional de Ciencias Sociales (CICS). Available online at http://unesdoc.unesco.org/images/0024/002459/245995s.pdf (accessed March 11, 2018).

Wallerstein, I. (2005). *Análisis del Sistema-mundo. Una introducción.* México: Siglo XX.

Part III
Ecological economy, political ecology and degrowth

6 Sustainable consumption and ecological sufficiency

Discourses and power relations

Marco Paulo Vianna Franco

Most of the luxuries, and many of the so-called comforts of life, are not only not indispensable, but positive hindrances to the elevation of mankind. With respect to luxuries and comforts, the wisest have ever lived a more simple and meagre life than the poor.

– Henry David Thoreau, *Walden*.

Introduction

Sustainability science relates to the rational use of scarce resources in a long-term perspective, with intrinsic uncertainty, seeking intertemporal satisfaction of human needs and justice in the relationship among humans and among humans and nature (Baumgärtner & Quaas, 2010). It is a discipline that encompasses ethical and moral aspects, in which not only efficiency, but also intra- and intergenerational justice is considered, i.e. a field concerned with possibilities and objectives in a biophysical and social context of the interactions between man and the natural world (Scerri, 2012).

The report of the World Commission on Environment and Development (1987, p. 8), a milestone in the establishment and dissemination of the concept of sustainable development, has unequivocally mentioned the need to promote sustainable consumption patterns, asserting that "sustainable global development requires that those who are more affluent adopt life-styles within the planet's ecological means - in their use of energy, for example". A similar idea has been presented in the 1970s, part of the argument of Paul Ehrlich, John Holdren and Barry Commoner, who have proposed that environmental impacts could be assessed according to the product of three factors: population, technology and affluence, whereas the latter would be given in terms of wealth per capita, individual material accumulation or even as production and consumption intensity (Ehrlich & Holdren, 1971). While the populational and technological factors have both received much attention in public and scholarly debates, little has been accomplished to alter the effects of excessive affluence or, more specifically, of overconsumption on the environment, at least until the beginning of the

1990s, when the discourse termed "ecological modernization" has emerged (Roepke, 2005).

Often considered as a similar concept to sustainable consumption, ecological sufficiency can be defined as the voluntary restriction of one's individual consumption motivated by an ecological concern or responsibility toward the future of human and non-human species (Heindl & Kanschik, 2016). Such assertion implies the reduction in absolute consumption levels, bearing in mind biophysical limits or the carrying capacity of the planet vis-à-vis the pressure made by the scale of human activities, materially and energetically.

In order to better understand the scope, limitations, meanings and consequences of the concepts of sustainable development and ecological sufficiency, the associated discourses need to be properly examined in the context of the power relations embedded in such a complex and controversial topic. Therefore, the ideas of sustainable consumption and ecological sufficiency must be thoroughly assessed, the former with its different interpretations and appropriations by technical and ideological discourses, the latter as part of a more precautious stance regarding sustainability, based on individual voluntarism and supported by various discourses, which include scientific theoretical frameworks, state policies, traditional knowledge and practices, resistance movements and moral or religious arguments.

Discourses on sustainable consumption

The concept of sustainable consumption carries many different meanings and interpretations, with the dominant vision of the term relating to

> the use of goods and related products which respond to basic needs and bring a better quality of life, while minimizing the use of natural resources and toxic materials as well as the emissions of waste and pollutants over the life cycle, so as not to jeopardize the needs of future generations.
> (United Nations Department of Economic and Social Affairs, 1995 as cited in OECD, 2002, p. 9)

Consumption-related issues have been one of the key aspects of the United Nations' post-2015 development agenda, as illustrated by the twelfth of the UN's Sustainable Development Goals: to "ensure sustainable consumption and production patterns". Sustainable consumption, along with a sustainable production, would be "about promoting resource and energy efficiency, sustainable infrastructure, and providing access to basic services, green and decent jobs and a better quality of life for all", a statement that corroborates the interpretation of "doing more and better with less" (United Nations, n.d.).

A more precise understanding of the term involves the concepts of weak and strong sustainable consumption. The former relates to efficiency gains in production and consumption processes in terms of matter and energy flows, seeking to minimize the rates of natural resource use and waste generation, while maintaining human material wellbeing. The latter, in turn, implies significant habit changes in consumption patterns of wealthier individuals, with a reduction in the absolute levels of matter and energy transformations (Sedacklo, Martinuzzi, Roepke, Videira, & Antunes, 2014).

According to Sedacklo et al. (2014), the widespread use of the expression "sustainable consumption" has not stimulated new research or public policies that engage in altering the lifestyle of the rich, i.e. in promoting strong sustainable consumption. Instead, the weak variant of the expression has increasingly gained ground as the predominant interpretation of the concept, in line with the discourse associated with ecological modernization theories. These theories advocate that ecological challenges might be successfully overcome through a reform of modern practices and institutions, based on the increasing relevance of an ecological perspective or rationality, induced by environmental problems (Mol, 2002). A continued industrial development would be the best option for escaping ecological crises while fostering employment, given the power of technological innovations to enhance economic competition by means of reduced resource use and waste generation (Andersen & Massa, 2000; Fisher & Freudenburg, 2001). According to Buttel (2000), it "hypothesizes that while the most challenging environmental problems of this century and the next have (or will have) been caused by modernization and industrialization, their solutions must necessary lie in more – rather than less – modernization and 'superindustrialization'". In such a view, sustainable consumption would be compatible with endless economic growth through the dematerialization of the economy. Constant technological innovations would allow for growth without significant rises in flows of matter and energy. Therefore, a sustainable consumption could be achieved by means of new "green" business opportunities in response to a higher demand for ecologically competitive products. A quantitative limit to consumption levels of the wealthy or provisions for the satisfaction of basic consumption needs of the poor play a secondary role in this approach. Economic growth, a condition for the social stability of capitalist societies, is thus treated as the solution to both ecological and social challenges. Such cornucopian view rests on dubious claims on the dematerialization of the economy, which focus on relative efficiency gains and disregard absolute levels of material and energy use by humans, making the case for further unlimited and unequal appropriation of resources.

Lorek and Fuchs (2013) have contributed to the analysis of discourses on sustainable consumption, claiming that research on this topic have little connection to other lines of inquiry on sustainable development, such as degrowth theories, despite the benefits that a systemic approach to sustainability might yield. The authors have attributed this circumstance to the dominance of the ecological modernization discourse applied to the issue of consumption, which shifts focus to efficiency gains through technological progress. Furthermore, governance modes based on weak sustainable consumption would be unable to provide adequate answers to challenges such as the limited carrying capacity of ecosystems or distributive conflicts inherent to capitalistic accumulation of wealth. Conversely, strong sustainable consumption would be a key element – although one that still lacks political power – to the fulfilment of sustainability science's purposes of intertemporally satisfying human needs and assuring justice in the relations among humans and among humans and nature.

Empirical studies that show an increasing decoupling of wealth from wellbeing (or happiness, with this line of research being commonly referred to as "happiness economics") as individual affluence grows, a phenomenon known as the "Easterlin paradox" (Easterlin, 1974), have not prevented the marginalization of the strong sustainable consumption discourse, mainly due to the opposition of influential social segments, such as corporations (Roepke, 2005). On the other hand, recent research results on the conditioning factors of wellbeing might assist political discourses in defense of a strong sustainable consumption. Feedback mechanisms between scientific research and social discourses (such as environmental science and environmentalist movements, respectively) have the potential to lead to the emergence of new political agendas, which nevertheless must compete with other – more or less antagonistic – agendas composed by different sets of research and social discourses. The challenge of the case for a strong sustainable consumption would then be to overcome the dominance of a political agenda driven by ideas and practices of ecological modernization.

The analysis of the power relations behind the appropriation of the meaning of sustainable consumption by conflicting discourses is frequently omitted from research and public policies on the issue (Fuchs et al., 2015). The lack of an explicit, comprehensive analysis of such relations hinders the proper understanding of the mechanisms that drive overconsumption, thus preventing the conception of policies that induce consistent changes in consumer's habits in line with the tenets of environmental sustainability and social justice. In this sense, Fuchs et al. (2015, p. 4) affirm that "sustainable consumption and absolute reductions research and action need to consider who sets the agenda, defines the rules and the narratives, selects the instruments of governance and their targets, and thus influences peoples' behavior, options, and their impacts". The dominance of the ecological modernization discourse ought to be understood as part of a wider hegemonic consensus (in a Gramscian sense) in the political and scientific spheres, beginning in the nineteenth century and intensifying in the post-war period, which legitimizes the universalization of capitalistic development. The market and its capacity to provide individuals with the necessary commodities for a "modern" way of life have become the unfaltering centre of a global agenda that inherently reproduces and expands such institutions through either civil or military power.

Scholarly and political debates on consumption and its associated discourses and power relations have repeatedly been subjected to the idea of consumer sovereignty (Fellner & Spash, 2014). One of the canons of neoclassical economics, the sovereignty of consumer preferences, enacted through the demand for goods and services, appeals to the idea that social and environmental degradation caused by market practices derive ultimately from the aggregate result of autonomous, individual actions, and are therefore justified. If individuals choose to consume excessively, to purchase highly polluting products, to reject "green" products or to disregard biodiversity loss, for example, markets should, according to this precept of consumer sovereignty, reflect these decisions and behaviours, maximizing human material welfare. Nevertheless, as Fellner and Spash (2014) refer to the "illusion of consumer sovereignty", consumers do not actually normatively control the economy, or even their own role in it. Their choices and preferences are social and cultural constructions, subject to dominant discourses imposed and spread by those who hold positions of political, intellectual or social power. The precept of individualism in the above-mentioned hegemonic capitalistic consensus, aided by a market-centred social order and a scientific ideal of human development, turns out to be a moral justification for such an ideology, with no direct correspondence to social reality. Legislative acts, advertising, investment decisions, orientation of technological innovation (including more questionable practices, such as planned obsolescence in product design) and scientific dogmatism are, among others, powerful instruments of propaganda or coercion tactics that may influence consumer habits. Road infrastructure, massive supply of fossil fuels, land transport legislation, automotive industry marketing and technical innovations in the sector, for example, compose a quite specific context in which individuals make daily decisions whether to buy a car or not, in a not very sovereign fashion. Producers can initiate changes in consumption patterns by channelling consumers' behaviour to new products. Hence, consumer sovereignty, a concept often used to obscure reality and avoid ruptures in the established order, turns to a myth when exposed to a thorough analysis of power relations (Latouche, 2007).

The efforts to introduce the strong sustainable consumption discourse, on the other hand, have been based on the belief that a reduced material consumption would lead to a correspondent workload reduction and therefore to an improved quality of life (the so-called "double dividends" of curbing consumption, with environmental and human welfare gains). Such efforts, although capable of balancing the power scale, are themselves bearers of moralistic ideological views (Alcott, 2008). Roepke endorses this assessment, stating that

> sometimes the promotion of the double dividend idea can get a moralistic touch: we should just give up all this bad and immoral consumerism and change our materialistic values, as it would simply make us better off – an idea lying in continuation of the old critiques of the consumer society.
>
> (2005, p. 11)

According to the author, achieving such state of affairs is not only difficult, but questionable, as consumption patterns are deeply ingrained in social and cultural life. Attempting to isolate and alter consumption behaviour affects and is affected by many other social variables, and to label it as strictly egoistic would be misleading (Miller 1995). These insights lead to yet another question: to what point should consumption be reduced, in absolute levels, if social purpose is to maximize the so-called double dividends? A conclusive answer still eludes researchers and policy makers alike.

The new discourse of ecological sufficiency

Ecological sufficiency (or eco-sufficiency) pledges a voluntary restriction of consumption at the individual level, motivated by a conscious concern about the current human-induced ecological challenges. The voluntarist character of such proposal has faced strong criticism, as a top-down, coercive agenda would probably lead to more effective results in the short term. However, such view would be incompatible with moral values of modern liberal societies, with bottom-up strategies replacing central planning as tools more in line with democratic processes. A voluntary approach that enables changes in consumption habits, even if not yet attested as an effective tool for environmental protection, is justified at least as a complementary effort to halt ecological degradation and their severe, uncertain consequences (Heindl & Kanschik, 2016). If associated with other public policies aiming sustainability in all forms of human activities, ecological sufficiency can not only reduce conspicuous consumption, but also channel resources to more environmentally friendly, nonmarket products that, in turn, enhance individuals' self-sufficiency and autonomy regarding their consumption needs.

Heindl & Kanschik (2016) stress four main aspects of ecological sufficiency: its ecological objective or concern; its individual approach, consumption-based actions and voluntarism. The authors argue that the voluntarism of ecological sufficiency would call for an implicit necessity to make public what are the actual local and global ecological limits, in order to have a clear target, quantitatively and non-arbitrarily assessed, by which people could willingly act upon through more or less thrifty choices. Such assessment, based on objective observations of biophysical conditions of the environment, could, nonetheless, mean that even the fulfilment of solely the most basic human needs, culturally determined, would be enough to exceed ecological limits. In this case, humanity would be faced with a moral dilemma not yet thoroughly explored in the literature.

The role of discourses and power relations is vital to a more comprehensive understanding of the social dynamics involving ecological sufficiency and individual liberties (Heindl & Kanschik, 2016). Public discourses strongly influence individual decisions to voluntarily adopt ecological sufficiency, which are often motivated by personal identity formation processes (Elliott, 2004), new opinions of what constitutes a good life (a simpler life, proximity to nature, leisure time, stronger community bonds and a sense of freedom from the oppression of consumerism) (Fischer & Grießhammer, 2013) and other intangible benefits. There are few studies on the impacts of public policies supporting the implementation of practices related to ecological sufficiency, both at the individual level or as part of more encompassing political programs. Even rarer are studies that seek to evaluate the negative interference of the dominant discourse of ecological modernization to the dissemination and operationalization of voluntary sufficiency principles.

The ecological concern embedded in the concept of ecological sufficiency contrasts with the anthropocentric view of nature, in which it is reduced into resources for the satisfaction of human needs, and therefore its preservation would only be of advantage if linked to positive outcomes in terms of material welfare. A genuine concern and responsibility toward nature, including future generations of human and non-human species, brings ecological sufficiency closer to biocentrism, with mankind considered as an inseparable part of its environment.

Discourses compatible with ecological sufficiency

The rise of discourses that promote ideas and practices in synch with the view of ecological sufficiency, although still far from equalling the powerful, dominant discourse of ecological modernization, can be illustrated by theoretical approaches and real-world public policies that foster actions contrary to conspicuous consumption habits. The analyses below focus on elements of a few selected initiatives that seek either to mitigate or provide alternatives to overconsumption and its social and environmental ill effects.

Theoretical approaches

Amartya Sen's capability approach

Amartya Sen (1992; 1999) has proposed a distinctive approach to the notion of sustainability, linking environmental conservation with the satisfaction of a culturally-determined set of the most basic human needs. Sen's well-known capability approach can be seen as a normative analysis of a sought-after balance between social welfare and environmental sustainability (Ballet, Koffi, & Pelenc, 2013), based on value judgements and individual freedom enjoyed by human beings acting not only egoistically, but also concerned with the well-being of others, including future generations and non-human species, in a social context that moves beyond the utilitarian view adopted by neoclassical economic theory. Sen's framework takes into account the restrictions to which human choices are subjected, as well as the lack of alternatives to exercise individual freedom. It is thus possible to better understand the relationship between man and the surrounding natural world, in a setting of social and technical evolution, and consequently formulate policies aiming at once human welfare and environmental sustainability. The search for new ways of social organization that point toward individual choices with milder environmental impacts constitutes, along with a consideration for intergenerational justice, a promising line of research in the field of sustainability science.

For an effective implementation of such framework, it is fundamental to assess the vulnerability, adaptation skills and resilience of individuals facing the challenges arising from a changing environment. Likewise, it is important to comprehend how the actions of such individuals influence such changes. Ballet, Bazin, Dubois and Mahieu (2011) illustrate these premises using choices relevant to the intergenerational aspects of deforestation. The absence of alternatives of local traditional communities to the utilization of wood as a source of subsistence is contrasted to other consumption patterns, such as those connected to deforestation for large-scale economic purposes, e.g. livestock or biofuel plantations. The former use would correspond more directly to basic human needs than the latter, if considered in terms of the intergenerational opportunities and restrictions by which the fulfilment of basic needs is conditioned.

Environmental justice

Environmental justice is one of the main subjects of political ecology, a field defined by Martinez-Alier (2002, p. 54) as "the study of ecological distribution conflicts". It analyzes the connections between power inequality and environmental degradation within the paradigm of economic growth. Given the ecological limits on a planetary level, developed countries would have to restrain their own consumption, releasing scarce resources for more vulnerable areas to have their most basic needs satisfied. In this sense, as argued by Heindl and Kanschik (2016), there would be a conflict between the principles of ecological sufficiency and social justice: the former proposes an upper limit and the latter a lower limit to consumption. These would correspond respectively to an ecological ceiling and a social foundation, as per Raworth's (2017) concept of "doughnut economics". Public policies should aim for the interval between these two boundaries, as meeting demands for social justice is essential to ensure public support for environmental issues, including actions in favour of sufficiency; and, in turn, the observance of ecological thresholds would prevent large-scale social degradation as a result from halting ecosystem services. Food and energy security represent, in this sense, key aspects of "socially inclusionary and environmentally sound development strategies" (Sachs, 2015, p. 13). The current global imbalances in food (Patel, 2012) and energy (Arto, Capellán-Pérez, Lago, Bueno, & Bermejo, 2016) consumption demonstrate how far mankind still is from becoming a sustainable society, hinting toward the role ecological sufficiency might play in this endeavour.

Research in environmental justice thus asks whether income redistribution and poverty eradication would lead to higher or lower environmental damages (Sawyer, 2002). The answer depends on a systemic understanding of populational dynamics and changes in consumption habits, also taking into consideration how direct and indirect impacts emerge from integrated productive economic cycles, determined by international relations between the global North and South, especially with reference to commodity exports as unidirectional – South to North –

energy and matter transferences with deteriorated terms of trade (Altvater, 1992). By acknowledging the complexity involved, a more simplistic view can be avoided, in which environmental havoc is caused by wealth in the North and poverty in the South, an easy target for discourses and powers related to ecological modernization, which attempt to justify economic growth and "green" business opportunities through social demands and ecological restrictions.

Economic degrowth

In the 1970s, a reinvigorated environmentalist movement, the oil crisis and the appearance of well-known academic books such as Club of Rome's Limits to Growth (Meadows, Meadows, Randers, & Behrens, 1972) and Rachel Carson's Silent Spring (Carson, 1968) have been accompanied by the works of economists arguing that economic processes are also natural processes, comprised ultimately of biological, physical and chemical transformations. Backed by recent developments in general systems theory and the laws of modern thermodynamics, they have tried to restore focus on biophysical constraints to economic growth on a finite planet, and on the role of flows and stocks of energy and matter in the life-supporting metabolic processes on earth (Ayres & Kneese, 1969; Boulding, 1966; Daly, 1968; Georgescu-Roegen, 1971). These and other economists sharing the same ideas have later been associated with ecological economics, a school of economic thought focusing on the human economy both as a social system and as a subset of the biophysical universe. The entropy law, formulated by Sadi Carnot back in 1850, was a key issue. According to Georgescu-Roegen (1971, p. 3), "the entropy law itself emerges as the most economic in nature of all natural laws". The fact that energy always gets deteriorated during physical transformations in closed systems (and therefore entropy always rises in closed systems) would imply that economic activity is bound to degenerate to levels compatible with a "solar budget", as the only thing keeping earth from being a closed system is the sun. Other implications are the irreversibility of time – something that mainstream economists have hardly taken into account – and the theoretical limits to the efficiency of recycling and other technological innovations, as well as the economy's dependence on finite resource reserves such as fossil fuels or heavy metals. The entropic argument, however, has not been able to draw much attention from mainstream growth theorists, whose scarce comments and replies have been persistently related to technological optimism in one way or another, mainly related to the possibility of perfect substitution between natural resources and other production factors.

The concept of economic degrowth has added strength and scope to the thermodynamic criticism to endless growth. As Kallis, Demaria and D'Alisa (2015, p. 3) state, degrowth "calls for the decolonization of public debate from the idiom of economism and for the abolishment of economic growth as a social objective". More specifically, it points to "a desired direction, one in which societies will use fewer natural resources and will organize and live differently than today. 'Sharing', 'simplicity', 'conviviality', 'care' and the 'commons' are primary significations of what this society might look like". Degrowth thus constitutes a theoretical framework, idea, project or movement embedded in diverse fields of knowledge, such as political ecology, ecological economics and moral philosophy, that encompasses the canons of ecological sufficiency.

The notion of a consumption-related voluntary sufficiency is vital to the attainment of a prosperous and fair degrowth, instead of social collapse. Although the belief that diminished consumption levels might lead to higher subjective wellbeing levels is controversial, with complex interactions taking place as the economy shrinks, some degrowth theorists argue that, even if not necessarily making individuals happier, the observance of proper policies could assure the fulfilment of basic human needs for all, and therefore a sustainable existence (Koch, Buch-Hansen, & Fritz, 2017). Still, fewer formal working hours, a stronger connectedness to other human beings and to the surrounding environment, widespread social equality leading to less envy, rivalry or isolation, and increasing personal free time and autonomy are some of the elements that might link degrowth to enhanced life satisfaction levels (Sekulova, 2015). In any case, the economic degrowth transition needs to abide by cultural values and practices and, therefore, in democratic societies it depends on planned, voluntary decisions to resist affluent lifestyles in favour of frugality (Alexander, 2015). Otherwise, ecological limits might impose a very different kind of degrowth, with significant human and non-human welfare losses.

Gandhian economic philosophy

The economic philosophy or political economy of M. K. Gandhi presents a different paradigm to Western economic thought. It is based on the intertwining of economics and ethics, with an anti-utilitarian view that replaces the infinitude of man's greed by the more plausible fulfilment of human needs within ecological boundaries. Policy should be focused on organizational and institutional changes, acknowledging the role played by power relations and observing the moral imperatives of truth, nonviolence (*ahimsa*) and labour (Gosh, 2002). Moving beyond these basic elements, Gandhi's philosophy also used the nomological notions of *anasakti*, "no desire for worldly possessions", and *sarvodaya*, "welfare to all" (Gosh, 2005, p. 62). Accumulation of wealth beyond the limit of basic human needs would be a moral deviation, leading to social instability. The rich would be mere trustees of such wealth, morally obligated to distribute resources and maximize community welfare (Gosh, 2005).

The combination of the principles above with *swaraj* – self-government, in the context of Indian emancipation from the British yoke, but also self-rule, self-restraint, spiritual, intellectual and political freedom, dignity and independence from external control, to be exercised by individuals or small communities and villages – and *swadeshi* – self-sufficiency, self-reliance, autonomy or also home economy – would naturally lead to the practice of civil disobedience (*satyagraha*) as a way to assert this philosophical outline. Disobedience contrasts with the understanding of nonviolence as sheer cowardice or "voluntary servitude", an expression used by Étienne de la Boétie (2012) in the sixteenth century. Inspired by Tolstoy, Thoreau and Emerson (Koshal & Koshal, 1973), Gandhi "considered nonviolent means the only way to convince the public that his ends were just and that the struggle should therefore be supported" (Renou, 2015, p. 162). Just ends would only be achieved through just means, a mix of direct action and conscientious objection supported by strong values, a conduct usually seen among activists for ecological sufficiency and their discourses based on constructive programs and positive alternatives for current global malaise (Renou, 2015). Real examples of nonviolent disobedience grounded on voluntary sufficiency principles include opposing large-scale capital ventures or biased legislation, as well as the refusal to repay high-interest bank loans, to pay unreasonable taxes or to comply with pro-market regulations.

Another development of Gandhi's economic philosophy is the "economy of permanence" of Kumarappa (1945). It centres economic analysis on small, democratic communities and how to make them self-sufficient in terms of basic human needs, mainly through subsistence agriculture and craftsmanship. Unlike the industrial development of Western societies, the economy of permanence would reflect nature's perennial capacity to sustain life. It takes into consideration environmental vulnerabilities, human creativity, spiritual values and altruistic behaviour (Corazza & Victus, 2015), thus serving as a complementary discourse to Gandhian economic philosophy in relation to ecological sufficiency.

Public policies

The buen vivir movement

A more practical discourse associated with the concept of ecological sufficiency, and inspired by old traditions of South American folk of Andean and Amazonian origins, *buen vivir* (Spanish expression adapted from the Quechuan *Sumak Kawsay*, meaning "to live in plenitude") is a social movement or political philosophy characterized by different views and values regarding concepts such as human development and welfare, which focus on community life and harmonious man-nature relationships (Acosta, 2015). Nature would not only present intrinsic value, but bear rights of its own. Environmental disruption arising from the creation of artificial needs, for instance, would breach the rights of *Pachamama* ("mother earth" or "mother nature") (Zaffaroni, 2011). Economic activity should support and be supported by elements such as solidarity, local autonomy, regenerative use of resources and the right of all peoples and communities to a self-assessed dignified existence.

Buen vivir advocates that social and economic regulation should be performed at the community level, reducing market and state power over individual and collective choices. Acosta (2015), however, acknowledges the need to confront power relations that are strongly unfavourable to *buen vivir*. The challenge to transform reality goes way beyond discourse implementation, even though some steps have already been taken in this direction, e.g. the incorporation of *buen vivir* as a constitutional principle of Ecuador. Having its economy based on commodity exports, the country's path toward the consolidation of *buen vivir* principles and practices still struggles to overcome the power of influential groups linked to large-scale extractive projects, which typically lead to social and environmental losses (Villalba-Eguiluz & Etxano, 2017).

The Bhutanese new development paradigm

The proposal of the Kingdom of Bhutan for a new global development paradigm is centred on the pursuit of happiness above all, questioning economic growth as an end in itself. According to the New Development Paradigm Steering Committee and Secretariat (2013), this initiative could foster meaningful societal changes, altering man-nature relationships and directing human attitudes toward more altruistic, cooperative and frugal values and practices. By challenging the old growth paradigm, Bhutanese policies provide a viable alternative to current human organizations based on industrial-level resource use and waste generation, with its harmful social and environmental collateral effects.

The hallmark of the proposed (post)development agenda is the adoption of the Gross National Happiness (GNH) index as a key measure of human progress. It is composed by social, cultural, political and ecological indicators that point to a holistic outline, reflecting the interconnectedness between human wellbeing, cultural values and ecological conservation. Its implementation framework combines bottom-up and top-down strategies, stressing the relevance of education at the local, regional, national and global levels, associated with governance mechanisms that could jointly lead to new behaviour and actions in line with the concept of ecological sufficiency. In this case, the notion of happiness, although broad and complex, is also firmly grounded in the fulfilment of basic human needs as a material foundation for contentment, harmoniously coupled with less tangible, psychological and spiritual elements. The needs of all would have precedence over the wants of a few, a more balanced and equitable vision of human progress or development that could potentially evince a way out of the trade-off presented between ecological boundaries and human wellbeing or happiness.

Final remarks

The concepts of sustainable consumption, in its weak and strong forms, and of ecological sufficiency have been presented above. The dominant discourse of ecological modernization, based on a hegemonic capitalistic consensus that deals with social and environmental problems by further expanding the reach of markets and bestowing on science the role of ultimate saviour, has been associated with weak sustainable consumption, based on efficiency gains, technological innovations and new "green" business opportunities. In contrast, it was shown that strong sustainable consumption and ecological sufficiency advocate for absolute reductions in matter and energy transformations, social justice and new perceptions related to wellbeing, quality of life, dignity, community and nature, supported by discourses such as Sen's capability approach, environmental justice, economic degrowth, Gandhian economic philosophy, the *buen vivir* movement and the Bhutanese new development paradigm. These and many other initiatives, such as Ubuntu philosophy, feminist economics, eco-communities, Pope Francis's encyclical letter *Laudato Si'*, alternative currencies, the Occupy movement and the several different currents of environmentalism, are expected to converge – possibly aided by social media – into the formation of a more powerful discourse in favour of ecological sufficiency. Either grounded on science, religion or ethics, and either motivated by environmental or social concerns, these views, taken as a whole, incorporate a wide array of forms in which the relations between happiness and the fulfilment of basic human needs are explored to face business-as-usual and modernization-like solutions to current global socioecological challenges.

The debate over the causes and consequences of contemporary consumer society is complex, plural, polemic and often contradictory. Different points of view can be found within the same group of interest, scientific discipline or culture. Economic, scientific, moral and political factors are juxtaposed in a social context in which discourses and power relations are as important as widely accepted scientific truths. The latter are appropriated by groups of interest with discourses that, weighed by their power or influence, are able to form and consolidate a determined worldview that, in turn, shapes social reality. A meaningful shift in current patterns of consumption – and of accumulation, a wider concept that more properly captures the capitalist claim for endless economic growth – depends fundamentally on the downfall of the dominant, powerful discourse of the hegemonic capitalistic consensus, either in a structured and consented way or tragically by the ecological collapse of the planet. As stated by Fuchs et al. (2016, p. 9), "it is time social scientists, natural scientists, and humanists, as well as those in applied fields such as business and engineering, study power, question power, and thereby challenge power. Consumption cannot be sustainable or reductions absolute with anything less."

References

Acosta, A. (2015). El Buen Vivir como alternativa al desarrollo. Algunas reflexiones económicas y no tan económicas [Buen vivir as an alternative to development. A few economic and not so economic reflections]. *Política y Sociedad, 52*(2), 299–330. doi: doi:10.5209/rev_POSO.2015.v52.n2.45203
Alcott, B. (2008). The sufficiency strategy: would rich-world frugality lower environmental impact? *Ecological Economics, 64*, 770–786. doi:doi:10.1016/j.ecolecon.2007.04.015
Alexander, S. (2015). Simplicity. In G. D'Alisa, F. Demaria & G. Kallis (Eds), *Degrowth: A Vocabulary for a New Era* (pp. 133–136). Abingdon, UK: Routledge.
Altvater, E. (1992). *Der Preis des Wohlstands: oder Umweltplünderung und neue Welt(un)ordnung* [The price of wealth: or the environmental plundering and the new world (dis)order]. Münster, Germany: Verlag Westfälisches Dampfboot.

Andersen, M.S., & Massa, I. (2000). Ecological modernization — origins, dilemmas and future directions. *Journal of Environmental Policy & Planning, 2*(4), 337–345. doi: doi:10.1080/714852820

Arto, I., Capellán-Pérez, I., Lago, R., Bueno, G., & Bermejo, R. (2016). The energy requirements of a developed world. *Energy for Sustainable Development, 33*, 1–13. doi: doi:10.1016/j.esd.2016.04.001

Ayres, R.U., & Kneese, A.V. (1969). Production, consumption, and externalities. *American Economic Review, 59*(3), 282–297.

Ballet, J., Bazin, D., Dubois, J.L., & Mahieu, F.R. (2011). A note on sustainability economics and the capability approach. *Ecological Economics, 70*, 1831–1834. doi: doi:10.1016/j.ecolecon.2011.05.009

Ballet, J., Koffi, J.M., & Pelenc, J. (2013). Environment, justice and the capability approach. *Ecological Economics, 85*, 28–34. doi:doi:10.1016/j.ecolecon.2012.10.010

Boétie, É. de la (2012). *Discourse on Voluntary Servitude.* Indianapolis, IN: Hackett Publishing Co.

Buttel, F.H. (2000). Ecological modernization as social theory. *Geoforum, 31*(1), 57–65. doi:doi:10.1016/S0016-7185(99)00044-5

Baumgärtner, S., & Quaas, M. (2010). What is sustainability economics? *Ecological Economics, 69*(3), 445–450. doi:doi:10.1016/j.ecolecon.2009.11.019

Boulding, K.E. (1966). The economics of the coming spaceship earth. In H. Jarret (Ed.), *Environmental Quality in a Growing Economy* (pp. 3–14). Baltimore, MD: John Hopkins University Press.

Carson, R. (1968). *Silent Spring.* Greenwich, CT: Crest Book.

Corazza, C., & Victus, S. (2015). Economy of permanence. In G. D'Alisa, F. Demaria & G. Kallis (Eds), *Degrowth: A Vocabulary for a New Era* (pp. 205–207). Abingdon, UK: Routledge.

Daly, H.E. (1968). On economics as a life science. *Journal of Political Economy, 76*(3), 392–406.

Easterlin, R.A. (1974). Does economic growth improve the human lot? Some empirical evidence. In P.A. David & M.W. Reder (Eds), *Nations and households in economic growth: essays in honor of Moses Abramovitz* (pp. 89–125). New York: Academic Press, Inc.

Ehrlich, P.R., & Holdren, J.P. (1971). Impact of population growth. *Science, 171*(3977), 1212–1217. doi:doi:10.1126/science.171.3977.1212

Elliott, R. (2004). *Making up people: consumption as a symbolic vocabulary for the construction of identity.* InK.M. Ekström & H. Brembeck (Eds) *Elusive Consumption.* Oxford: Berg.

Fellner, W., & Spash, C.L. (2014). The illusion of consumer sovereignty in economic and neoliberal thought [SRE-Discussion Paper 2014/02]. WU Vienna University of Economics and Business, Vienna, Austria.

Fischer, C., & Grieβhammer, R. (2013). When less is more – sufficiency: terminology, rationale and potentials [Working Paper n. 2/2013]. *Öko-Institut*, Freiburg, Germany. Available online at www.oeko.de/oekodoc/1879/2013-007-en.pdf (accessed January 20, 2018).

Fisher, D.R., & Freudenburg, W.R. (2001). Ecological modernization and its critics: assessing the past and looking toward the future. *Society and Natural Resources, 14*(8), 701–709. doi:doi:10.1080/08941920119315

Fuchs, D., Di Giulio, A., Glaab, K., Lorek, S., Maniates, M., Princen, T., & Roepke, I. (2016). Power: the missing element in sustainable consumption and absolute reductions research and action. *Journal of Cleaner Production, 132*, 298–307. doi: doi:10.1016/j.jclepro.2015.02.006

Georgescu-Roegen, N. (1971). *The Entropy Law and the Economic Process.* Cambridge, MA: Harvard University Press.

Gosh, B.N. (2002). Gandhian political economy: the methodological structuration. *Humanomics*, 18(1), 9–28. doi:doi:10.1108/eb018869

Gosh, B.N. (2005). The ontological principles of Gandhian political economy. *Humanomics*, 21(1), 60–87. doi:doi:10.1108/eb018901

Heindl, P., & Kanschik, P. (2016). Ecological sufficiency, individual liberties, and distributive justice: implications for policy making. *Ecological Economics*, 126, 42–50. doi: doi:10.1016/j.ecolecon.2016.03.019

Kallis, G., Demaria, F., & D'Alisa, G. (2015). Introduction: degrowth. In G. D'Alisa, F. Demaria & G. Kallis (Eds), *Degrowth: A Vocabulary for A New Era* (pp. 1–19). Abingdon, UK: Routledge.

Koch, M., Buch-Hansen, H., & Fritz, M. (2017). Shifting priorities in degrowth research: an argument for the centrality of human needs. *Ecological Economics*, 138, 74–81. doi:doi:10.1016/j.ecolecon.2017.03.035

Koshal, R.K., & Koshal, M. (1973). Gandhian economic philosophy. *American Journal of Economics and Sociology*, 32(2), 191–209.

Kumarappa, J.C. (1945). *Economy of Permanence*, Varanasi, India: Sarva Seva Sangh Prakashan.

Latouche, S. (2007). Sustainable consumption in a "de-growth" perspective. In E. Zaccaï, (Ed.) *Sustainable Consumption, Ecology and Fair Trade.* New York: Routledge.

Lorek, S., & Fuchs, D. (2013). Strong sustainable consumption governance – precondition for a degrowth path? *Journal of Cleaner Production*, 38, 36–43. doi: doi:10.1016/j.jclepro.2011.08.008

Martinez-Alier, J. (2002). *The Environmentalism of the Poor: A Study of Ecological Conflicts and Valuation.* Cheltenham, UK: Edward Elgar.

Meadows, D.H., Meadows, D.L., Randers, J., & Behrens, W.W., III. (1972). *The Limits to Growth: A Report for the Club of Rome's Project on the Predicament of Mankind.* New York: Universe Books.

Miller, D. (Ed.) (1995). *Acknowledging Consumption. A Review of New Studies.* London: Routledge.

Mol, A.P.J. (2002). Ecological modernization and the global economy. *Global Environmental Politics*, 2(2), 92–115. doi:doi:10.1162/15263800260047844

New Development Paradigm Steering Committee and Secretariat (2013). *Happiness: Towards a New Development Paradigm* [Report of the Kingdom of Bhutan]. Available online at www.newdevelopmentparadigm.bt/wp-content/uploads/2014/10/Happ inessTowardsANewDevelopmentParadigm.pdf (accessed March 9, 2018).

Organization for Economic Co-operation and Development (2002). *Policies to Promote Sustainable Consumption: An Overview* [Policy Case Studies Series ENV/EPOC/ WPNEP(2001)18/FINAL]. Paris: OECD.

Patel, R. (2012). *Stuffed and Starved: The Hidden Battle for the World Food System* (2nd edn). Brooklyn, NY: Melville House Publishing.

Raworth, K. (2017). *Doughnut Economics: Seven Ways to Think like a 21st Century Economist.* White River Junction, VT: Chelsea Green Publishing.

Renou, X. (2015). Disobedience. In G. D'Alisa, F. Demaria & G. Kallis (Eds), *Degrowth: A Vocabulary for a New Era* (pp. 162–164). Abingdon, UK: Routledge.

Roepke, I. (2005). *Consumption in Ecological Economics.* Internet Encyclopaedia of Ecological Economics. Available online at www.isecoeco.org/pdf/consumption_in_ee. pdf (accessed February 5, 2018).

Sachs, I. (2015). Entering the Anthropocene: the twofold challenge of climate change and poverty eradication. InF. Mancebo & I. Sachs (Eds), *Transitions to Sustainability* (pp. 7–18). Dordrecht, Netherlands: Springer.

Sawyer, D. (2002). Population and sustainable consumption in Brazil. In D. J. Hogan, E. S. Berquo & H. S. M. Costa (Eds), *Population and environment in Brazil: Rio+10* (pp. 255–276). Campinas, Brazil: CNPD-ABEP-NEPO/UNICAMP. Available online at www.nepo.uni camp.br/publicacoes/livros/rio+10/rio10p225a254.pdf (accessed January 14, 2018).

Sekulova, F. (2015). Happiness. In: G. D'Alisa, F. Demaria & G. Kallis (Eds), *Degrowth: A Vocabulary for a New Era* (pp. 113–116). Abingdon, UK: Routledge.

Sen, A. (1992). *Inequality Reexamined*. Oxford: Oxford University Press.

Sen, A. (1999). *Development as Freedom*. Oxford: Oxford University Press.

Scerri, A. (2012). Ends in view: the capabilities approach in ecological/sustainability economics. *Ecological Economics, 77*, 7–10. doi:doi:10.1016/j.ecolecon.2012.02.027

Sedacklo, M., Martinuzzi, A., Roepke, I., Videira, N., & Antunes, P. (2014). Participatory systems mapping for sustainable consumption: discussion of a method promoting systemic insights. *Ecological Economics, 106*, 33–43. doi:doi:10.1016/j.ecolecon.2014.07.002

United Nations (n.d.). *Goal 12: Ensure Sustainable Consumption and Production Patterns*. Available online at www.un.org/sustainabledevelopment/sustainable-consumption-p roduction/ (accessed February 20, 2018).

Villalba-Eguiluz, C.U., & Etxano, I. (2017). Buen vivir vs development (II): the limits of (neo-)extractivism. *Ecological Economics, 138*, 1–11. doi:doi:10.1016/j.ecolecon.2017.03.010

World Commission on Environment and Development (1987). *Our Common Future*. Oxford: Oxford University Press.

Zaffaroni, E.R. (2011). La Pachamama y el humano [Pachamama and the humane]. In A. Acosta & E. Martínez (Eds), *La naturaleza con derechos: de la filosofía a la política* (pp. 25–137). Quito, Ecuador: Abya-Yala.

7 Holistic peace

A new paradigm for business

Tilman Bauer

Introduction

Our economic world is mired in a crisis of values. We see that greed, an emphasis on short-term profits, and general apathy towards human needs and the environment are commonplace. Even as economies become increasingly interconnected and interdependent, the consciousness within business appears to not have moved much beyond an exploitation paradigm. Global sustainability and wellbeing require a new mindset where business creates value for all, as systemic problems require systemic solutions. This mindset entails a holistic vision of business fostering peace. Accordingly, this article explores a theoretical framework, which allows for a new mindset of corporate leadership for peace to emerge where business can climb a ladder of morality. The relationship between business and peace is explored from the perspective of individual companies and their potential to contribute to peace.[1]

For centuries, classical philosophers such as Immanuel Kant (1795), Charles de Montesquieu (1748), and Adam Smith (1776) have recognized the broader role of business, or commerce, trade, and international cooperation in general, in creating peace and stability.[2] The connection was already studied in the seventeenth century by Éméric Crucé (1623), who foresaw a peaceful worldwide union characterized by free trade and commerce. However, connecting business and peace – and assigning business the role of fostering peace (Fort and Schipani, 2004) – is also of emerging contemporary importance. Luk Bouckaert and Manas Chatterji comment in their book *Business, Ethics and Peace*:

> We believe that 'business for peace' expresses an option for an emerging future that on the one hand is not yet realized but on the other hand is already present as a potential and necessary reality. The emerging future manifests itself as a historical movement calling for a deliberate moral commitment.
>
> (2015: xvi)

This movement has been the focus of a steadily increasing number of scholars such as Timothy Fort, who argues that it is in the interest of business to foster peace (Fort, 2015). Moreover, the United Nations Global Compact's "Business for Peace" initiative, the UK-based non-profit organization *International Alert*, and the recently founded *Business, Peace and Sustainable Development* journal are some important fora of, and for, the debate. In particular, the growing literature on "Peace Through Commerce" – for example, Fort (2007), Williams (2008), Oetzel et al. (2010), and Fort (2011) – has linked business practices to reduced violence and to a number of positive contributions to peace.

In line with the literature introduced above, it is well established that peace has a "negative" definition (the absence of physical violence) and a "positive" definition (the absence of structural violence or the presence of justice), as put forward by Johan Galtung (1965, 1967, 1969) – generally regarded as one of the "fathers" of Peace Studies. However, the concept of peace can be further expanded because the negative/positive framework may not sufficiently describe the large realm of the concept. For example, peace and spirituality are tightly interlinked – and at the core of the "transrational" school of thought as advocated by Wolfgang Dietrich (2008, 2012). In fact, the broader the definition of peace, the more intertwined it is with spirituality (Bauer, forthcoming). As Laszlo Zsolnai posits, spirituality is a non-materialistic lifestyle (Zsolnai and Flanagan, forthcoming; Zsolnai, 2004; Bouckaert and Zsolnai, 2011), going beyond the perceivable. It recognizes phenomena that may not be otherwise recognizable and has the potential to connect with a higher wisdom or a higher purpose for the common good. Therefore, as expounded in the next section, peace can serve as a goal for some of the highest forms of human endeavor, as those endeavors transcend self-interest and fuse with the experience of spiritual bliss. These facets are directly relevant to the domains of Peace Studies and of Responsible Business, as well as to the nexus of these fields.

The concept of business as a force for peace may seem counterintuitive when considering its often-negative impact on local communities, not to mention how the business of war has continually rewarded corporate interests. However, it can be argued that ethical business does have the potential, and perhaps the responsibility, to foster peace by assuming a more responsible and ethical role in society. At the core of this re-envisioning lies the understanding that we are undergoing a paradigm shift, as suggested by Fritjof Capra (1982; 1996) among others. The severity of our systemic global problems – poverty, world population growth, species extinction, unsustainable debt, environmental degradation, etc. – underscores the need for a new paradigm, as no systemic problem can be solved on its own. Here, the importance of a corporate contribution to peace is perceptible, with *Forbes* magazine ranking peace as one of five areas of major importance in the future of corporate responsibility (Guthrie, 2014).

The aim of this article is to better understand how the business-peace relationship can be conceptualized and why it is relevant today. What follows is a theoretical and conceptual exploration of the idea that the expanded concept of peace can form the philosophical basis for a framework where business can, and perhaps should, foster peace. Peace is referred to as lower or higher contributions to the spiritual development of society. Proponents of Corporate Social

Responsibility represent the initial outcry that business should *somehow* contribute positively to society; yet, no consensus has been found regarding a definition of the substance of that expected contribution. Therefore, the goal here is to sketch a new, emerging paradigm for business that addresses this question. The basic reasoning is that, if we agree that the purpose of business is to create positive impact for society, and if we agree that the concept of peace can be seen as the substance of positive impact, then the purpose of business is to foster peace. The implication is that some of our fundamental assumptions about the nature and role of business in society are challenged. Here, *being ethical* is distinguished from merely *not being unethical*. The notion of climbing up the ladder of morality, or fostering greater levels of peace, is at the core of the framework that this article puts forward. The article concludes that corporate leadership for peace describes a transrational paradigm in which the well-being of all, including nature, is at the forefront of corporate attention. The ultimate vision is to confront all entrepreneurs and business professionals with the question how their companies contribute to peace.

Business and peace

The need for an overarching notion of positive impact

Hereinafter, a central assumption is that it is in the inherent interest of companies to be ethical, to be responsible, and to contribute positively to society.[3] It has been established that business is "more likely to flourish when societies practice integrity virtues" (Fort and Schipani, 2004: 21). Conversely, failing to practice these virtues can lead to legal/regulatory, ethical, and societal consequences. Fort and Schipani (2004 :21) continue: "if virtues are a component to justice, then flourishing commerce benefits from virtuous behavior and is threatened by non-virtuous behavior."

Ethical products/services meet human needs in a socially, environmentally, and economically sustainable way. Therefore, ethical business is when "human beings can meaningfully connect their self-interest with the welfare of others" (Fort and Noone, 2000: 546). In fact, creating *some* kind of positive impact has been suggested as an alternative conceptualization of the purpose of business (Lankoski and Smith, 2017). But what exactly does "positive impact" mean? Etymologically and practically, "creating positive impact" and "being responsible" are mostly devoid of meaning, as there is no general answer or agreement as to what the essence of "positive impact" or "corporate responsibility" is.[4] Nor do they dictate any concrete practices or specific logic *per se* – leading to a plethora of definitions and guidelines for Corporate Social Responsibility (Dahlsrud, 2006). The notion is abstract and context-bound. Promoting the mere idea of fostering positive impact (as practiced in sustainability circles) is worthwhile – but logically insufficient without a substantial definition of its content. To suggest minimizing negative impact (such as CO_2 emissions) is logically viable because it is identifiable upon existence. Yet, being less bad is not good enough (McDonough and Braungart, 2002).

In order to provide an overarching notion to serve as the substance of "responsibility" and "impact" and to seal this logical gap, a new vision for twenty-first century business needs to be defined. Such a vision needs to be sufficiently broad and encompassing to be useful in any context. The notion of peace may be apt and useful here.

Beyond nonviolence: defining the concept of peace

The etymology and meaning of the word *peace* extends far beyond the absence of war. It includes the Anglo-French *pes*, or "freedom from civil disorder," the Old French *pais*, or "peace, reconciliation, silence, permission," and the Latin *pax* meaning "compact, agreement, treaty of peace, tranquility, absence of war." However, the meaning is dependent on the interpretive context – geographic, cultural, and historic – and, in fact, a very rich history of peace philosophy is revealed. As Wolfgang Dietrich (2008; 2012) finds, the plurality of "peaces" manifests in the "Five Families" that cover the philosophical and cultural richness of understandings of peace in the world (Dietrich et al., 2014; Lederach, 2005). For example, the pre-imperial Goddess Pax and her male counterpart Mars are the source of the word peace in the energetic world (Dietrich, 2008, 2012). This important insight helps to see through the patriarchal redefinition of the singular concept. To understand this dynamic, Dietrich's (2008, 2012) "Five Families" are paraphrased below:

- *Energetic Peace* originates from an understanding that matriarchal monotheism is a source of harmonious primordial energy and that everything is connected with everything through a manifestation of energy. "Peace out of harmony," a central statement, refers to the unification of dualities/ opposites, such as yin and yang. "[E]nergetic peace [is] an achievement of humanity, which derives from man's archaic experience of being nourished by Mother Nature, often enough worshiped as the Great Mother" (Dietrich, 2006: 1), beginning in the inner self and extending, by way of harmonious vibrations, through society, nature, and the universe. In other words, when polarities are in balance, peace is experienced. However, as energies are always dynamic, peace is, therefore, not a stable state but a continuous expression of relations.
- *Moral Peace* is the patriarchal "peace out of the one truth" idea, resting on the introduction of dualism as an element for norms. This brings forth notions such as justice ("peace through justice"), because peace is the satisfaction of basic needs through divine reconciliation. However, "my justice" may not be the same as "your justice" – leading to a problematic understanding of peace, as in the concept of a "just war." Moral peace was promoted by strong institutions (religion) that translated norms into universal truths. This coincided with the emergence of city states (polis), and

hence, the understanding of *pax* as an agreement of civil order. "Peace thus does not float anymore within the harmonious relation of things but is rooted in the *One Order*, the *One Truth*, which is guaranteed by power" (Dietrich, 2006: 4).

- *Modern Peace* rests on ideals such as reason, humanitarianism, equality, technological progress, free trade, and federalism. Rational thinking replaces theistic thinking in moral interpretations, referring to a materialistic/mechanistic understanding of the Newtonian/Cartesian world in which the whole is understood by its parts. The notion of "development" became the twin of "peace" (Dietrich, 2006; Dietrich and Sützl, 2006), and security resurfaced as the substance of a universal imperative for nation-states with the central statement being "peace out of security."

- *Postmodern Peace* doubts the teachings of modernity, challenging Hobbes, Descartes, Newton, and Kant, the founding fathers of modern thinking. This also supports the founding of the discipline of Peace Studies. Postmodern peace is not a function of governmental action or reductionist clockwork thinking; its interpretations acknowledge networks, perceiver-constructed structures, fields, systems, chaos, and complexity: the celebration of the incomplete, small, mundane, and unspectacular "many peaces" (Dietrich and Sützl, 2006) through the plurality of truths, opposing the structural and cultural violence of modernity.

- *Transrational Peace* amalgamates the previous four families. The aim is to transcend the limits of reason by combining it with the energetic understanding of life (as suppressed by the modern view) – without forgetting modernity's and postmodernity's lessons. Moreover, spirituality is a part of the human experience, as postulated by humanistic, transpersonal, or positive psychology, without denying rationality. "Peace through harmony" is complementary to reasonable thinking, that is, to the peaces through justice, security, and truth. Transrational interpretations start with, and go beyond, the individual and expand consciousness to include collective systems. Transrational peaces require a perceiving subject, and analysis of the perceiving self. Thus, there is no one absolute truth, as relational aspects of subjects and objects abound. Transrational peace is the lifelong quest for a dynamic balance: harmony is a function of security, security is a function of justice, justice is a function of truth, and truth can only exist in harmony. The notions of spirituality, love, and harmony are, again, part of the academic vocabulary, as they form integral parts of the transrational peace concept.

Dietrich's (2008, 2012) Five Families of Peaces, paraphrased above, is a seminal pillar supporting the theory of holistic peace and its connection to spirituality – and offers scholarly understanding far beyond a positivist approach. But how exactly does it contribute to our understanding of peace? To answer this question, we turn first to the works of Johan Galtung (1965; 1967; 1969), who distinguished the field of Peace Studies from Conflict Studies in the 1960s by coining the notions of "negative peace" and "positive peace." In his seminal paper, Galtung (1969) established negative peace as the absence of physical violence, and positive peace as the absence of structural violence, or as the presence of justice, conveyed as something that "amounts to [no] less suffering than personal violence" (Galtung, 1969: 173). Galtung (1990: 291) adds "cultural violence" to his theoretical arsenal as "any aspect of a culture that can be used to legitimize violence in its direct or structural form." Galtung (1990: 292) also develops the concept of violence so that any "avoidable insults to basic human needs" (cf. Galtung, 1980; 1996) – survival needs, wellbeing needs, identity needs, and freedom needs – are considered either physical, structural, or cultural violence.

Galtung's negative and positive peace is a basic but fundamental and highly useful conceptualization of peace, and has generally been adopted by the field of Peace Studies (albeit not without criticism, see, for example, Lawler, 1995; Dietrich, 2008; 2012; and Coady, 2008; Galtung is, however, defended, for example, by Vorobej, 2008). We learn that we can distinguish between the absence of negative notions and the presence of positive notions. This brings forth the following definitions adopted in this article, slightly modified from Galtung:[5] *Weak peace* is defined as the absence of *any* type of systematic violence (whether physical, structural, or cultural). It is a quasi-nonspiritual starting point, limiting itself to calmness and the absence of stress. In this framework, it is the lowest level, or stage, of peace. *Strong peace*, on the other hand, refers to the effect of the presence of positive values, ideals, or virtues that we want to have in society, such as justice, health, happiness, education, prosperity, sustainability, wellbeing, and so on. All these are aspects of strong peace. It corresponds to spiritual practice and virtue. These points exemplify the need for sound structures in society, ranging from individual to political and organizational abilities, to cope peacefully with each other. This understanding of peace goes beyond the absence of physical or structural violence, as it promotes the presence of any positive values that enable the sound functioning of society on the basis of a balance of power, legitimate and transparent decision-making, interdependent relationships that foster cooperation, the ability to deal with conflicts, and respectful behavior, despite often-arising (perceived) incompatibilities (Miller, 2005). In other words, strong peace is the result of a well-functioning society on all levels.

However, there are aspects of peace that go beyond this distinction, as we can define peace in a wider and more holistic sense. This is a major insight from Dietrich's transrational philosophy of peace, as discussed above. Jeong (2000: 30) states: "A holistic conception of peace links the ideal of the human spirit to the harmony between different components of the earth system and even universe." It is the extension of inner peace to outer peace and the realization of the interconnectedness of beings (Fox, 2014; Dalai Lama, 2009a; Dalai Lama, 2009b; Dalai Lama, 2002). Jeong (2000) points out that harmony with the universe also includes the concept of living in harmony with nature. Danesh (2011: 65) notes that "peace is a psychosocial and political as well as moral and spiritual condition requiring a conscious approach, a universal out-look, and an integrated, unifying strategy." From these points, *holistic peace* is defined as a transrational vision for humanity and moral excellence. Essentially, it is the highest fathomable form of peace closely connected to, and intertwined with, spirituality. It speaks to a higher purpose of human endeavor, inter-connectedness, and spiritual bliss or enlightenment.

With this framework in mind, we can discuss peace as a necessary part of our relationship with society. The three levels, or stages, of peace – weak, strong, and holistic peace – are compared with negative and positive peace in Table 7.1. The discussion above has painted a picture of peace that ranges from the cold, mini-malistic, and narrow to one that embraces what might be the full potential of the human family. Peace becomes the ultimate substance of collective ethical visions. It serves as a fundamental goal of human activity, and yet as a source of ambi-guity – *and* as an inspiration for the better. It has the potential to guide – to offer a red thread guiding us through the jungle of imperatives towards creating a virtuous impact.

Why Discuss Peace in the Context of Business?

Companies are faced with ever-increasing pressure to become "sustainable" and "responsible" while being "corporate citizens." Numerous models, theories, tools, indices, and frameworks have been developed to push companies into certain conceptual and practical molds (see, for example, Carroll, 1979; 1991; Freeman, 1984; and Porter and Kramer, 2011). Corporate Social Responsibility "captures the most important concerns regarding the relationship between

Table 7.1 Weak peace, strong peace, and holistic peace compared to negative peace and positive peace

	Absence of physical or direct violence or war	*Absence of any systematic (physical, structural, or cultural) violence*	*Presence of positive values, ideals, or virtues (e.g. health, wellbeing, justice, prosperity, etc.)*	*A transrational vision and higher purpose for humanity, moral excellence, interconnectedness.*
Negative peace	✔			
Positive peace		✔	✔	
Weak peace		✔		
Strong peace			✔	
Holistic peace				✔

Source: author's own elaboration.

business and society" (Moura-Leite and Padgett, 2011: 536). Therefore, any endeavor that addresses the role of business in and towards society must speak to this discourse.

"Sustainability," a recent buzzword, gained mainstream prominence through the "Brundtland Report" (World Commission on Environment and Development, 1987), which coined the idea that the needs of future generations should not be compromised. Such "sustainable development" essentially "square[s] the circle of competing demands of environmental protection and economic development" (Dresner, 2008: 1). Lo and Sheu define corporate sustainability as

> a positive multi-faceted concept covering areas of environmental protection, social equity, community friendship and sustainable development in corporate governance [...] that creates long-term shareholder value by embracing opportunities and managing risk from economic, environmental and social dimensions.
>
> (2007: 345)

These three dimensions – economic, environmental, and social – are often called the three pillars of sustainability, or sustainable development, and go back to the Triple Bottom Line concept in John Elkington's (1998) work. However, as Gemma Burford et al. (2013) discuss, there has been a debate around the fourth "missing pillar." What could be missing from the economic, environmental, and social dimensions? The cultural-aesthetic discourse suggests that culture is the fourth pillar. Conversely, a political-institutional point of view emphasizes the fourth pillar as good governance with a formal system of rules. And, finally, a third perspective suggests the religious-spiritual aspect connects sustainability with the global ethical consciousness awakening to a spiritual moral awareness – which has been missing in the past. While distinct, these three perspectives all revolve around human values. Such human values include respect and care for the community of life, ecological integrity, social and economic justice, democracy, nonviolence, and, quintessentially, peace. As Burford et al. (2013) note, mainstream sustainability discourse such as the Rio +20 rhetoric does not address such ethical values.

Rather than suggesting peace as the fourth pillar, this article proposes that peace is the missing foundation of *all* pillars, as it is a prerequisite to a thriving and sustainable civilization. Peace is, therefore, related to social sustainability, referring to a society where social tensions are limited, and conflicts settled in a peaceful and civilized manner (Dillard, Dujon, and King, 2009). Hence, it follows that working for sustainability – when defined more broadly, as above – correlates with working for peace. This also applies to the environmental and economic dimensions of sustainability, as there is a clear link between, for example, climate change and peace, and livelihood creation and peace.

From a Business Ethics perspective, there is a moral duty to create "shared value" for society (Porter and Kramer, 2011) by adhering to "principles and virtues that create space for the multiplicity of human goods" (Fort, 2001: 304;

Fort, 2007). To argue that fostering peace is in one's self-interest, one must understand that long-term self-interest is always more satisfactory than short-term self-interest (Hosmer, 1994a). Moreover, if we assume that "acting in ways that can be considered to be 'right' and 'just' and 'fair' is absolutely essential to the long-term competitive success of the firm" (Hosmer, 1994b: 192), then such moral behavior must be in line with behavior that benefits society. If it "pays" to be moral in the long term (Fort, cited in Shaw and Corvino, 1996: 382), it must also pay to foster peace in society. It is in the interest of business to operationalize peace (Bauer, 2016) – because the concept of peace will replace what sustainability represents today; i.e. "peace is the new sustainability," as Per Saxegaard from the Business for Peace Foundation advocates (personal communication, 2016).

Companies that accept an ethical path should, therefore, be concerned. Turning to a normative rationale from Galtung's *Peace Business* (Santa Barbara, Dubee, and Galtung, 2009: 17): "Why should business also be concerned with peace? Because the present alignment of economic forces in favor of economic growth is too narrow, too misleading, too dangerous and destructive to all parties." If we look at the extended understanding of violence (Galtung, 1969; Galtung, 1990; Santa Barbara et al., 2009), we notice that "business as usual" can foster inequality, lead to unsustainable practices, and exploit human and natural resources. If we believe in the virtue of nonviolence – and agree that violence is bad and to be avoided – then business should not foster violence.

Scholars following Milton Friedman (1962) have conceptualized the purpose of a corporation as limited to maximizing profits, thereby effectively precluding it from a peace-fostering purpose. Yet, few companies can avoid their social responsibilities on some level. Today, companies are expected to create profits while, at the same time, creating value for stakeholders. Michael Braungart (2005) argues that "the real responsibility of corporations is purely to do good work." Marilise Smurthwaite (2008) further argues that a corporation's purpose is to make profits, serve the common good, be a good citizen, contribute to the community, and be socially responsible (for example, through projects to relieve poverty). All those "purposes," in fact, relate to the three stages of peace – even profit making, as its absence would create trouble: structural violence in layoffs and loss of purpose, welfare, etc.

To conclude this section, and to illustrate the relationship between business and weak, strong, and holistic peace identified earlier, the following offers a rough (and partly overlapping) overview of what companies can do. Companies can contribute to *weak peace*, for example, by designing non-harming products/services, adhering to laws, self-regulating to avoid being the cause of violence, instilling clear standards against bribery and corruption, and involving the community to engage in an honest and respectful dialog with relevant stakeholders to act as a convener for the sake of peace and stability. *Strong peace* efforts may entail activities that positively contribute to the evolution of society through instilling positive values and ideals; for example, respecting and supporting human rights, promoting gender equality, taking responsibility for the

environment, or contributing to the economic development of an impoverished area. Finally, *holistic peace* leads towards interconnectedness and the
inherent wellbeing of society, emphasizing balance within oneself, with others,
with nature, and with the universe. Fostering holistic peace in business rests on
moral excellence in leadership, while seeking a higher purpose and nurturing a
global consciousness that fosters compassion and collaboration. The conceptual
framework presented here is summarized in Figure 7.1 (Bauer, 2015).

The transrational business paradigm

Climbing up the ladder of morality

Truly successful companies should simultaneously grow profits and create social
good (Kanter, 2009), that is, foster peace. This entails going beyond *merely
ethical* (i.e., not unethical) actions to become *more ethical* and perhaps to strive
towards moral excellence. This refers to climbing a "ladder of morality," which
is defined as moving from lower to higher commitments to, or stages of, promoting peace.[6] As Fort and Westermann-Behaylo (2008) recognize, companies
today may not always possess the required moral maturity to foster peace
through corporate activities. Does an organization have a moral obligation
(Moore, 1999) to foster peace? One could argue that business has the power,
potential, and, therefore, the moral obligation to do good. Geoff Moore (1999:
339) finds that: "acceptance of the concept of corporate moral agency is
becoming the norm."

   However, companies do not always take moral responsibility seriously.
Therefore, the distinction between active and passive moral agency is necessary.
An active stance entails acting upon one's responsibility, such as actively instilling a sense of fostering peace throughout an organization. Passive corporate
moral agency, on the other hand, does not deny responsibility in the sense of
legal/ethical duty and does, therefore, not fear negative consequences, as it
does, thus far, comply with mainstream expectations of doing no harm. It does,
however, fail to base decisions on a moral consciousness. If a company wants to
develop a stronger reputation in the field of creating positive social impact, that
is, of fostering peace, then an active stance exhibits leadership. Essentially,
business has the moral obligation to contribute positively to society *if* it takes an
active stance on corporate moral agency. Merely conceptualizing a company's
products and services as being capable of contributing to peace in society can
lead to a "tipping point" (van Tulder et al., 2014) towards more responsible
business practices by encouraging the development of moral maturity.

   Corporate Social Responsibility and Business Ethics were, until recently,
largely absent from, or under-valued in, business education. Now, growing
interest in social/ethical issues can be observed. As Subhabrata Bobby Banerjee
(2008) points out, the hegemony of capitalism's market ideology has produced
a type of discourse – a systemic structure or paradigm – that does not foster
responsible behavior. Thus, "changing the discourse" is the collective business

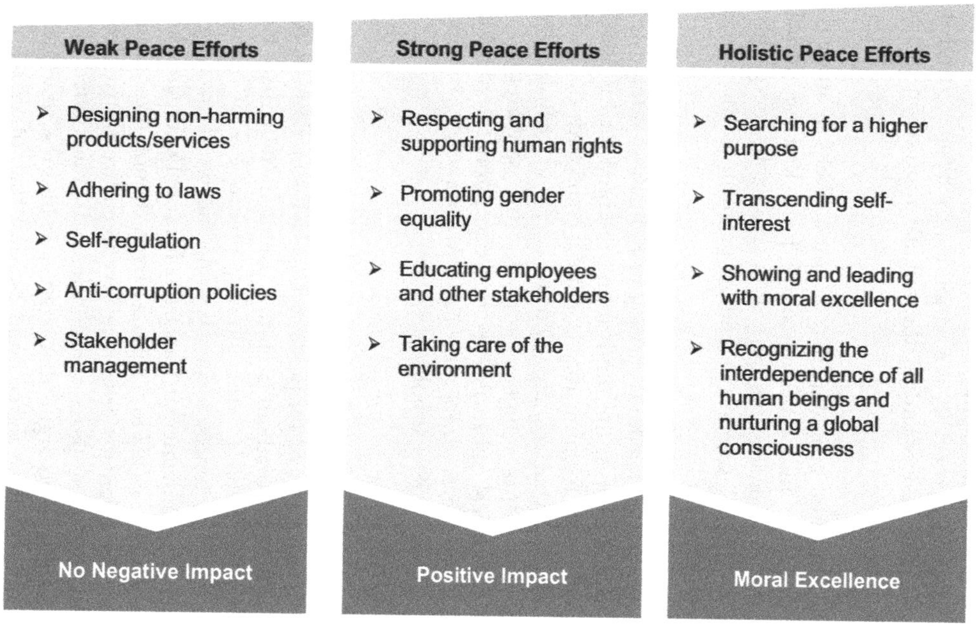

Weak Peace Efforts

➤ Designing non-harming products/services

➤ Adhering to laws

➤ Self-regulation

➤ Anti-corruption policies

➤ Stakeholder management

No Negative Impact

Strong Peace Efforts

➤ Respecting and supporting human rights

➤ Promoting gender equality

➤ Educating employees and other stakeholders

➤ Taking care of the environment

Positive Impact

Holistic Peace Efforts

➤ Searching for a higher purpose

➤ Transcending self-interest

➤ Showing and leading with moral excellence

➤ Recognizing the interdependence of all human beings and nurturing a global consciousness

Moral Excellence

Figure 7.1 Examples of what business can do for weak, strong, and holistic peace
Source: Author's own elaboration

agenda. It can be argued that the solution must be market-based. After all, if markets are culture, "explicitly moral projects, saturated with normativity" (Fourcade and Healy, 2007: 299–300), then we must take care not to prescribe or impose "our" solution on others; rather, the solution must come from "within." Hence, a new paradigm is needed where corporate action for holistic peace is normatively embedded. The more moral and responsible a company wants to be, the higher it goes up the ladder of fostering peace.

A high position on the ladder of morality is exemplified by business magnate Elon Musk (2013) in his *TED Talk* regarding the original motivation behind his work:

> I thought about, what are the problems that are most likely to affect the future of the world or the future of humanity? I think it's extremely important that we have sustainable transport and sustainable energy production. That sort of overall sustainable energy problem is the biggest problem that we have to solve this century.

These words portray deep concern for the wellbeing of humanity. While Musk has been criticized on many accounts, the motivation presented for his endeavors suggests a transrational vision for humanity because it transcends the "what can I do?" question by asking "what actually needs to be done?" Musk showcases wisdom and true passion for a higher purpose. This is, therefore, an example of the type of practical spirituality – or "exceptional leadership" (Chaudhry, 2011) – that connects deeper meaning with moral excellence (Dalai Lama and Muyzenberg, 2008; Fairholm, 1998).

Towards holistic peace

The discourse of business being a force for peace requires a distinction between the prevailing business-as-usual paradigm and the paradigm described here, with peace as the "*telos*" (Fort, 2001) – the ultimate objective – of business. These mindsets portray vital differences to justify using the word "paradigm" (Kuhn, 1970), as it requires a fundamental leap from Milton Friedman's heritage to argue today that business *should* foster peace. Even though the business-peace connection historically originates from the seventeenth century idea of international cooperation facilitating peace through trade (as mentioned in the introduction), it may be difficult to argue that aggressive business strategies of the prevailing mainstream paradigm foster good beyond that of shareholder benefit. Therefore, as Fort and Schipani (2004) recognize, it is only *ethical* business that fosters peace in its communities.

More precisely, ethical business can refrain from causing violence (Haufler, 2001), contribute to stopping war (Sweetman, 2009), and help prevent violence (Nelson, 2000). In these cases, whether direct or structural violence, business fosters *weak peace* through its ordinary activities: industry self-regulation, economic growth and development, stakeholder management, diversified hiring, etc. One can recognize the trajectory of business thinking, as activities that foster *strong peace* have only recently entered the mainstream responsible business agenda: with the advent of the United Nations Global Compact, activities such as supporting human rights, promoting gender equality, and respecting the environment have contributed to a new understanding of responsibility. Finally, business activities that foster *holistic peace* – nurturing a higher purpose, for example, or transcending self-interest, and embodying moral excellence – are starting to emerge. Holistic peace efforts include hitherto isolated examples that revolve around, for example, alternative models of generative ownership (Kelly, 2012), mission-centered governance, and aligning the organizational purpose to peace-generating outcomes or activities.

With reference to Bouckaert and Chatterji (2015: xvi), business as a force for peace is not a "purely subjective and normative viewpoint expressing what *ought* to be done independent of what *is*" but rather "an option for an emerging future." This emerging "transrational turn" (Dietrich, 2013: 187, 2011) has the potential to transcend the economic growth maxim (as already postulated by Boulding, 1945), overcome inherent conflicts of capitalism (as put forward by Karl Marx, Immanuel Wallerstein, and others), and offer individual actors the satisfaction of contributing to a greater good. Essentially, transrational business seeks to find the golden middle way between communism and capitalism, thereby paving the way for holistic peace: business contributes to the common good while preserving the individual's right (and motivation) to free enterprise. To better understand a holistic peace mindset, characteristics of the emerging transrational business paradigm are elucidated next.

Fritjof Capra (1982; Capra and Luisi, 2014) discusses the shift from the old to a new paradigm for science and society. The old paradigm refers to a Newtonian/Cartesian reductionist way of thinking: the world functions like a machine and that, by understanding all parts of a system, we also understand the whole system. What does it imply to go through a paradigm shift? While Thomas Kuhn (1970) refers to paradigm shifts within one field or discipline, Capra (1982: 15) recognizes that "today our society as a whole finds itself in a [...] crisis." Accordingly, the *new* paradigm is a "new vision of reality, a fundamental change in our thoughts, perceptions and values" (Capra, 1982: 16; cf. Wheatley, 2006). Capra continues:

> The new vision of reality we have been talking about is based on awareness of the essential interrelatedness and interdependence of all phenomena – physical, biological, psychological, social, and cultural. It transcends current disciplinary and conceptual boundaries and will be pursued within new institutions. At present there is no well-established framework, either conceptual or institutional, that would accommodate the formulation of the new paradigm, but the outlines of such a framework are already being shaped by many individuals, communities, and networks that are

developing new ways of thinking and organizing themselves according to new principles.

(1982: 265)

Capra's 1982 statement is still relevant today. Holistic peace, based on Dietrich's (2008, 2012) transrationality, offers one framework for this new paradigm – showing that prevailing interpretations of peace mirror the prevailing general paradigm, both in science and in society. In fact, the conceptual framework of why and how business should foster weak, strong, and holistic peace respectively seems to suggest the emergence of new values for business. Linda Groff and Luk Bouckaert write:

> Since the postwar period, the nature of business has undergone a permanent evolution because the conditions in its environment are in continuous change. Although many business leaders do not realize fully the new conditions [...], they are yet confronted with the ecological, psychological and social effects of the change. More enlightened entrepreneurs are aware of the paradigm shift from a capitalistic towards a holistic and post-capitalistic idea of doing business. It is striking how this paradigm shift in business follows a parallel track as the evolving concept of peace.
>
> (2015: 9)

In the new paradigm, everything is interconnected and affects everything. What matters are the relationships between units in a network. According to Capra (1982: 266), "systems are integrated wholes whose properties cannot be reduced to those of smaller units." This systems theory approach is directly related to chaos theory for which "an underlying interconnectedness that exists in apparently random events" (Briggs and Peat, 1999: 2) is essential. Dee Hock (2005: 13) defines "chaordic" organizations as "the behavior of any self-organizing and self-governing organism, organization, or system that harmoniously blends characteristics of chaos and order [or as the] characteristic of the fundamental, organizing principle of nature." One might say that the new paradigm follows this chaordic approach. Coupling this with transrationality, a new awareness of unity emerges between the cosmos, nature, human beings, and all systems within and between.

Exemplified by ecosystems in nature (Capra, 1982), it may be conducive to set the agenda towards more ethical collaboration and interconnectedness as opposed to old-school competition.[7] David Korten (2015: 279) states, "[i]n the ecological era, people will be unified globally not by the mutual insecurity of global competition, but by a global consciousness that we share on Earth and a common destiny." Perhaps the most fundamental change would be shifting from controlling an organization as one does a machine, with every part designed to maximize profits, to a systems mindset. In the new paradigm, organizations are considered as "living" systems (Capra, 2002: 102) where creativity emerges through chaos and self-organization from the bottom up.

This entails, for example, a strong emphasis on networking and communities of practice. Given the novelty of the emerging paradigm, it cannot yet be defined with certainty. Its principles may feature notions of systems thinking, chaos theory, self-organization, transrationality, transcending duality, interconnectedness, interdependence, and stronger collaboration.

The depiction above is merely illustrative, in line with literature that includes both *a priori* conceptual analyses and *a posteriori* empirical analyses of cases where evidence of an emerging paradigm can be observed – such as in "teal organizations" studied by Frederic Laloux (2014), in which a higher purpose, empowerment, self-management, and creativity of employees are emphasized. What is proposed here is that holistic peace can be declared as the ultimate objective in the new paradigm because the expanded concept of peace offers universal inspiration to all of humanity. This forms the basis for a transrational paradigm of business and peace.

Conclusion

This chaper presents a new paradigm for business that fosters holistic peace. By recognizing that peace – including its spiritual aspects – is relevant to all business, not just in societies facing outright conflict, can we better identify and address intrinsic ethical challenges and welcome a more responsible and peaceful future. Business has the potential, and acknowledges the societal expectation, to be a major force for good in society – and corporate leadership for peace can answer that call.

The basis of this study is the philosophical and theoretical foundation of the meaning of peace. Peace entails three stages: *Weak peace* (the absence of war or any systematic violence); *strong peace* (the presence of positive ideals such as justice, health, happiness, education, prosperity, sustainability, wellbeing, etc.); and *holistic peace* (a transrational vision for humanity, an ultimate higher purpose, interconnectedness, and moral excellence). Business *can* and *should* foster peace, because it is in the interest of business and society to have a symbiotic relationship. Accordingly, creating positive impact – fostering peace – can be construed as the *raison d'être* of the corporation. Drawing a conceptual framework, and a trajectory, of business vis-à-vis weak peace, strong peace, and holistic peace enables us to distinguish between activities that business can engage in. Business can not only contribute to weak peace and strong peace through responsible and ethical business practices, but also to holistic peace through a new mindset that transcends self-interest for a better future towards a greater good. This involves, for example, nurturing a higher organizational purpose, embodying moral excellence, and aligning business models and ownership structures to a higher consciousness conducive to fostering peace. Ideas can then evolve through the transcendence of reason, as spirituality is acknowledged to be a source of inspiration and power.

Transrational business is a new, emerging paradigm that enables business to climb the ladder of morality by reaching higher levels of positive contributions to society. The criteria of weak, strong, and holistic peace form a ladder of morality because each higher level represents, contains, or entails activities that require a higher level of moral maturity. Such a paradigm is centered around holistic peace as the ultimate objective of business and brings to the fore the general weal and wellbeing of all stakeholders, including nature. Even though holistic peace efforts may seem radical or even insurmountable, they may be the future norm, just as today's innovative strong peace efforts were radical only a few decades ago to Milton Friedman and others. Whether this new type of business thinking – where fostering holistic peace forms the pinnacle of corporate success – leads to reduced or to increased profits remains an open question. While it may be necessary to curtail the greed for profit, new business models and innovative products/services that foster holistic peace may, in fact, offer unprecedented opportunities for visionary leaders (Rifkin, 2015). Be that as it may, the ideas put forward in this article raise the question of how we, as society, want to deal with industries that are shown not to foster peace. For example, do we want to tolerate arms production in the hands of private companies?

The core argument is that business should foster peace – in accordance with moral maturity. This argument rests on the assumptions that society's expectations towards sustainable and ethical business will remain and deepen; that peace can be seen as the cornerstone and substance of positive societal impact; that the purpose of the corporation should not be restricted to mere profit maximization; and that realizing the human potential of living in peace is a sovereign maxim which enables the evolution of society. As it has been shown that the concept of peace is relevant for business, the goal is to elevate the Responsible Business discourse to a new level. Here, enlightened business leaders will play a major role.

Acknowledgments

I would like to thank Professor Wolfgang Dietrich, Professor Matti Häyry, Professor Eero Vaara, Assistant Professor Ville-Pekka Sorsa, as well as my researcher colleagues Marleen Wierenga, Thomas Taussi, and Anu Penttilä for helpful comments on earlier versions of this article.

Notes

1 This chapter is based on the author's two Masters' theses (Bauer, 2015; 2016).
2 It is not the aim of this chapter to investigate the various definitions of the expanded concept of business. More nuanced research is needed on different types of business fostering peace.
3 While discussing this assumption in detail is beyond the scope of this article, it is critical because business can only be a force for peace in a context in which the assumption holds that the fundamental purpose of business is defined and understood as ethical value creation.
4 One notable exception is William McDonough and Michael Braungart's (2000; 2013) concept of "Cradle to Cradle" where products are expected to deliver "positive nutrients" to the "biosphere" and/or to the "technosphere."

5 The terminology of weak and strong peace is adapted from Webel's (2007: 11) "Spectral Theory of Peace."
6 It is worth noting that the ladder of morality is not a ladder of ethics: there is no external source proclaiming that being higher on the ladder is better, as not every company is expected to be at the top. Rather, opting for a higher or lower position on the ladder is an internal, or intrinsic, question of the felt morality of the individual manager/organization. In other words, it should be a conscious decision. Being on the lower end is not to be judged as being inferior (as long as one does not slip to the very bottom, i.e. being outright immoral). On the other hand, being higher on the ladder does not exclude activities associated with lower levels of the ladder.
7 Tuure Parkkinen (2015) analyzes dependence on economic growth and points out that competition for customers and employees can be in the interest of these stakeholders.

References

Banerjee, S.B. (2008). Corporate Social Responsibility: The Good, the Bad and the Ugly. *Critical Sociology*, 34(1), 51–79.

Bauer, T. (2015). Business – A Force for Peace: Why and What? A Theoretical Study. Unpublished Master's Thesis. Aalto University School of Business, Helsinki, Finland. Available online at http://epub.lib.aalto.fi/en/ethesis/pdf/14325/hse_ethesis_14325.pdf (accessed April 9, 2018).

Bauer, T. (2016). Operationalizing Peace: Criteria for a Holistic Business Peace Index. Unpublished Master's Thesis. Rotterdam, The Netherlands:Erasmus University Rotterdam School of Management.

Bauer, T. (forthcoming). Spirituality and Peace. In Zsolnai, L. & Flanagan, B. (Eds) *International Handbook of Spirituality and Society*. Oxford: Routledge.

Bouckaert, L. & Chatterji, M. (Eds) (2015). *Business, Ethics and Peace. Contributions to Conflict Management, Peace Economics and Development*, Volume 24. Bingley, UK: Emerald Group Publishing Limited.

Bouckaert, L. & Zsolnai, L. (Eds) (2011). *The Palgrave Handbook of Spirituality and Business*. Houndmills: Palgrave Macmillan.

Boulding, K.E. (1945). *The Economics of Peace*. New York: Prentice-Hall, Inc.

Braungart, M. (2005). It´s time for corporations to move beyond guilt management. *Corporate Responsibility Management*, 1(6), 3.

Briggs, J. & Peat, F.D. (1999). *Seven Life Lessons of Chaos: Spiritual Wisdom from the Science of Change*. New York: HarperPerennial.

Burford, G., Hoover, E., Velasco, I., Janoušková, S., Jimenez, A., Piggot, G., Podger, D., & Harder, M.K. (2013). Bringing the "Missing Pillar" into Sustainable Development Goals: Towards Intersubjective Values-Based Indicators. *Sustainability*, 5(7), 3035–3059.

Capra, F. (1982). *The Turning Point: Science, Society, and the Rising Culture*. New York: Bantam.

Capra, F. (1996). *The Web of Life: A New Scientific Understanding of Living Systems*. New York: Anchor Books.

Capra, F. (2002). *The Hidden Connections: A Science for Sustainable Living*. New York: Anchor Books.

Capra, F. & Luisi, P.L. (2014). *The Systems View of Life: A Unifying Vision*. Cambridge: Cambridge University Press.

Carroll, A.B. (1979). A Three-Dimensional Conceptual Model of Corporate Performance. *The Academy of Management Review*, 4(4), 497–505.

Carroll, A.B. (1991). The Pyramid of Corporate Social Responsibility: Toward the Moral Management of Organizational Stakeholders. *Business Horizons*, 34(4), 39–48.

Chaudhry, R. (2011). *Quest for Exceptional Leadership: Mirage to Reality*. New Delhi, India: SAGE Response.

Coady, C.A.J. (2008). *Morality and Political Violence*. New York: Cambridge University Press.

Crucé, E. (1623, 1909 Edition). *Le Nouveau Cynée* (The New Cyneas, edited and translated by Willing Balch, T.). Philadelphia: Allen, Lane and Scott.

Dahlsrud, A. (2006). How Corporate Social Responsibility is Defined: An Analysis of 37 Definitions. *Corporate Social Responsibility and Environmental Management*, 15(1), 1–13.

Dalai Lama (2002). *How to Practice: The Way to a Meaningful Life*. New York: Atria Books.

Dalai Lama (2009a). *The Dalai Lama's Little Book of Inner Peace: The Essential Life and Teachings*. New York: Hampton Roads Publishing.

Dalai Lama (2009b). *The Art of Happiness: A Handbook for Living*, 10th edn. New York: Riverhead Books.

Dalai Lama & Muyzenberg, L. (2008). *The Leader's Way: The Art of Making the Right Decisions in our Careers, our Companies, and the World at Large*. London: Nicholas Brealey Publishing Ltd.

Danesh, H.B. (Ed.) (2011). *Education for Peace Reader*. Education for Peace Integrative Curriculum series, volume 4. Available online at http://efpinternational.org/wp-con tent/uploads/2011/11/efp_reader.pdf (accessed May 11, 2018).

Dietrich, W. (2006). *A Call for Trans-Rational Peaces*. Available online at http://www. uibk.ac.at/peacestudies/downloads/peacelibrary/transrational.pdf (accessed May 11, 2018).

Dietrich, W. (2008). *Variationen über die Vielen Frieden. Band 1: Deutungen* (Variations on the Many Peaces. Volume 1: Interpretations). Wiesbaden: VS Verlag für Sozialwissenschaften.

Dietrich, W. (2011). *Variationen über die vielen Frieden, Band 2: Elicitive Konflikttransformation und die transrationale Wende in der Friedenspolitik* (Variations on the Many Peaces. Volume 2: Elicitive Conflict Transformation and the Transrational Shift in Peace Politics). Wiesbaden: VS Verlag für Sozialwissenschaften.

Dietrich, W. (2012). *Interpretations of Peace in History and Culture, Many Peaces Volume 1*. London: Palgrave Macmillan.

Dietrich, W. (2013). *Elicitive Conflict Transformation and the Transrational Shift in Peace Politics, Many Peaces Volume 2*. London: Palgrave Macmillan.

Dietrich, W., Echavarría, J., Esteva, G., Ingruber, D., & Koppensteiner, N. (Eds) (2014). *The Palgrave International Handbook of Peace Studies: A Cultural Perspective*. London: Palgrave Macmillan.

Dietrich, W. & Sützl, W. (2006). A Call For Many Peaces. In Dietrich, W., Echavarría, J. & Koppensteiner, N. (Eds) *Key Texts of Peace Studies/Schlüsseltexte der Friedensforschung / Textos Claves de la Investigación para la Paz* (pp. 282–302). Vienna: LIT-Verlag.

Dillard, J., Dujon, V. & King, M.C. (2009). *Understanding the Social Dimension of Sustainability*. New York: Routledge.

Dresner, S. (2008). *The Principles of Sustainability*. London: Earthscan.

Elkington, J. (1998). *Cannibals with Forks: The Triple Bottom Line of 21st Century Business.* Gabriola Island: New Society Publishers.

Fairholm, G.W. (1998). *Perspectives on Leadership: From the Science of Management to its Spiritual Heart.* Westport, CT: Praeger Publishers.

Fort, T.L. (2001). Corporate Makahiki: The Governing Telos of Peace. *American Business Law Journal*, 38(2), 301–361.

Fort, T.L. (2007). *Business, Integrity and Peace: Beyond Geopolitical and Disciplinary Boundaries.* Cambridge: Cambridge University Press.

Fort, T.L. (Ed.) (2011). *Peace Through Commerce: A Multisectoral Approach.* Dordrecht: Springer.

Fort, T.L. (2015). *The Diplomat in the Corner Office: Corporate Foreign Policy.* Stanford, CA: Stanford University Press.

Fort, T.L. & Noone, J.J. (2000). Gifts, Bribes, and Exchange: Relationships in Non-Market Economies and Lessons for Pax E-Commercia. *Cornell International Law Journal*, 33(3), 515–546.

Fort, T.L. & Schipani, C.A. (2004). *The Role of Business in Fostering Peaceful Societies.* Cambridge, UK: Cambridge University Press.

Fort, T.L. & Westermann-Behaylo, M. (2008). Moral Maturity, Peace Through Commerce, and the Partnership Dimension. In Williams, O.F. (Ed.), *Peace Through Commerce: Responsible Corporate Citizenship and the Ideals of the United Nations Global Compact* (pp. 55–74). Notre Dame, IN: University of Notre Dame Press.

Fourcade, M. & Healy, K. (2007). Moral Views of Market Society. *Annual Review of Sociology*, 33, 285–311.

Fox, M.A. (2014). *Understanding Peace: A Comprehensive Introduction.* New York: Routledge.

Freeman, R.E. (1984, 2010 Edition). *Strategic Management: A Stakeholder Approach.* Cambridge: Cambridge University Press.

Friedman, M. (1962, 2002 Edition). *Capitalism and Freedom.* Chicago: The University of Chicago Press.

Galtung, J. (1965, 2003 Edition). International Programs of Behavioral Science Research in Human Survival. In Schwebel, M. (Ed.) *Behavioral Science and Human Survival* (pp. 226–247). Lincoln: iUniverse, Inc.

Galtung, J. (1967). *Theories of Peace: A Synthetic Approach to Peace Thinking.* International Peace Research Institute, Oslo. Available online at www.transcend.org/files/Galtung_Book_unpub_Theories_of_Peace_-_A_Synthetic_Approach_to_Peace_Thinking_1967.pdf (accessed May 11, 2018).

Galtung, J. (1969). Violence, Peace, and Peace Research. *Journal of Peace Research*, 6(3), 167–191.

Galtung, J. (1980). The Basic Needs Approach. In Lederer, K., Galtung, J., & Antal, D. (Eds) *Human Needs: A Contribution to the Current Debate* (pp. 55–125). Cambridge, MA: Oelgeschlager, Gunn & Hain.

Galtung, J. (1990). Cultural Violence. *Journal of Peace Research*, 27(3), 291–305.

Galtung, J. (1996). *Peace by Peaceful Means: Peace and Conflict, Development and Civilization.* International Peace Research Institute Oslo. London: SAGE Publications Ltd.

Groff, L. & Bouckaert, L. (2015). The Evolving View on Peace and its Implications for Business. In Bouckaert, L. & Chatterji, M. (Eds) *Business, Ethics and Peace. Contributions to Conflict Management, Peace Economics and Development* (pp. 3–23). Bingley, UK: Emerald Group Publishing Limited.

Guthrie, D. (2014). A Conversation on Corporate Social Responsibility. *Forbes*. Available online at www.forbes.com/sites/dougguthrie/2014/01/09/a-conversatio n-on-corporate-social-responsibility/ (accessed May 11, 2018).

Haufler, V. (2001). *A Public Role for the Private Sector: Industry Self-Regulation in a Global Economy*. Washington, DC: Carnegie Endowment for International Peace.

Hock, D. (2005). *One From Many: VISA and the Rise of Chaordic Organization*. San Francisco: Berrett-Koehler Publishers, Inc.

Hosmer, L.T. (1994a). *Moral Leadership in Business*. Homewood: Richard D. Irwin, Inc.

Hosmer, L.T. (1994b). Why be Moral? A Different Rationale for Managers. *Business Ethics Quarterly*, 4(2), 191–204.

Jeong, H-W. (2000). *Peace and Conflict Studies – An Introduction*. Hants, UK: Ashgate Publishing Ltd.

Kant, I. (1795, 2013 Edition). *Zum Ewigen Frieden: Ein Philosophischer Entwurf* (Perpetual Peace: A Philosophical Sketch). Berlin: Michael Holzinger.

Kanter, R.M. (2009). *Supercorp: How Vanguard Companies Create Innovation, Profits, Growth, and Social Good*. New York: Random House, Inc.

Kelly, M. (2012). *Owning Our Future: The Emerging Ownership Revolution – Journeys to a Generative Economy*. San Francisco, CA: Berrett-Koehler Publishers, Inc.

Korten, D.C. (2015). *When Corporations Rule the World*. Oakland, CA: Berrett-Koehler Publishers, Inc.

Kuhn, T. (1970). *The Structure of Scientific Revolutions*. Chicago: University of Chicago Press.

Laloux, F. (2014). *Reinventing Organizations: A Guide to Creating Organizations Inspired by The Next Stage of Human Consciousness*. Brussels, Belgium: Nelson Parker.

Lankoski, L. & Smith, N.C. (2017). Alternative Objective Functions for Firms. *Organization & Environment*, Special Issue, Creating Value for Stakeholders. Available online at http://journals.sagepub.com/doi/10.1177/1086026617722883 (accessed May 11, 2018).

Lawler, P. (1995). *A Question of Values: Johan Galtung's Peace Research*. Colorado: Lynne Rienner Publishers, Inc.

Lederach, J.P. (2005). *The Moral Imagination: The Art and Soul of Building Peace*. New York: Oxford University Press.

Lo, S.-F. & Sheu, H.-J. (2007). Is Corporate Sustainability a Value-Increasing Strategy for Business? *Corporate Governance: An International Review*, 15(2), 345–358.

McDonough, W. & Braungart, M. (2000, May-June). A World of Abundance. *Interfaces*, 30(3), 55–65.

McDonough, W. & Braungart, M. (2002). *Cradle to Cradle: Remaking the Way We Make Things*. New York: North Point Press.

McDonough, W. & Braungart, M. (2013). *The Upcycle: Beyond Sustainability – Designing for Abundance*. New York: North Point Press.

Miller, C.E. (2005). *A Glossary of Terms and Concepts in Peace and Conflict Studies*, 2nd edn. Addis Ababa: University for Peace Africa Program.

Montesquieu, C. de (1748, 1752, 2001). *The Spirit of the Laws* (translated by Nugent, T.). Ontario, Canada: Kitchener, Batoche Books.

Moore, G. (1999). Corporate Moral Agency: Review and Implications. *Journal of Business Ethics*, 21(4), 329–343.

Moura-Leite, R.C. & Padgett, R.C. (2011). Historical Background of Corporate Social Responsibility. *Social Responsibility Journal*, 7(4), 528–539.

Musk, E. (2013, February). Elon Musk: The Mind Behind Tesla, SpaceX, SolarCity. *TED Talks*. Available online at www.ted.com/talks/elon_musk_the_mind_behind_ tesla_spacex_solarcity (accessed May 11, 2018).

Nelson, J. (2000). *The Business of Peace: The Private Sector as a Partner in Conflict Prevention and Resolution*. London: The Prince of Wales Business Leaders Forum, International Alert, Council on Economic Priorities.

Oetzel, J., Westermann-Behaylo, M., Koerber, C., Fort, T.L., & Rivera, J. (2010). Business and Peace: Sketching the Terrain. *Journal of Business Ethics*, 89(4): 351–373.

Parkkinen, T. (2015). *Fixing the Root Bug: The Simple Hack for a Growth-Independent, Fair and Sustainable Market Economy 2.0*. Reparodigm Publishing.

Porter, M. & Kramer, M.R. (2011). Creating Shared Value. How to Reinvent Capitalism – And Unleash a Wave of Innovation and Growth. *Harvard Business Review*.

Rifkin, J. (2015). *The Zero Marginal Cost Society: The Internet of Things, the Collaborative Commons, and the Eclipse of Capitalism*. New York: Palgrave Macmillan.

Santa Barbara, J., Dubee, F., & Galtung, J. (2009). *Peace Business: Humans and Nature Above Markets and Capital*. Kolofon Press/Transcend University Press.

Saxegaard, P. (2016, May 4). Personal Interview with T. Bauer. Oslo, Norway.

Shaw, B. & Corvino, J. (1996). Hosmer and the 'Why Be Moral?' Question. *Business Ethics Quarterly*, 6(3), 373–383.

Smith, A. (1776, 1937 Edition). *An Inquiry into the Nature and Causes of the Wealth of Nations* (edited by E. Cannan). New York: The Modern Library, Random House Inc.

Smurthwaite, M. (2008). The Purpose of the Corporation. In Williams, O.F. (Ed.) *Peace Through Commerce: Responsible Corporate Citizenship and the Ideals of the United Nations Global Compact* (pp. 13–54). Notre Dame, IN: University of Notre Dame Press.

Sweetman, D. (2009). *Business, Conflict Resolution, and Peacebuilding: Contributions from the Private Sector to Address Violent Conflict*. Routledge Studies in Peace and Conflict Resolution. Abingdon, Oxon: Routledge.

Van Tulder, R., Van Tilburg, R., Francken, M., & Da Rosa, A. (2014). *Managing the Transitions to a Sustainable Enterprise*. New York: Routledge.

Vorobej, M. (2008). Structural Violence. *The Canadian Journal of Peace and Conflict Studies*, 40(2): 84–98.

Webel, C.P. (2007). Introduction: Toward a Philosophy and Metapsychology of Peace. InWebel, C.P. & Galtung, J. (Eds) *Handbook of Peace and Conflict Studies* (pp. 3–13). Abingdon, Oxon: Routledge.

Wheatley, M. (2006). *Leadership and the New Science: Discovering Order in a Chaotic World*. San Francisco: Berrett-Koehler Publishers, Inc.

Williams, O.F. (Ed.) (2008). *Peace Through Commerce: Responsible Corporate Citizenship and the Ideals of the United Nations Global Compact*. Notre Dame, IN: University of Notre Dame Press.

World Commission on Environment and Development (1987). *Report of the World Commission on Environment and Development: Our Common Future. The Brundtland Report*. Available online at www.un-documents.net/our-common-future.pdf (accessed May 11, 2018).

Zsolnai, L. & Flanagan, B. (Eds) (forthcoming). *International Handbook of Spirituality and Society*. Oxford: Routledge.

Zsolnai, L. (Ed.) (2004). *Spirituality and Ethics in Management*, 2nd edn. Dordrecht: Springer.

Part IV

Gandhian and Buddhist political economy

8 Gandhi, economics, and the new story

Michael N. Nagler

When the shocking news of Mahatma Gandhi's assassination on January 30, 1948 spread throughout India the outpouring of grief was so overwhelming that Western journalists were hard put to it to comprehend what they were experiencing. One of them, Edward Snow, turned to an Indian friend who told him, "You know, the people feel that there was a mirror of the Mahatma in which everyone could see the best in himself, and when the mirror broke, it seemed that the thing in oneself might be fled forever" (Shirer, 1979, p. 227).

Gandhi was, considered from any point of view, one of the most remarkable figures of the twentieth century. Satyagraha, the nonviolent method of struggle that he invented, or rather resuscitated from ancient sources and some social practices of his own time, has revolutionized civil resistance, and its potential is far from exhausted. But this is only one example of the not-inconsiderable contributions he was able to make to many widespread fields of human endeavor, from health care to religion, including some, like economics, in which he had no formal training. How was he able to do this?

There is no reason to doubt his own claim that his life was an indivisible whole and that all his activities ran into one another and they all had their rise from his "insatiable love of mankind." Yet in this age of reductionism and compartmentalization there are aspects of that claim that deserve some explanation. In this chapter we will focus on his contribution to economics, but it should not be lost sight of that we would miss something essential to consider that contribution as a separate or, as we say today, "siloed" offering that can be understood apart from its connection to, for example, religion. As he himself said, "Religion to be true must satisfy what may be termed humanitarian economics, that is, where the income and the expenditure balance each other." (Tendulkar, 1969, vol. 2, p. 268). Similarly, connecting one of the main tenets of his economic thought with nonviolence, he wrote, "All my experiments in ahimsa (nonviolence) convince me that nonviolence in practice means common labour with the body." (*ibid.*, vol. 5, p. 225).

Some background

Western economic theory, indeed almost all contemporary fields of inquiry (as Goethe would add, "and alas, even theology") have had a pervasive problem of compartmentalization. In the case of economics its "specialization" has led to considering wealth and market processes apart from their impact on actual human well being. This is what prompted E.F. Schumacher to subtitle his ground-breaking book *Economics As Though People Mattered* (Schumacher, 1975) and the King of Bhutan more recently to come up with his catchy revision of the guiding criterion for economic success GNH, or "Gross National *Happiness*."

It is, of course, necessary to specialize, but as knowledge multiplies it can mean the loss of *context*. The last of our species who was said to have mastered all the fields of knowledge of his time was Aristotle. When specialization entails a piecemeal approach it becomes, especially at times like these when the whole story of reality is shifting, a woefully inadequate approach to solving problems, including the most pressing problems that we are facing. One of these (or one aspect of all contemporary dilemmas) is certainly violence, and as John Burton has said of that problem (Burton, 1997, p. 10), "In so far as specific problems are being tackled by authorities as though they were separate problems, there can be no lasting cures for any of them." It is timely, indeed necessary, then, to understand, as far as we can, Gandhi's ability to find a liberating simplicity amid the welter of issues with which we have to deal. What did he mean when he said, for example, that "all mental and physical ailments are due to one common cause"? (Tendulkar, 1969, p. 81).

If we apply Thomas Kuhn's influential model to the contemporary crisis (Kuhn, 1962), we are caught in an incomplete "paradigm shift" that leaves us suspended between two versions of reality: an "old story" (OS) in which the universe consists essentially of inert matter acted upon by chance forces and a "new story" (NS) that sees the universe made of consciousness, energy, *and* matter which seems to exhibit a driving purpose that is discernible throughout the evolution of life, namely the rise of that consciousness. The old story is essentially one of separateness. All material reality is by nature particulate, separate, and all living beings are existentially separate so that competition, an endless depletion of natural resources, and various (other) forms of violence are inevitable. In the story struggling to emerge, by contrast, there is a subtle connectedness among all living things such that competition and violence are not only unnecessary but constitute direct violations of that driving purpose, and cannot be sustained as permanent features of our lived reality for that reason.

There is, to be sure, a bit of misnomer in these popular terms: the OS is usually traced back to Descartes, Bacon, and the birth of the industrial revolution, which is not very old in the scale of these major civilizational shifts, while the so-called NS is identical in most of its features with what Huxley aptly called the perennial philosophy (*philosophia perennis*) that has been around for millennia across many cultures, East and West. Saint Augustine, in a lyrical outburst, refers to the God he has at last seen as a *pulchritudo tam antiqua et tam nova*, a "beauty so ancient and so new" (St Augustine, 1960, X. 27). One is tempted to say the same about the "new" vision of reality, which has sources in both the perennial wisdom tradition common to many indigenous and advanced cultures and the astonishing developments across virtually all fields of science that began at the turn of the last century. While we will not have the scope here to go into this development in detail,[1] the features of the NS that are most useful for our purposes, all in stark contrast to the "old," or prevailing paradigm, are:

- We do not live in a meaningless universe.
- The basic reality of the universe is not matter, but consciousness.
- All life is an interconnected whole.
- Human beings can (and a few have) take charge of their own destiny.

While the still incomplete shift to this worldview represents perhaps the greatest transformation of Western culture since the advent of monotheism and it affects every aspect of our experience, there does seem to be single idea, or focus underneath its bewildering complexity, and that is the perennial question of philosophy: *who are we?* The heart of our present dilemma between two paradigms was well brought out in an observation of the late religion scholar, Huston Smith, who put his finger on a deficiency that bids fair to being central to the shift some years ago at a conference: "For our culture as a whole, nothing major is going to happen until we figure out who we are. The truth of the matter is, that today we haven't a clue as to who we are. There is no consistent view of human nature in the West today" (quoted in Glazer, 1999).

The thesis of the present chapter is that Gandhi's "insatiable love of mankind" provided him with such a view – or indeed arose from it – and that this is what furnished him with a ground from which he was able to make not-inconsiderable contributions to so many fields.

Despite his self-presentation as a political and social activist, there can be little doubt that Gandhi stood squarely in the lineage of the ancient sages who developed India's version of the "new" story. The story goes that once a British missionary in India claimed spiritual kinship with him saying, "we're both men of God, Mr. Gandhi, aren't we." His epic reply was, "I am a man of God disguised as a politician;" "You are a politician disguised as a Man of God." The decision to downplay his "mahatmaship" (*mahatma* meaning "great soul") seems to have been not only a matter of modesty but a strategic decision to prevent people from putting him on a pedestal and dismissing his achievements as beyond the reach of ordinary mortals. Yet, as he was no doubt aware, the Indian people on the whole certainly took him as a representative of their ancient spiritual tradition, i.e. a "mirror in which one could see the best in him (or her-)self;" and that recognition did not by any means lead to his dismissal as a political force of rare power.

It is fashionable to claim that he got his nonviolence from Tolstoy and Thoreau, which is perhaps reassuring to us in the West, but Gandhi explicitly stated that he had hit upon nonviolence and civil disobedience before he read either of them. He traced it instead, to the sages of India's past, who he claimed were "greater geniuses that Newton" (Gandhi, 1927). This put him into conflict, in fact, with the prevailing Western worldview that was making inroads into India's faith in herself and her extraordinary heritage. He was aware from his early days in South Africa that he was up against nothing less than what we'd call today a "clash of civilizations," or rather, of two *ideas* of civilization. He puts into the mouth of the Colonial Secretary of the Transvaal, General Smuts, the attitude of the Europeans who opposed him:

> South Africa is a representative [aka colony] of Western civilization while India is the centre of Oriental culture. Thinkers of the present generation hold that these two civilizations cannot go together... The West is opposed to simplicity while Orientals consider that virtue to be of primary importance.... Western civilization may or may not be good, but Westerners wish to stick to it... They have shed rivers of blood for its sake.... It is therefore too late for them now to chalk out a new path for themselves.
>
> (Gandhi, 1928, pp. 83f)

His political struggle, vast in scope as it was even in itself, was a tool for the much larger effort to, as we would say now, shift the whole story of humanity: "Through realization of freedom of India", he explained, "I hope to realize and carry on the mission of brotherhood of man." (Tendulkar, 1969, vol. 2, p. 353).

The new story, in other words, is rooted in a simplicity that cannot be easily conceptualized in a material worldview. Matter is by nature multiform and divided − objects are by nature separate − which cannot but be carried over into our conception of who we ourselves are and how we are related to the rest of life, indeed of all existence. The human image that runs through the mature Gandhi's speaking, writing, and action is identical to the new story on which ancient wisdom and modern sciences are converging. In it each of us is:

- body, mind, and spirit − in reverse order of importance. We are in fact spiritual beings in search of unity with all that lives;
- deeply interconnected with other human beings and indeed all of life, and therefore
- cannot be fulfilled, in the final analysis, by the consumption of things and physical experiences. Moreover,
- security can never be realized within societies by punishing offenders, but by rehabilitating them and restoring broken relationships, or between nations by defeating "enemies."

Gandhi was quite aware, for example, of the racist attitude that threw him off the train at Maritzburg in April, 1893, but already at that time, a good year before his public career began, he sensed that the insult was not to be taken personally or as an Indian but was yet another example of "man's inhumanity to man." Racism, which still so disfigures our world, is a virulent form of that inhumanity, but not the only one. Later he would resist with all his heart and soul the similar tensions among Indians themselves, whether Hindu against Muslim or caste Hindu against "untouchable."

What he faced in South Africa was really a tension between two visions of human nature, resting on what Augustine called two *amores*, or drives: the instinct for self-preservation that flows naturally from a materialist worldview and the instinct for self-sacrifice in service to a higher cause that is an expression of our yearning for unity and relationship to a larger whole — in his vocabulary, for God. In other words, the underlying conflict he faced is not really between two civilizations but two *ideas* of civilization, two "stories"; one that has us as physical beings inescapably locked into competition and violence and another that acknowledges our spiritual nature and the unity of consciousness. In this sense he anticipated the struggle in which we find ourselves today – of which, as we say, racism vs. inclusivity is only a particularly compelling example. If you cannot see beyond the physical dimension of the human being you are doomed to fall victim to racist feelings. Conversely if you *can* see that we have another, much deeper nature that is not in itself physical, racism becomes absurd, along with any other form of exclusivity. In the new story, they fall away almost by themselves.

We might clarify here, because of its relevance to his economic thinking, that Gandhi's love of mankind was a kind of shorthand for a love of all creatures, indeed all of life (which is why the voluntarily poor man of India has often been compared to the voluntarily poor man of Assisi). His aching concern for the way cows and bullocks were treated in the destitute villages of India seems to equal his loving concern for the villagers themselves, though he was horrified by the abuse of the noble concept of cow-protection, originally meant to stand for stewardship of the earth and all its life forms, as a shibboleth to produce hatred for Muslims. The cow is, of course, the symbol of the earth's bounty and the token of natural wealth in all Indo-European and many other cultures; in India in particular she became also the symbol of God's bounty and ahimsa. His strict vegetarianism was originally an inheritance, later consciously adopted as an aspect of the same ahimsa when the latter became the core of his political and economic work.

The belief that we can only be fulfilled by material possessions prevents us from recognizing the evidence, which increases day by day, that beyond a certain point wealth does *not* lead to greater happiness (e.g. McRaney, 2012) and that war, or any manifestations of competition and violence do not make us secure. Unfortunately, it is precisely this underlying belief that is upheld and reinforced on a daily basis by the mass media in most industrialized societies.

While he repudiated this belief system to its core, Gandhi was never for a wholesale rejection of any institution (not even caste, famously and controversially), but always asked, in a Socratic spirit,[2] what is the legitimate purpose of this institution, custom, or profession. He would assess how well it was performing that function, and that would lead to a kind of triage in which the institution would be deemed functional as it stood, in need of reform, or (as in the case of untouchability or colonialism) removal.

What then, we may ask with him, is the real function of an economy, one that arises from the larger, more complete image he held of the human being?

First and foremost, he reasoned, it would be designed for fulfilling human *needs* and not, as at present, require an artificial multiplication of *wants*. Gandhi saw close to a century ago that this could not in principle be the basis of a sustainable economy:

> I do not believe that multiplication of wants and machinery contrived to supply them is taking the world a single step nearer its own.
>
> (Gandhi, 1927)

Note the implication that an economy should talk us "nearer our own," that is, facilitate a kind of self-realization. He goes on to urge his countrymen, even more strongly:

> So do not be lifted off your feet, do not be drawn away from the simplicity of your ancestors. A time is coming when those, who are in the mad rush today of multiplying their wants, vainly thinking that they add to the real substance, real knowledge of the world will retrace their steps and say: What have we done.
>
> (Gandhi, 1962, p. 5)

What, indeed. Speaking not only to Indians here, but through India to all of us, Gandhi saw that the artificiality of modern economies' multiplication of wants is not only a slender reed on which to try to base such a vital function of human society but is damaging to the human spirit. In this, as elsewhere, his outlook was squarely in the age-old spiritual tradition of India. A well-known and much revered contemporary and admirer of Gandhi, who did not, by contrast, make any attempt to downplay her spiritual identity, once said in no uncertain terms:

> Man appears to be the embodiment of want. Want is what he thinks about, and want indeed is what he obtains. Contemplate your true being or else there will be want, wrong action, helplessness, distress, and death.
>
> (Chaudhuri, 1998, p. 133)

The last thing that a modern advertiser wants is for you to "contemplate your true being," because you would soon discover that you have untapped inner resources and what you are really seeking is connectedness with others, and eventually, as Einstein said, with "all of nature in its beauty." Gandhian economics, then, as even the Wikipedia article points out, is, "a school of economic thought based on the *spiritual and* socio-economic principles expounded by Indian leader Mahatma Gandhi." And it goes on,

> It is largely characterised by rejection of the concept of the human being as a rational actor always seeking to maximize material self-interest that underlies classical economic thinking. Where Western economic systems were (and are) based on what he called the "multiplication of wants," Gandhi felt that this was both unsustainable and devastating to the human spirit. His model, by contrast, aimed at the fulfillment of needs – including the need for self-realization, for meaning and community ...[it] also aim to promote spiritual development and harmony with a rejection of materialism.[3]

Simplicity, Smuts's secretary saw, was an essential feature of the Asian outlook of his day. If this is more than a stereotype, it was because a complicated external environment, a life surrounded by and dedicated to the accumulation of *things*, distracts the person from exploring his or her "true being," an exploration that is primarily within. Properly understood, simplicity need not lead to uniformity; it can foster localized *diversity*. Putting simplicity and diversity together, Gandhi came up with the need for *svadeshi,* or localism, which can be taken as the antidote to centralization and the "globalization from above" that has come to characterize the "international community" today.

Svadeshi was one of the guidelines for building an economy that would "promote spiritual development" as well as restore prosperity and meaningful lives to impoverished Indian masses. Its iconic project was khadi, which while working toward those goals enabled all Indians to wear with pride the homespun cloth (*khadi* or *khaddar*). Alongside these other advantages, khadi would level social distinctions among rich and poor in Indian society. In his plan, which for a time largely succeeded, the wealthiest and highest in social status, the lawyers and statesmen, would both spin and wear khadi along with the simplest villager. But there's more: even the physical act of turning the spinning wheel, the *charkha*, was at least potentially, if done in the right spirit, a spiritual practice:

> The turning of the charkha in a lifeless way will be like the turning of the beads of the rosary with a wandering mind, turned away from God.
> (Tendulkar 1969, vol. 5, p. 242)

We would be tempted to call this today "mindful spinning"; but Indian readers would have recognized it as the first step in a classic series for yogic practice: concentration on an outside object or activity (*dhāraṇa*), concentration then on a single thought (*dhyāna*), and finally meditation proper (*nididhyāsana*). For all these reasons hand-spinning became the "sun" in the solar system of his famous "Constructive Programme" (CP) which was designed to rebuild Indian society from the ground up and by doing so provide a powerful platform from which to launch, where still required, the direct, obstructive acts of non-cooperation and disobedience that struck off the thus loosened grip of the Raj. By 1927 the

charkha, or hand-spinning campaign, included "50,000 spinners in 1,500 villages besides weavers, washermen, printers, dyers, and tailors" (Gandhi, 1927) as
well as the distributors and consumers who proudly wore what Nehru called
"the livery of our freedom." Yet it should not be overlooked that this
rebuilding or restoration of India's economy and social order was at the same
time aimed at the spiritual uplift of the human individual. The human being
cannot thrive or realize him or herself without service to a larger whole. Thus,
all activities within his economic program answered to the three purposes of
human work later described by another Gandhi admirer (and one who, like
himself, kept something of a distance from formal economic theory), E. F.
Schumacher:

> First, to provide necessary and useful goods and services; second, to enable
> everyone of us to use and thereby to perfect our gifts like good stewards;
> and third, to do so in service to, and cooperation with, others so as to
> liberate ourselves from our inborn egocentricity.
>
> (Schumacher, 1979, p. 123)

Schumacher's "inborn egocentricity" could almost be a quote from the Bhagavad
Gita, Gandhi's beloved "spiritual reference book," which declares that all human
beings fall under the spell of *māyā*, the delusion of separateness, at birth (vii.27).

In all its features, then, Gandhi's economic vision derived from his contrast-
ing, indeed challenging image of the human being as a spiritual being seeking
community rather than a primarily material being seeking personal gratification
(Edgeworth, see note 3, above). The fulfilling of needs of necessity *included* our
"higher" needs (à la Maslow) for mutual service and community. The artificial
multiplication of wants, by contrast, not only leaves us more and more frustrated but alienates us from ourselves, from one another (since we come to be
regarded as "markets" for various degrees of exploitation), and of course the
natural world. Our material needs are actually modest and the planet we live
on (in this view ours is not a random universe) contains all the resources
necessary to fulfill them for all persons, in a renewable cycle. That would be
true even of the burgeoning populations that today are putting such a burden
on the earth and its resources – though of course those populations would stop
burgeoning if more people realized where our gratification and fulfillment
really lie! He held that no one should rest until everyone had enough of food,
clothing, and shelter (and we would add today, healthcare). Although Gandhi
fought shy of appeals to "rights," as they can become a slogan for wants and a
cover for self-centered demands, he did allow that every person has a right to
fulfill these basic needs.

Our non-material needs, on the other hand, are greater and – once the basic
needs are guaranteed – more important. It is interesting to note that that other
great apostle of nonviolence, Martin Luther King, also took it as self evident
that we are body, mind, and spirit and require fulfillment on all three levels. In
his powerful speech on "The Other America" he spoke of the "millions of

(privileged) people … who have food and material necessities for their *bodies*, culture and education for their *minds*, freedom and human dignity for their *spirits*" (King, 1968).

With this background we can turn to the question of natural resources. The remarkable thing about higher needs is that despite their even greater importance in making us fully human, they require next to nothing from the outer environment. Indeed, often they are more than just renewable, they *increase* with use. When in a conflict I "offer dignity" to my opponent (a definition of "nonviolence" in the Tagalog language) I do not diminish my own dignity; on the contrary. I raise the level of human dignity overall, including my own. This is why King said, famously, "injustice anywhere is a threat to justice everywhere" (King, 1963). Things like justice and dignity, compassion or – by contrast – hatred, are not mere abstractions; they are non-material forces whose existence, and primary importance, is a central feature of the new story.

The presence of these not-otherwise-visible forces helps to explain how nonviolence creates useful change even when it doesn't "work." As Chenoweth and Stephan discovered in their landmark study of regime changes in the last century – the first systematic study of nonviolent action in modern political science (Chenoweth & Stephan, 2011), not only are nonviolent insurrections ten times more likely to lead to democratic institutions than violent insurrections, they are four times more likely to do so even when they "fail" – that is, fail to dislodge the authoritarian regime (Prof. Chenoweth, personal communication, 2016). The very act of "offering dignity" implicit in the adoption of nonviolent means raises human dignity, which can ultimately make totalitarianism, which ultimately depends on the devaluing of the person, impossible.

Some features of his economic scheme might not seem to have this deeper, or spiritual valence at first sight, for example, "bread labour." This plank in the platform of CP that he adopted from Ruskin meant that each person, regardless of his or her place in the social and economic system, was to be engaged in producing enough in the way of food, clothing, or shelter for her or his own upkeep. The point was first of all to raise the inherent dignity of labor by lowering the psychological boundary, the inevitable sense of superiority, that comes with any such division of social roles. This is particularly important for us at this time, when inequalities of wealth have been exaggerated to an extreme – some would say, obscene – degree. It is not surprising, then, that some version of bread labor seems to recommend itself to many, often to young people, who have "opted out" of the present economy and taken to farming or similarly basic crafts. Gandhi's strenuous objection to the unnecessary accumulation of wealth was, again, based fundamentally in terms of the spiritual alienation it caused even (or particularly) for the wealthy. In a strikingly penetrating, and equally strikingly prescient observation he identified something that people really want when they pursue wealth beyond any conceivable need: "What is really desired, under the name of riches is, essentially power over men.… In accurate terms it is 'the art of establishing the maximum inequality in our own favour'" (Gandhi, 1956 [1951], p. 57). That is, the maximum material and social separateness.

No wonder he felt that "a non-violent system of government is clearly an impossibility as long as the wide gulf between the rich and the hungry millions persists" (Prabhu & Rao, 1969, p. 157). Recently Richard Wilkinson and Kate Pickett have illustrated at length how inequality downgrades every measure of democracy and human well-being (2009). In the last analysis, however, bread labor was a requirement not only of social healing and the bringing in of "beloved community," but (as always) of individual self-realization, or what Anandamayi Ma would call the discovery of one's true being: "To forget how to dig the earth and tend the soil is to forget ourselves" (Gandhi, 1946, p. 282).

If one gets to the bottom of any part of Gandhi's economic platform, then, one finds that its root value is in the fulfillment of the human being, as an individual *and* as a member of a society. It is not that all his followers were consciously aware of this. *Svadeshi,* or "localism," for example, which envisions the fulfilled individual contributing to the well being of society in ever-widening circles, had in the meantime, for many, the strictly pragmatic application of boycotting foreign imports. Many individuals enthusiastically participated in the boycotts as their way of helping gain independence from foreign rule without bothering with the wider interpretation. In the same way, he explained, despite the astonishing success of nonviolence at dislodging a long-entrenched imperial domination – and thereby signaling the downfall of the colonial era worldwide – this was only the beginning of the power it was destined to exert in human affairs. We were seeing, in his terms, the "nonviolence of the weak," i.e., those who refrained from violence because they understood the strategic value of doing so without having in view the actual welfare of the oppressor. The "nonviolence of the strong," when it was taken to a large scale, would build a different foundation for the world order.

For Gandhi and those who followed his vision more closely, *svadeshi,* too, was based on the concept of a self-sufficient, empowered individual, immune to the blandishments of the advertising that is today the main driver of the "multiplication of wants." In this sense it is closely parallel to *trusteeship,* the answer to ownership that he took from English law, whereby a person holds things in trust for the well-being of the community rather than regarding him- or her-self as its actual owner. Alongside its obvious usefulness in leveling economic inequality, trusteeship ultimately rested on the spiritual principle that, as one of his favorite scriptures says, we really do not own anything, but "all belongs to the Lord" (Easwaran, 2007, p. 57).

Trusteeship gave one an ennobling responsibility over rather than subjection to things and other people. If carried out on a large scale (which it never was) it would even provide a nonviolent alternative to dispossession as a means of leveling material inequalities. One statement of this feature can be quoted at some length:

> Nature produces enough for our wants from day to day, and if only everybody took enough for himself and nothing more, there would be no pauperism in this world. ... I do not want to dispossess anybody. I should

then be departing from the rule of ahimsa. If somebody possesses more than I do, let him. But so far as my own life has to be regulated, I do say that I dare not possess anything which I do not want.

(Gandhi, 1933, p. 184)

Conclusion and applications

When Gandhi moved to the village of Uruli Kanchan in 1946 to carry out his experiments in nature cure, he claimed that "all mental and physical ailments are due to one common cause" (Tendulkar, 1969, p. 81) so that, for example, the fully conscious adoption of nature cure would not only make perfect medical and economic sense, in effect solving the health care problems of India's poor villagers, but would lead to the end of crime in those villages (*ibid.*, p. 192). The deeper one looks into Gandhi's thoughts and experiments, and the more one explores their wider implications, the more clearly they converge on a simple, though profound, vision of the human person as a spiritual being destined to seek a higher purpose and, as Augustine said, by his very nature compelled to seek unity with others (St Augustine, 1958, xix: 12). This is a practical way to think about the "insatiable love" he laid claim as the basis of his varied efforts. We stand in need today, in the welter of problems facing us, of the simplicity and practicality of what we might call this Grand Unified Theory of positive social change.

A surprising thing about the fulfillment of what we are calling higher needs – corresponding to the higher image Gandhi held of the human being – in the process first-order or material needs are satisfied more or less automatically. Individuals who take no more than they really need in the way of food, clothing, and shelter and look to fulfill their second-order needs for service, responsibility, and trust, etc., automatically relieve the burden we are placing on the earth and our fellow creatures. As Indian physicist, turned environmental and food activist, Dr. Vandana Shiva says, "Take care of the pollution of the human mind and they will take care of the pollution in the environment."[4] Conversely, those who overuse material resources in the attempt to find fulfilled on that level (which is impossible), letting higher needs, if there be any, take care of themselves, end up satisfying neither. As Wilkinson and Pickett point out, "the evidence shows that happiness is not increased even over periods long enough for real incomes to have doubled" (Wilkinson and Pickett, 2009, p. 8).

Since Gandhi grounded his economic – and other thinking – in what he saw as the essential characteristics of the human being, needs and wants that would be the same in any cultural setting, his experiments can be applied, with relatively minor adjustment, to our own time and place. That is extremely important. Gandhi, as we have seen, predicted that the path the industrialized nations had taken was leading to a dead end when we would need to retrace our steps and say, "what have we done." For Wilkinson and Pickett, that time has now come:

Economic growth, for so long the great engine of progress, has, in the rich countries, largely finished its work. Not only have measures of well being and happiness ceased to rise with economic growth but, as affluent societies have grown richer, there have been long-term rises and rates of anxiety, depression and numerous other social problems. The populations of rich countries have got to the end of a long historic journey.

(2009, pp. 5/6; italics added)

End times can be catastrophic. Fortunately, there are experiments in a new economic order already being tried here and there that can help make the transition be, as Sally Goerner says, "gentle, not catastrophic" (Goerner, 2004, p. 165). Within the profession itself we have economists like Claire Brown, my colleague at Berkeley, whose "Buddhist Economics" stands squarely in the tradition of E.F. Schumacher (Brown, 2017), and in that way goes somewhat further than the work of Amartya Sen, Paul Krugman, and others. More radical departures, many of which come even closer to Gandhi, are represented by economists like the Chilean Manfred Max-Neef, whose emphasis on "human scale development" and recognition of the finitude of the earth's resources are in perfect harmony with Gandhian principles (including democracy, and at least implicitly nonviolence), and most recently Kate Raworth and her model of "doughnut economics" (Raworth, 2017). Thinking of economics "as if people mattered," as Schumacher would say, has been stimulated consciously or otherwise by the King of Bhutan's abovementioned revolutionary revision of that sacred cow of the materialist paradigm into Gross National *Happiness*.

Perhaps even more importantly, quite a number of experiments are underway that aim at living out a more or less Gandhian alternative "on the ground." These range from ambitious (and highly successful) enterprises like the Mondragon cooperatives in northern Spain and numerous B-Corporations worldwide that hold themselves to the "triple bottom line" of people, planet, and profit, to the numerous individuals and communities living "off the grid" all over the industrialized world.

All these efforts contain the seeds of a peaceful revolution that can embrace not only economics but everything that depends on an enhanced vision of what it means to be a human being – which is everything. These efforts are at present rather piecemeal and uncoordinated. That difficulty, which is certainly limiting their effectiveness, has begun to be addressed. The term current for this effort among progressive activists and theorists is "intersectionality." But intersectionality is still multiplicity. The connection among all the aspects of violence and inequality in the world will elude us until we have the courage and imagination to see how "all mental and physical ailments are due to one common cause." A greater familiarity with the Gandhian experiments that sought to address that cause, only a few of which have been touched on here, can very much help in this process. The trick is not only to see, and implement the experiments themselves but to understand the exalted and unifying image of the human being on which they are based.

Notes

1 In addition to the growing literature on the New Story, including Nagler, 2001, and deal with it at length in *The Third Harmony* (available for publication).
2 I am not referring to the Socratic *method,* but to Socrates's dictum that every profession has its original, legitimate purpose and its characteristic corruption – almost always money.
3 "Gandhian Economics," Wikipedia *ad loc.* Diwan and Lutz (1987) entirely agree that his economics take off from an entirely different principle than the one to "maximize material self-interest that underlies classical economic thinking," e.g. F.Y. Edgeworth, "The first principle of economics is that every agent is actuated only by self-interest." (*ibid.*, p. 13).
4 Lecture delivered in Oakland, CA, 2005.

References

Brown, C. (2017). *Buddhist Economics: An Enlightened Approach to the Dismal Science.* New York:Bloomsbury Press.

Burton, J.W. (1997). *Violence Explained: The Sources of Conflict, Violence and Crime and Their Prevention.* Manchester: University of Manchester.

Chaudhuri, N. (1998). *That Compassionate Touch of Ma Anandamayee.* Delhi: Motilal Benarsidass.

Chenoweth, E., & Stephan, M. (2011). *Why Civil Resistance Works: The Strategic Logic of Nonviolent Conflict.* New York: Columbia University.

Diwan, R. K., & Lutz, M. A. (1987). *Essays in Gandhian Economics.* New York: Intermediate Technology Development Group, North America.

Easwaran, Eknath. (2007). *The Upanishads.* Berkeley: The Blue Mountain Center of Meditation.

Gandhi, M.K. (1927, March 17). Young India.

Gandhi, M.K. (1928). *Satyagraha in South Africa.* Ahmedabad: Navajivan.

Gandhi, M.K. (1933). "Sarvodaya," in *Speeches and Writings of Mahatma Gandhi*, 4th edn. Madras: Natesan & Co.

Gandhi, M.K. (1946, August 25). Harijan.

Gandhi, M.K. (1956 [1951]). *Sarvodaya,* paraphrase of Unto This Last (V. G. Desai, Trans.). Ahmedabad: Navajivan.

Gandhi, M.K. (1962). *Industrialise and Perish.* Ahmedabad: Navajivan.

Glazer, S. (1999). *The Heart of Learning.* New York:Tarcher/Putnam.

Goerner, S. (2004). "Creativity, Consciousness, and the Building of an Integral World" in D. Loye (Ed.), *The Great Adventure: Toward a Fully Human Theory of Evolution* (pp. 153–180). Albany: SUNY Press.

King Jr., M.L. (1963). "Letter from Birmingham Jail." Available online at http://www.africa.upenn.edu/Articles_Gen/Letter_Birmingham.html (accessed November 11, 2017).

King Jr., M.L. (1968). "The Other America." Retrieved from Available online at www.gphistorical.org/mlk/mlkspeech/ (accessed November 11, 2017).

Kuhn, Thomas. (1962) *The Structure of Scientific Revolutions.* Chicago: Chicago University Press.

McRaney, D. (2012). "The Fascinating Scientific Reason why 'Money Doesn't Buy Happiness'" *Alternet.* Available online at www.alternet.org/story/153887/the_fascinating_scientific_reason_why_%22money_doesn%27t_buy_happiness%22 (accessed January 20, 2018).

Nagler, Michael. (2001). *The Search for a Nonviolent Future*. Novato, CA: New World Library.

Natesan, G.A. (1933). *Speeches and Writings of Mahatma Gandhi*. Madras: Natesan and Company.

Prabhu, R.K., & Rao, U.R. (Eds). (1969). *The Mind of Mahatma Gandhi*, Ahmedabad: Navajivan.

Raworth, K. (2017). *Doughnut Economics: Seven Ways to Think Like a 21st Century Economist*. White River Junction: Chelsea Green.

Schumacher, E.F. (1979). *Good Work*. New York: Harper & Row.

Shirer, W. (1979). *Gandhi: A Memoir*. New York: Simon and Schuster.

St. Augustine. (1958). *The City of God*. New York: Doubleday, Image Books.

St. Augustine. (1960). *The Confessions of St. Augustine*. New York: Image Books.

Tendulkar, D.G. (1969). *Mahatma: Life of Mohandas Karamchand Gandhi*, Vol. 7. New Delhi: Publications Division, Government of India.

Gandhi, Mahatma (1999). *The Collected Works of Mahatma Gandhi*. (Vol. 25). New Delhi: Publications Division, Government of India. Available online at www.gandhia shramsevagram.org/gandhi-literature/collected-works-of-mahatma-gandhi-volum e-1-to-98.php (accessed January 23, 2018).

Wilkinson, R., & Pickett, K. (2009). *The Spirit Level: Why Greater Equality Makes Societies Stronger*. New York: Bloomsbury Press.

9 Buddhist principles for a non-violent economy

Gábor Kovács

The chapter explores the Buddhist contribution to establish a non-violent political economy. It introduces the development of the conceptions of Buddhist economics from the perspective of non-violence. It reviews the works of the four most influential authors from the field of Buddhist economics that gave centrality to the conception of non-violence in economy: the observations on non-violent economy by Gandhi; the conception of "small is beautiful" by Schumacher; the main economic ideas of Payutto, a Thai Buddhist monk; and the conceptions of Buddhist economic strategy by Zsolnai. The chapter introduces the main Buddhist principles and the core values that make Buddhism a unique approach to the subject of economics.

Buddhist teachings could be the sources and essential components of the presence of non-violence in the economy. The development of the conceptions of Buddhist economics testifies that the expansion of Buddhist views in the field of economics is a bottom up initiative, which is not yet an economic system, but rather a problem-solving strategy that is able to give guidance for establishing non-violent business models and to implement business practices in the spirit of non-violence.

The present chapter explores the possible Buddhist contribution to establishing a non-violent political economy. It introduces the development of the conceptions of Buddhist economics through a particular lens – from the perspective of non-violence. The aim of the study is to present the evolution of this concept, along with the development of Buddhist economics more generally. In doing this, the chapter utilizes a definition of the non-violent political economy suggested by the editors, Fredy Cante and Wanda Torres, in the preface to this book, which has been interpreted by the authors of the various chapters of the present book. Namely,

> the study of the complex relations and interactions among political, economic, ideological, and organizational power that do not generate devastating and/or harming impacts on nature and human life.… A non-violent political economy aims to generate social relations of production,

appropriation, distribution, exchange, expenditure and consumption with minimal destructive impacts on both society and nature.

(p. xix)

Furthermore, the chapter treats Buddhism as a spiritual tradition that aims to alleviate suffering, with the main goal of liberation. Buddhism aims to improve three synergistic abilities that assist with achieving perfection on the path of purification. The pursuit and practice of Buddhist virtues plays an important role on the Buddhist path. It is the departure point for leading a whole life that is geared to the alleviation of suffering. A virtuous livelihood makes meditation practice fruitful. The consequence of fruitful spiritual practice is deepening mindfulness and the emergence of wisdom, which in turn contributes to the further perfection of virtues. The first and foremost precept for Buddhists who seek to travel the path to liberation and lead their life according to the virtues is to refrain from doing harm or violence.

This chapter explores the opportunities that exist for Buddhist economics to contribute to the establishment of a non-violent political economy. It does not present a general summary of the development of the discipline, although there is much research which has a focus on various dimensions of the subject (Kovács, 2013). The study has the specific goal of analyzing the place of non-violence in the history of Buddhist economics.

Given the centrality of non-violence in the analysis, the chapter reviews four influential contributions from the field of Buddhist economics, all of which strongly emphasize the importance of the principle of non-violence in economics. First, it presents the thoughtful observations on the economy of Mahatma Gandhi, who made a determining contribution to the emergence of Buddhist economics. It then reviews the most important thoughts contained in *Small is Beautiful*, the classic work of E. F. Schumacher, who used the expression "Buddhist economics" for the first time in history. Then, the chapter summarizes the main ideas about economics of a Thai Buddhist monk, P. A. Payutto, from his book *Buddhist Economics: A Middle Way for the Market Place*. Finally, it introduces the works of Zsolnai about the Buddhist way of business from his paper *Buddhist Economic Strategy*. In parallel with this investigation, the chapter introduces the main principles and core values of Buddhism that make the application of Buddhism a unique approach to the subject of economics. The chapter's concluding remarks describe the extent to which we may talk about a non-violent Buddhist political economy, or rather about the Buddhist approach to the role of non-violence in economic practices.

Non-violence, the creed of Mahatma Gandhi

Mahatma Gandhi (1869–1948), from India, was one of the most influential political leaders of his time, and one who put non-violence at the center of his political philosophy and applied a non-violent approach to all areas of life. As a child he was influenced by the virtue of non-violence contained in the teachings of Jainism and Buddhism, which spiritual traditions stimulated his abhorrence of violence in his practice of Hinduism (Gandhi, 1957). His childhood memories about the importance of non-violence lasted throughout his life, and determined his career as an "apostle of non-violence" (Fischer, 1950).

Non-violence became Gandhi's creed: "Non-violence is the first article of my faith. It is also the last article of my faith" (Prabhu and Rao, 1968). Gandhi considered the need to lead by example as an important principle, thus of fundamental importance in his life was the everyday practice of voluntary simplicity. This can be understood as leading a moderate, frugal life that incorporates the deep, personal practice of non-violence (Richards, 1982). As Bouckaert, Opdebeeck and Zsolnai (2008) have clarified, frugality means living a simple lifestyle with low material consumption that opens the mind to spiritual goods.

Gandhi also devoted his life to perfecting and extending the principle of non-violence in society: his practice of non-violence was thus socio-centric (Gandhi, 1957; Schweitzer, 1936). His work testifies to the fact that non-violence is not merely a principle, but a strategy for dealing with social difficulties. He practiced the concept of "peaceful resistance," a form of non-cooperation with the British Empire that played a role in liberating India from its colonizers. Furthermore, he fought for the emancipation of women, for the rights of untouchables in India, and against poverty (Fischer, 1950; Gandhi, 1957; Richards, 1982).

In his fight against poverty, Gandhi sought to operationalize non-violence in the economy. His main economic objective was to alleviate rural poverty in India by increasing the minimum standard of living, incorporating the imperative that individuals also have the right to express their personality. Gandhi believed that implementing the principle of non-violence in the economy would have a direct impact on creating social well-being (Gandhi, 1957).

Some say that Gandhi was an economist rather than a politician, as he aimed at the alleviation of the difficulties of poor people in rural areas of India through economic means. Based on the principle of non-violence, his economic philosophy was self-sufficiency, implying locality and the application of small-scale technology. Economic self-sufficiency aims at the satisfaction of standards of living using local resources by creating local job opportunities, and by applying socially and ecologically appropriate technology. Gandhi also recognized the importance of the preservation of natural resources at the expense of industrial production. In line with his notions about economic self-sufficiency, he believed that individual requirements should be linked with local production in the spirit of co-operation in order to create a solid, well-knit rural economy (Koshal and Koshal, 1973; Kumarappa, 1951).

The concept of economic self-sufficiency may be the driving force behind a more just, equitable and decentralized social and economic order. It can contribute to the realization of true well-being, and keeping economic wealth within moderate limits. From a Buddhist standpoint, self-sufficiency allows people to alleviate the suffering encountered on the material plane of their existence, and allows them to practice the virtue of moderation in their everyday life. Furthermore, through the non-violent approach of self-sufficiency, independent self-sustaining communities can come into being at the village level that contribute to the revitalization of rural economics (Kumarappa, 1951). Thus, as Koshal and Koshal (1973) assert, the practical implementation of Gandhian economic philosophy could contribute to rural reconstruction, to the decentralization of the economy, and to the realization of environmental sustainability; developments that are also called for by Georgescu-Roegen (1971).

Gandhi's notions about the non-violent, political economy were influenced by his childhood experiences with Jainism and Buddhism. As a consequence of these experiences, non-violence obtained a central role in his social and economic philosophy through the practice of voluntary simplicity in everyday life. Later, Gandhi's thoughtful observations about the non-violent political economy inspired many people and contributed to the emergence of Buddhist economics.

Small Is Beautiful

Gandhi had a major influence on the way of thinking of succeeding generations of heterodox economists. The Gandhian spirit of non-violence in the field of economics inspired Ernst Friedrich Schumacher, a German-born English economist, writer, economic thinker, and philosopher (Opdebeeck, 2011; Richards, 1982; Schumacher 1973). Schumacher was originally an economic adviser to the National Coal Board in England, but travelled to Asia where he met with Gandhi's ideas, learned eastern philosophy and the teachings of Buddhism. As a result, in later life he dedicated his career as a scholar of economics to the pursuit of non-violence in economics (Schumacher, 2011).

Gandhi approached economic issues through the principle of non-violence with the aim of alleviating poverty. Although he was not an economist, he indirectly broke with the metaphysical models of conventional neoclassical economics through his concept of economic self-sufficiency (Kumarappa, 1951). Schumacher also broke with the metaphysical models of the conventional neoclassical economy, but as the result of his thorough inquiry into the role of modern economics. Schumacher was originally an economist, fully aware of the metaphysical niche and blindness of traditional economics, and the limits to economic calculus (Schumacher, 1973; 1978). To create the lacking metaphysical foundation required to substitute Western materialism-based approaches to economics, he turned towards eastern philosophies, and specifically the teachings of Buddhism (although this choice was somewhat incidental: Schumacher stressed that the teachings of Christianity, Islam, or Judaism could have been used to ground the metaphysical background for economics, as well as any of the other great Eastern traditions) (Schumacher, 1973).

Influenced significantly by Gandhi's thinking (Schumacher, 2011), and after breaking with conventional neoclassical economic models, Schumacher (1973) established Buddhist economics as a people-centered economic philosophy by connecting it intuitively to the central teachings in the Noble Eightfold Path of

Buddhism. He claimed that "'Right Livelihood' is one of the requirements of the Buddha's Noble Eightfold Path. It is clear, therefore, that there must be such a thing as Buddhist economics" (Schumacher, 1973, p. 53).

Schumacher's ideas about Buddhist economics encompass three major areas, all of which were investigated in detail in his book *Small is Beautiful – Economics as if People Mattered*. He investigated the issue of work, together with technology and employment, the issue of localization, and natural resources (Schumacher, 1973).

Although Schumacher (1979) summarized his ideas about the notion of work in his book *Good Work*, he also re-examined the role and the content of work in the light of Buddhist economics. He identified the threefold function of work as "[giving] a man a chance to utilize and develop his faculties; [enabling] him to overcome his ego-centredness by joining with other people in a common task; and [bringing] forth the goods and services needed for a becoming existence" (Schumacher, 1973, p. 54). Schumacher concluded that, in order to utilize and develop the faculties of man, the application of an "intermediate technology" was needed. Poor people require technologies that are positioned midway between traditional but uneconomical practices and the costly high-tech solutions which only provide work for a few (Schumacher, 2011). Such small-scale technology is non-violent, has a human face, and contrasts with the mainstream approach of automatization that destroys human capacities and the soul of the worker, and transforms human work into meaningless activity (Schumacher, 1973). Schumacher's vision includes a culture of non-violence, which implies promoting co-operation as opposed to competition. No single person, however talented or educated, can be complete by himself or herself. Life is ordered in such a way that everyone is interdependent and is designed to live and work harmoniously in a community (Schumacher, 2011). The three functions of work contribute to Schumacher's conviction that Buddhist economic planning can create full employment, unlike the Western practice of maintaining a minimum rate of unemployment (Schumacher, 1973).

The second area of investigation encompasses the most important characteristics of Buddhist economics and their consequences for economic scaling. According to Schumacher (1973), these are the principles of simplicity and non-violence. Both of these are fundamental Buddhist virtues that are closely related: an optimal, but relatively low rate of consumption that produces a high degree of human satisfaction, thereby allowing people to live without pressure, fulfills the primary injunction of Buddhist teaching: "Cease to do evil; try to do good." Simple, non-violent, Buddhist behavior that does not accept man's superiority over other species and the environment implies responsibility and compassion towards every sentient being; a position which affects economic life as well. Furthermore, the principles of simplicity and non-violence assume localization: the restriction of production to that which involves the use of local resources for satisfying only local needs, and the avoidance of large-scale commerce, which is a source of external dependence and justifiable only in exceptional cases and on small scale (Schumacher, 1973).

Finally, Schumacher drew the attention to the fact that modern economics does not distinguish between renewable and non-renewable materials and resources as it operates through a process of quantification, although non-renewable resources are fundamentally different from renewable resources. In a spirit of non-violence, a reverent attitude must be established not only towards all sentient beings, but also towards the scarce resources of nature, which must be handled with the greatest care. Following this approach, non-renewable resources must be consumed only if their use is indispensable, with the greatest care, and in the spirit of non-violence (Schumacher, 1973).

Although Schumacher's way of thinking was greatly inspired by Gandhi, he improved and more accurately operationalized the economic component of the Gandhian spirit of non-violence. He showed how voluntary simplicity and non-violence can contribute to lowering the level of consumption and to localization. Furthermore, he corroborated the *raison d'etre* of non-violence as the metaphysical foundation for economics, thus defining Buddhist economics in opposition to the Western economic calculus which lacks metaphysical foundations. Schumacher (1973) called Buddhist economics the systematic study of how to attain given ends with the minimum means.

A Middle Way for the Market Place

The third important work that awarded special importance to non-violence in the field of Buddhist economics was written by a Thai Buddhist monk, the Venerable P. A. Payutto, who was the most influential author on the subject in the mid-1990s. The starting point of the discussion in his book *Buddhist Economics: A Middle Way for the Market Place* is an analysis of the lack of any ethical dimension in Western economics. Payutto (1994) warns that its moral neutrality and its isolation from other sciences make economics a narrow discipline that is not capable of managing the emerging social and environmental problems of modernity. Avoiding consideration of ethics and moral values is evidence that economics lacks a metaphysical background, as also claimed by Schumacher (1973).

Payutto (1994) continues his analysis by differentiating two kinds of desires that fuel economic activities, according to the teachings of Buddhism. The desire or craving for pleasurable objects leads to seeking objects of satisfaction. On the other hand, the desire for well-being or aspiration is directed towards attaining benefits, and leads to right effort. The former is a negative approach, as the desire to acquire pleasurable objects is limitless, and cannot be satisfied. This idea was also outlined by Schumacher (1973) in a reference to Gandhi, who wrote that "The Earth provides enough to satisfy every man's need, but not every man's greed" (Schumacher, 1973, p. 33). Aspiration, on the other hand, is a positive desire, which is worth promoting as it seeks the realization of well-being (Payutto, 1994).

In line with Buddhist teachings, Payutto (1994) recommends distinguishing between economic activities based on their driving forces. The ethicality of economic activities can be evaluated by determining whether a given act originates from negative desires and aims at the satisfaction of craving, or originates from positive desires and aspires at promoting the benefit of those involved. In cases where negative desires are the driving forces behind economic decisions, behavior tends to be morally unskillful. When positive desires or the aspiration for well-being are the driving forces for behavior, it is morally skillful.

Besides making an evaluation of the driving forces behind economic behavior, Payutto (1994) drew attention to another dimension of the ethicality of economic activities: the role of responsibility. Another crucial way to evaluate the ethical quality of economic decisions is to investigate its effects in all three planes of existence. Decision-makers should be responsible for their actions as these relate to the individual, the social and the environmental planes of existence. Economic activities must strive to create harmony and promote well-being on all these planes.

One of the most remarkable innovations of the author was his reinterpretation of various conventional economic concepts in the light of Buddhist ethics, and the introduction of some further Buddhist-economic concepts. Payutto's work investigates and reframes the conceptions of "value," "consumption," "work," "production," "competition," and "choice" by utilizing the notions of positive and negative desires and responsibility. Furthermore, it introduces the conceptions of "moderation," "non-consumption," "overconsumption," "contentment," "non-production," "cooperation," and "life-view as the contextualization of economics" (Payutto, 1994). It is apparent from this attempt to create these profound economic conceptions that, similarly to Schumacher (1973) – his predecessor in the field of Buddhist economics – Payutto (1994) also refuted the mainstream economic notion of "more is more."

Schumacher's conception of Right Livelihood (1973) was further detailed in Payutto's (1994) paper, which suggests that Right Livelihood is determined by the well-being that economic actions generate. The realization of well-being presupposes making a distinction between wants and needs by means of identifying positive and negative desires. Unlike the mainstream approach, economic activities should have little to do with limitless consumption and economic growth. Economic activities must rather aim to satisfy basic necessities that are conceptualized broadly as standards of living by Gandhi (Kumarappa, 1951). These basic necessities are sufficient food, clothing, housing, proper health care, and education (Payutto, 1994).

Payutto (1994) defined two major characteristics of Buddhist or middle-way economics: the realization of true well-being, and the non-harming of oneself and others. An important component of well-being is the practice of moderation, as only this form of consumption brings benefits. In line with the practice of moderation, Buddhist economics does not strive for maximization, but rather the satisfaction of basic needs by optimal economic means. Non-harming or non-violence is extended and interpreted to all three planes of existence, as economic activities must take place in a way, which does not harm oneself by causing a decline in the quality of life, and does not harm others by causing problems for society or imbalance in the environment.

A fundamental, but less well recognized assertion of Payutto (1994) is that "one need not be a Buddhist or an economist to practice Buddhist economics," suggesting that Buddhist economics is not an economic system in a narrow sense, but rather an alternative approach to economics that may be practiced by anyone.

Buddhist economic strategy

The fourth contribution in this investigation explores Buddhist economic strategy (Zsolnai, 2007; 2008; 2011), and synthesizes many components of the work of Gandhi, Schumacher and Payutto, but includes further important innovations in the field of Buddhist economics. As a significant outcome it expounds, specifies and operationalizes the assertion that "one need not be a Buddhist or an economist to practice Buddhist economics" (Payutto, 1994) by introducing the five principles of Buddhist economics.

The related papers start by expounding their starting points: teachings about "no-self," a central tenet of Buddhism that was not previously mentioned in the field of Buddhist economics. Based on empirical and philosophical foundations, Buddhism refutes the existence of a permanent, non-changing self, which idea has been verified using evidence from modern neuroscience. The idea of no-self represents a radical challenge to fundamentally egocentric mainstream economics, and its pursuit would have two major consequences: it could foster and justify genuine, altruistic behavior in economics, and it could promote an understanding of interdependence that would foster mindfulness about the consequences of economic activities on others and on nature (Zsolnai, 2007; 2008; 2011).

The papers introduce five principles that make Buddhist economics a genuine alternative to the mainstream economic position by challenging its basic principles: the latter include profit-maximization, cultivating desires, introducing markets, instrumental use of the world, and self-interest-based ethics. The alternative principles of Buddhist economics include minimizing suffering, simplifying desires, non-violence, genuine care, and generosity (Zsolnai, 2007; 2008; 2011).

The goal of mainstream economics is profit-maximization. The goal of Buddhism is the minimization of suffering, a position which is also applicable in the field of economics. The significance of suffering (or loss-minimization) is underpinned by psychological evidence about sensitivity to loss (Zsolnai, 2007; 2008; 2011). Mainstream economics cultivates desire, which is a prerequisite for profit-making, although psychological evidence shows that an excessively materialistic value orientation undermines well-being. In opposition to this, the Buddhist economic approach simplifies desires. Reducing one's desires to the level of satisfying basic necessities is wise, as wanting less can bring benefits for individuals, the community, and for nature. Furthermore, psychological evidence shows that people with fewer desires have greater well-being (Zsolnai

2007; 2008; 2011). Thus, the practices of contentment, moderation, and frugality in connection with meeting basic necessities and the practice of mindfulness in connection with desires and wants can play a major role in reducing consumption, thus promoting sustainability. The marketization of mainstream economics may be seen as a form of violence, a phenomenon by which society and the environment become subordinated to market mechanisms that are promoted as the solution to all emerging problems. In opposition to this, the guiding principle of Buddhist economics regarding problem solving is non-violence, which requires that an act does not cause harm to anybody. According to Buddhist economics, cutting down the influence and the reach of the market to a size commensurate with functioning in accordance with the conception of non-violence is necessary. Keeping the magnitude of markets within limits can contribute to increasing fairness, locality, and the maintenance of community economics (Zsolnai 2007; 2008; 2011). Mainstream economics rationalizes value production by defining marginal contributions to production output. Buddhist economics proposes an ethic of genuine care instead of employing a calculative approach. Evidence from the field of business ethics shows that caring organizations are rewarded for the higher costs of their caring behavior among owners, managers, employees, customers, and subcontractors (Zsolnai 2007; 2008; 2011). There is little room for ethics in mainstream economics, as value-creating activity incorporates the interests of others only so far as it serves self-interest, although there is evidence that such an opportunistic approach usually fails. In opposition, Buddhist economics encourages generosity in economic relationships, which usually works even as an economic strategy because psychological evidence shows that individuals reciprocate to a greater extent than what they receive (Zsolnai 2007; 2008; 2011).

Based on these five principles, Buddhist economics can be seen not as a system but a strategy that can be applied in any economic setting at any time, and one which "helps to create livelihood solutions that reduce the suffering of all sentient beings through the practices of want negation, non-violence, caring and generosity" (Zsolnai 2008, pp. 298–299). As is clear from the arguments presented above, the conceptions of a Buddhist economic strategy can be corroborated and verified by the scientific achievements of various disciplines, thus permitting a more humanistic understanding of the role of economics. They confirm the assumption of Payutto (1994) that, from a Buddhist perspective, economics cannot be separated from other branches of knowledge because economics is not a self-contained science, but one of a number of interdependent disciplines that are working to remedy the problems of humanity and promote well-being.

Buddhist economics is a radical alternative to the mainstream economic mindset as it represents a minimizing framework and is thus opposed to the mainstream maximizing paradigm (Zsolnai 2007; 2008; 2011). Buddhist economic strategy is based on the conception of no-self, and is built around five principles, in which non-violence plays a fundamentally important role. The Buddhist approach to economics encompasses altruism and reciprocity, and testifies that the practice of non-egoistic behavior in economics makes sense, even if it contradicts the mainstream market belief that everything has a price and a substitute.

Conclusions: from non-violent business practices to a non-violent political economy

The history of Buddhist economics includes attempts to create various kinds of political economies based on different Buddhist teachings. These initiatives were not based on the principle of non-violence, but rather built around the practice of the faculties of mind in economic behavior. One of these initiatives was mindful economics (Magnuson, 2008), constructed on the practice of right mindfulness for building mindful economic institutions. The other was pannaism (Puntasen, 2004), an economic system based on wisdom. The GNH initiative of Bhutan is also a remarkable Buddhist project in the field of the political economy. This is implemented in a Buddhist society, based on Buddhist values, and has the aim of directing and measuring the performance of the country along various social dimensions. GNH is above all a complex economic policy and a macroeconomic index (Tideman, 2011). Such initiatives show that there is an opportunity to talk about a Buddhist political economy from a Buddhist point of view, although the main purpose of the present chapter is rather to introduce the place of non-violence in Buddhist economics, and to explore its role in creating a non-violent political economy.

The chapter has demonstrated through the analysis of four influential works from the related field of research that non-violence plays a crucial role in the Buddhist way of approaching the subject of economics. The concluding part of the chapter reviews the opportunities for establishing a non-violent political economy according to the working definition of the present book by approaching Buddhist economics from the perspective of non-violence. Nevertheless, the earlier-presented, non-violent component of Buddhist economics also has a practical dimension, ultimately limited to one institution in society: business. One can use the principles of Buddhist economic strategy to assess whether any economic activity conforms to relevant Buddhist values, especially that of non-violence. Furthermore, these principles stimulate and inspire us to do business in a non-violent way that alleviates suffering.

From the contributions of Gandhi's economic self-sufficiency to Zsolnai's Buddhist economic strategy, conceptual development in the reverse direction has been experienced so far, from the wider approach of the political economy to the more practical utilization of Buddhist tenets about economic practice. Gandhi applied the term economic self-sufficiency to a whole economic system, based on non-violence, aimed at satisfying the living standards of individuals or providing the basic necessities of life (Kumarappa, 1951). Schumacher (1973) defined the metaphysics of the related economic approach by utilizing the Buddhist philosophy of non-violence, but also began to practically operationalize this by investigating its effect on work, technology, employment, localization, and resources. Payutto (1994) further broadened the scope of the theoretical conceptions of Buddhist economics by redefining the terms "value," "production," and "competition," and especially by introducing the terms "moderation," "non-consumption," and "non-production." More importantly, Payutto also firmly alluded to the notion that Buddhist economics is not exclusively for Buddhists, as anyone can practice it. Ultimately, Zsolnai (2007; 2008; 2011) articulated in his description of Buddhist economic strategy that it is thus not an economic system, but rather a problem-solving strategy within which one can implement the spirit of non-violence in business and management.

This chapter has introduced the idea that Buddhist teachings could be the source and an essential component of the inclusion of non-violence in the economy. Non-violence is a major element of Buddhist economics, along with the conception of no-self and the need for the reduction of suffering. The development of Buddhist economics with its conception of non-violence shows that the expansion of Buddhist views into the field of economics will involve a bottom up approach not in the shape of an economic system – yet – but rather a problem-solving strategy.

With its philosophical background and its core values, Buddhism may be able to contribute to the establishment of a non-violent political economy in the near future in which "the complex relations and interactions among political, economic, ideological, and organizational power do not generate devastating and/or harming impacts on nature and human life." Perhaps more importantly, it is even now able to provide guidance about how to establish business models and implement business practices that operate in the spirit of non-violence.

References

Bouckaert, L., Opdebeeck, H., and Zsolnai, L. (Eds) (2008). *Frugality: Rebalancing Material and Spiritual Values in Economic Life*. Frontiers of Business Ethics. Oxford: Peter Lang.

Fischer, L. (1950). *The Life of Mahatma Gandhi*. New York: Harper and Brothers.

Gandhi, M.K. (1957). *An Autobiography or the Story of My Experiments with Truth*. Boston: Beacon Press.

Georgescu-Roegen, N. (1971). *The Entropy Law and the Economic Process*. Cambridge: Harvard University Press.

Koshal, R.K., and Koshal, M. (1973). "Gandhian economic philosophy". *American Journal of Economics and Sociology* 32, 2, pp. 191–209.

Kovács, G. (2013). "Buddhist Economics". In Opdebeeck, H. (ed.) *Responsible Economics. E. F. Schumacher and his Legacy for the 21st Century* (pp. 33–53). Bern: Peter Lang.

Kumarappa, J.C. (1951). *Gandhian Economic Thought*. Bombay: Vora.

Magnuson, J.C. (2008). *Mindful Economics: How the U.S. Economy Works, Why it Matters, and How it Could Be Different*. New York: Seven Stories Press.

Opdebeeck, H. (2011). "Schumacher's People-Centered Economics". In Bouckaert, L. and Zsolnai, L. (Eds) *Handbook of Spirituality and Business* (pp. 171–179). Houndmills: Palgrave Macmillan.

Payutto, P. (1994). *Buddhist Economics: a Middle Way for the Market Place*. Bangkok: Buddhadhamma Foundation.

Prabhu, R.K., and Rao, U.R. (Eds). (1968). *Mind of Mahatma Gandhi*. Ahmedabad: Navajivan Publishing House.

Puntasen, A. (2004). *Buddhist Economics: Evolution, Theories and Its Application to Various Economic Subjects*. Bangkok: Amarin Press.

Richards, G. (1982). *The Philosophy of Gandhi. A Study of his Basic Ideas*. London: Curzon Press.

Schumacher, D. (2011). *Small is Beautiful in the 21st Century. The Legacy of E. F. Schumacher*. Dartington: Green Books.

Schumacher, E.F. (1973). *Small is Beautiful: Economics as if People Mattered*. New York: Harper and Row.

Schumacher, E.F. (1978). *A Guide for the Perplexed*. New York: Harper and Row.

Schumacher, E.F. (1979). *Good Work*. New York: Harper and Row.

Schweitzer, A. (1936). *Indian Thought and its Development*. Boston: Beacon Press.

Tideman, S. (2011). "Gross National Happiness". In Zsolnai, L. (Ed.) *Ethical Principles and Economic Transformation – A Buddhist Approach* (pp. 133–155). Dordrecht: Springer.

Zsolnai, L. (2007). "Western Economics versus Buddhist Economics". *Society and Economy*, 29, 2, pp. 145–153.

Zsolnai, L. (2008). "Buddhist Economic Strategy". In Bouckaert, L. and Opdebeeck, H. and Zsolnai, L. (Eds) *Frugality* (pp. 279–304). Bern: Peter Lang.

Zsolnai, L. (2011). "Buddhist Economics". In Bouckaert, L. and Zsolnai, L. (Eds) *Handbook of Spirituality and Business* (pp. 88–95). Houndmills: Palgrave Macmillan.

Disarmament, post-military systems of defense and transition towards a nonviolent social order

10 Civilian-based defense systems

Leveraging economic power to fulfill security treaty obligations

James F. Powers

Sovereign States currently face challenges unlike those of yesteryear. No longer are domestic issues euphemistically-referred to as *internal matters*. All States feel the indirect repercussions from transnational organized crime, hunger/famine, genocide, human rights abuses, economic/infrastructure decline, religious/ethnic/racial persecution, illiteracy, illegal immigration, refugee issues, illegal immigration, lack of governmental services, and even international treaties, etc.

States formally meet as signatory members of various treaties/agreements to discuss/debate collective political, security, economic, environmental, humanitarian assistance, human rights, transnational crime, trade issues, etc. When the *common* interests become so acute as to require collective solutions/collaboration, States create legal arrangements as members or *State parties* to treaties. As defined by the United Nations (1999),

> a "State party" to a treaty is a country that has ratified or acceded to that treaty, and is therefore legally bound by the provisions in the instrument. A "treaty" is a formally concluded and ratified agreement between States. The term is used generically to refer to instruments binding at international law, concluded between international entities (States or organizations). Under the *Vienna Conventions on the Law of Treaties*, a treaty must be (1) a binding instrument, which means that the contracting parties intended to create legal rights and duties; (2) concluded by states or international organizations with treaty-making power; (3) governed by international law and (4) in writing.

Using the UN and these instruments as fora to either publicly air grievances against or support one another, each State brings its unique core values, beliefs, traditions, culture, ethos,[1] national interests and politics to the discussions. According to Jablonsky (1997), States consider their inherent *determinants of power* (natural and social) to influence discussions. Regardless of the degree to which the *natural* determinants of power (i.e., geography, population and natural resources) or *social* determinants of power (i.e., economic capacity, military strength, political, psychological and informational resources) exist, every State wields these powers – *either directly or indirectly* – to influence/coerce other states for their own benefit. It is a *game* played and understood by all – some better than others. Political scientists, economists, academics and military strategists often refer collectively to these inherent State strengths/capacities as *elements of national power*. For scholars and military strategists, these *elements* refer to four general descriptors: diplomatic, informational, military, and economic.[2] When the *nonviolent* elements (e.g., diplomatic, informational and economic) fail to produce the desired effect, States tend to see no alternative than to exercise the *violent* element (military). This *legitimate use of physical force by States* is a political science and sociology concept regarded by many as the defining characteristic of a modern State – legitimacy being the key descriptor.[3] Whether your analysis of world events is micro or macro, ignoring reality is not an option. When distinguishing *right* from *wrong*, legitimate States clearly understand sovereignty, international human rights, and what constitutes lawful/unlawful acts and practices. Nonetheless, disputes/quarrels among States still exist – usually arising when one State tries to prove that the actions of another are in the *wrong*. C. S. Lewis (1952), Fellow and Tutor in English Literature at Oxford University, characterized arguments in the following way:

> There would be no sense in trying ... unless you and he had some agreement as to what Right and Wrong are.... But taking the race as a whole ... the human idea of decent behaviour was obvious to everyone.
>
> (pp. 4–5)

Although the rights/protections and responsibilities afforded by *sovereign* status are clear, there is growing UN (2010) concern/support to intervene when States fail to protect their populace, condone violations of human rights, etc. According to the UN Special Adviser on the Prevention of Genocide (2010), "Sovereignty no longer exclusively protects States from foreign interference; it is a charge of responsibility that holds States accountable for the welfare of their people" (p. 4).

Other responsibilities/obligations, however, seem less obvious; particularly, fulfilling signatory/member obligations of treaties/agreements. Although transitioning from a *military/paramilitary-based defense* (hereafter MBD)[4] to a *civilian-based defense* (hereafter CBD) system is a sovereign decision, treaty/agreement obligations remain firm. In general terms and to enhance clarity, Sharp describes CBD as,

> a policy [in which] the whole population and the society's institutions become the fighting forces. Their weaponry consists of a vast variety of forms of psychological, economic, social, and political resistance and counter-attack. This policy aims to deter attacks and to defend against them by preparations to make the society unrulable by would-be-tyrants and aggressors. The trained population and the society's institutions would be prepared to deny the attackers their objectives and to make consolidation of political control impossible. These aims would be achieved by

applying massive and selective noncooperation and defiance. In addition, where possible, the defending country would aim to create maximum international problems for the attackers and to subvert the reliability of their troops and functionaries.

(1990, pp. 2–3)[5]

According to Sharp (1990), "Instead of military weaponry, civilian-based defense applies the power of society itself to deter and defend against internal usurpations and foreign invaders ... [the weapons] are wielded by the general population and the institutions of the society" (p. vii).[6] Sharp and Jenkins (1990) provided further clarification of the word *weapons* (psychological, social, economic, and political) as "those tools or means, not necessarily material, that may be used in fighting whether in military or nonviolent conflicts ... used to wage widespread noncooperation and to offer massive public defiance" (p. 6). From a psychological perspective, *communications*, in whatever form one chooses, can also be considered a weapon (Fowler, Fowler and Allen, 2016).[7]

In layman's terms, then, *nonviolent political tactics* generally comprise civilian-orchestrated measures designed to influence governmental policies, programs and strategies. According to the Albert Einstein Institution (1973), these tactics are "classified into three broad categories: nonviolent protest and persuasion, noncooperation (social, economic, and political), and nonviolent intervention" (par. 1).[8] Notwithstanding the myriad reasons to embrace CBD, how States leverage these internal, *nonviolent political tactics* to fulfill signatory treaty/agreement responsibilities in some capacity will remain a major consideration and potentially-limiting factor toward transition.

The number of scholarly works touting the benefits of CBD is numerous. This article offers no argument/objections to the rationale but rather posits some considerations and observations related to fulfilling treaty/agreement obligations. Using the research/findings of Schelling, Boulding, and Sharp as the foundational basis, this article explores five questions:

1   How helpful is CBD in countering potential security threats?
2   If/when States transition from MBD to CBD, what are the likely impacts?
3   How can CBD be better used?
4   What are the main challenges in implementing CBD?
5   Are there any inspirational case studies?

Although both denotative and connotative definitions exist, those used herein are the most pertinent, generally-accepted, and widely-used by the UN, legitimate States, academia, militaries and the community of nonviolent political action proponents.

Transitioning to CBD inherently requires the consideration of many dynamic and interrelated factors (e.g., sovereign responsibilities, domestic priorities, territorial/border disputes, regional security issues, crime, welfare of the populace, influx of refugees, and denial of criminal safe havens to name but a few). This article neither supports nor rebuts any suggestions to destroy dangerous/expensive weaponry (from light weapons to weapons of mass destruction);[9] nor does it debate the degree of effectiveness of *weapons of communication* [10] and *tactics of nonviolent political action*. Readers need not worry about interpreting any economic/fiscal projections. One, simple assumption provides the article's basis: The elimination of MBD *might* foster an *increase* in economic power and, thus, more affordable bargaining options for outsourcing security assistance.[11]

Negotiating/bargaining for security assistance *via* a treaty/agreement is a reasonable and viable option. But how might would-be *protectors/proxies* view their fellow *protectorates (signatories)*? The insights of Schelling, Boulding, Sharp *et al.* continue to inform strategists and suggest options for achieving policy objectives.[12]

Economic well-being vs. security: a priority dilemma

Ensuring territorial integrity is arguably the primary sovereign responsibility. Territorial security measures establish the conditions for human well-being, economic prosperity, domestic policies/programs, and State-funded programs/services designed to support the populace. How States design and manage their security apparatus is also a sovereign right. Several options seem obvious:

Option 1: Rely on *State* military/paramilitary police forces.
Option 2: Rely on *international* military/paramilitary polices forces.
Option 3: Rely on a *hybrid* combination.

Option 1 requires State-derived resources and, thus, *adversely* impacts the allocation of resources for domestic programs/services, which is not favorable to the CBD proponents. Option 2 leverages the military/paramilitary capabilities found in treaties/agreements while rendering other State resources as compensation – a *quid pro quo* – favorable to the CBD proponents. Option 3 leverages the strengths of options 1 and 2 but incurs the angst/weaknesses associated with alliance decisions, membership costs, and timely dissuasion/deterrence against external aggression, which would likely get mixed reactions by the CBD proponents. Perhaps the most notable example of Option 3 lies within The North Atlantic Treaty:

> *Article 5*: The Parties agree that an armed attack against one or more of them in Europe or North America shall be considered an attack against them all and consequently they agree that, if such an armed attack occurs, each of them, in exercise of the right of individual or collective self-defence recognised by Article 51 of the Charter of the United Nations will assist the Party or Parties so attacked by taking forthwith, individually and in concert with the other Parties, such action as it deems necessary,

including the use of armed force, to restore and maintain the security of the North Atlantic area.

(North Atlantic Treaty Organization, 1949)

Considering these *options*, the works of Schelling, Boulding, and Sharp provide perspectives, insights, analyses, and rational considerations. Depending on the degree of risk that the States are willing to accept, all *options* appear suitable.[13] Lest we forget: no State currently uses CBD as its primary security apparatus.

How helpful is CBD in countering potential security threats?

Neither Schelling nor Boulding provided examples of *how* economic power has empowered CBD to counter security threats via security treaties/agreements effectively. Their works, however, do provide the basis for State bargaining/ negotiations to that end. Although Sharp and Jenkins provided prime examples of successful, nonviolent struggles, none of them resulted from State CBD systems; each occurred as dynamic, popular responses to illegitimate/unlawful actions:

> During the 1980s, we witnessed the most important worldwide expansion of the practical use of nonviolent struggle that has ever occurred. From Tallinn to Nablus, Rangoon to Santiago, Pretoria to Prague, Beijing to Berlin, people around the world are ever more employing non-violent struggle to assert their rights for freedom, independence, and justice.
>
> (1990, p. viii)

Sharp and Jenkins (1990) also categorized these examples by *type conflict/context*. They mention internal oppression and colonial rule; external aggression is not: "Nonviolent action has played a major role in resistance against dictatorships, in struggles for achieving greater freedom, in campaigns against social oppression, in opposition to unwanted political changes, and in struggles against colonial rule and for national independence" (p. 8).

The following examples (pp. 4–5) indicate successful, although episodic, nonviolent struggles; each proves, depending on the context, that CBD remains a viable option:

- the American colonial nonviolent revolution (1765–1775);
- the Hungarian passive resistance against Austrian rule (1850–1867);
- Finland's disobedience/political noncooperation against Russia (1898–1905);
- the major aspects of the Russian Revolution of 1905, and the February Revolution of 1917 (before the October Bolshevik coup d'état);
- the failed Korean, nonviolent protest against Japanese rule (1919–1922);
- several Gandhi-led, Indian independence campaigns (1930–1931);
- Polish movements of 1956, 1970–1971, and 1976;

- the Polish workers' movement, 1980–1989, for an independent trade union and political democratization;
- the 1944 nonviolent revolutions in El Salvador and Guatemala against established military dictatorships;
- the civil rights struggles led by Reverend Martin Luther King in the USA in the 1950s/1960s;
- the 1978–1979 revolution against the Shah Mohammad Reza Pahlavi in Iran;
- the 1953 East German Rising;
- the 1956–1957 Hungarian revolution nationwide revolt against the government of the Hungarian People's Republic and its Soviet-imposed policies;
- the 1963 Buddhist campaign against the Ngo Dinh Diem Government in South Vietnam and the 1966 Buddhist campaign against the Saigon regime;
- the 1953 strike movement at Vorkuta and other prison camps in the Soviet Union; and
- the civil rights and Jewish activist struggles in the USSR in the 1970s/1980s.

The following 24 States have no regular military forces: Andorra, Costa Rica, Dominica, Grenada, Haiti, Iceland, Kiribati, Liechtenstein, Marshall Islands, Mauritius, Micronesia, Monaco, Nauru, Palau, Palestine Territories, Panama, St. Lucia, St. Vincent and the Grenadines, Samoa, San Marino, Solomon Islands, Tuvalu, Vanuatu, and Vatican City.[14] Perhaps the decisions to not establish a military were fiscal-based or perhaps risk-based. It is anyone's guess whether the natural determinants previously-mentioned by Jablonsky (1997) or Le Billon (2005) informed decision-makers to *outsource* security mechanisms *via* a treaty/alliance.

If/when States transition to CBD, what are the likely impacts?

Schelling's insight/experience reflected in *game theory* and *bargaining*, coupled with his experience in national security affairs, provide a practical and holistic basis for *how* States *might* leverage economic power in return for collective defense. However, in the "Introduction" to Sharp's *The Politics of Nonviolent Action, Part One: Power & Struggle* (1973), Schelling warns of the consequences of actions – whether violent or nonviolent:

> The violent actions and the nonviolent are different methods of trying to make it unrewarding for people to do certain things, and safe or rewarding to do other things. Both can be misused, mishandled, or misapplied. Both can be used for evil or misguided purposes.

(p. xx)

Schelling (1980) also referred to the various methods used by States to conduct disarmament as *schemes*.[15]

"Disarmament" has covered a variety of schemes, some ingenious and some sentimental, for cooperation among potential enemies to reduce the likelihood of war or to reduce its scope and violence. Most proposals have taken as a premise that a reduction in the quantity and potency of weapons, particularly of "offensive" weapons and of weapons that either deliberately or incidentally cause great civilian agony and destruction, promotes this purpose. Some schemes have been comprehensive; others have sought to identify particular areas where the common interest is conspicuous, where the need for trust is minimal, and where a significant start might be made which, if successful, would be a first step toward more comprehensive disarmament.

(p. 230)

Although Schelling's masterpiece, *The Strategy of Conflict* (1980), does not specifically state that *economic power* influences CBD, it does beget understanding the influences of behavioral economics in bargaining for/negotiating collective defense. Insofar as references to security treaties/agreements are concerned, Schelling posited: "We may wish to control or influence the behavior of others in conflict, and we want, therefore, to know how the variables that are subject to our control can affect their behavior" (pp. 1–2).

Those "variables" include domestic economic conditions; trade balances/imbalances; embargos; restrictions; and existing/emerging, governmental, social programs. *But what about deterrence? Can a State security strategy realistically envision/address every potential contingency? Is CBD a panacea for all contingencies; is this the weakest link that belies CBD as a realistic option?*

Possibly. Schelling's insight into *deterrence* may also raise another question: *Is it prudent to eliminate any deterrence option?* And this, logically, leads to yet another question: *Can CBD realistically offer the same degree of deterrence as MBD?* Schelling's views on this question appear clear: "Deterrence is concerned with the exploitation of potential force. It is concerned with persuading a potential enemy that he should in his own interest avoid certain courses of activity" (p. 9).

Schelling's (1966) assertion that military strategy is more now the art of coercion, of intimidation, and of deterrence would support outsourcing security assistance *via* a treaty/agreement (pp. 1–34). Where no treaty/agreement exists, however, there is risk; disregarding deterrence options is not only strategically unsound but also negligent. By inference, Schelling suggested that eliminating the military option becomes the catalyst/basis for empowering another element of power (e.g., economic). As Schelling (1984) posited, deterrence, surrender, most limited-war strategies, and notions like accidental war, escalation, pre-emptive war, brinksmanship, alliance relationships, arms-race phenomena, and arms control, are all meaningless. "War hurts … not all the losses of war are recoverable … whether budgets are rigidly fixed or not" (p. 269).

In a rational world, where States abide by the principles founded in the Peace of Westphalia (1648) and Charter of the UN (1945), CBD appears a pragmatic option. Where mutual trust is absent, unintended consequences occur. As Schelling (1980) advised:

> We tend to identify peace, stability, and the quiescence of conflict with notions like trust, good faith, and mutual respect. To the extent that this point of view actually encourages trust and respect, it is good. But where trust and good faith do not exist and cannot be made to by our acting as though they did, we may wish to solicit advice from the underworld, or from ancient despotisms, on how to make agreements work when trust and good faith are lacking and there is no legal recourse for breach of contract.
>
> (p. 20)

Schelling's ideas on *bargaining/coercion* also continue to influence States during strategic negotiations; surrendering any sovereign authority in return for collective defense will bring consequences – some *positive*, some *negative* – depending on the perspective. Security treaties/agreements primarily address security issues/concerns common to *all* signatory members – not internal, political, or criminal matters. Thus, resolving potential, external security threats/concerns (seen as a *benefit*) will come at some *cost*. Treaty organizations bargain with/coerce perceived adversaries. As Schelling (1966) reminded us, "Coercion requires finding a bargain, arranging for him [adversary] to be better off doing what we want-worse off not doing what we want-when he takes the threatened penalty into account" (p. 4).

Boulding (1989) suggested three forms of power, categorized by the *consequences* of exercising each: *destructive, productive (economic)*, and *integrative*. The linkage between *destructive* and MBD is obvious. *Productive/economic* and *integrative power* deductively lend themselves toward creating a greater synergy and stronger partnerships. Not surprisingly, Boulding urges strengthening these two forms of power while marginalizing the destructive form (par.1). According to Bogdonoff (1982), Boulding offered not only nonviolent resistance as an alternative but also possibly the first use of the term *transarmament*: "The process of changeover from a military defense policy to a civilian-based defense policy.... In transarmament, military forces and weaponry are gradually replaced with psychological, social, economic, and political weapons" (par. 4).

Integrative power is particularly useful when discussing either the redistribution of resources (a possible result of CBD) or bargaining/negotiating for collective defense (i.e., treaty/agreement). Integrative power, as Boulding acknowledged, is "both the most difficult to define and yet potentially the most significant form of power" (par. 7).

Unlike many proponents though, Boulding is not so quick to disregard *destructive power*. As Schelling touted the need for a deterrence capability, Boulding asserted that it is the synergy derived from *integrative* organizations that ultimately prove that destructive power does indeed play a role: "While destructive power is needed to make threats, threats are most effective when they are made in an integrative context which legitimates the demand for submission" (par. 9).

Using examples of defeated States experiencing periods of cultural/economic development after war/conflict, Boulding questioned the need/benefit of MBD. Americans realize this – perhaps more so than any other State. Following WWII, the USA orchestrated nation-building support toward the lead belligerents – Japan and Germany; both were severely-restricted in the subsequent peace agreements[16] from developing any offensive military capability. These *rebuilt/retooled* States are now economic powerhouses. While MBD proponents are quick to highlight the obvious economic benefits (e.g., technical/scientific/medical developments, defense/deterrence capabilities), Boulding suggested that "economic benefits would almost certainly be greater had the resources devoted to the military been directed directly toward economic development" (par. 10). These "economic benefits" might include lower tax rates and the resultant increase in discretionary income, income derived from investment, greater employment positions, increased revenue due to increased business income, increased governmental services, etc.

Sharp, perhaps the most well-known CBD advocate, skillfully explained the mechanics of his theories. Most are well-suited for either geographically-isolated or smaller States/territories having no credible adversaries with any *strategic-reach* capability.[17] Readers may assume that the 24 States previously mentioned have concluded that CBD is their best option, as a result of some type of strategic appraisal process. That decision, however, may have had more to do with fiscal limitations and less with the theories of Schelling, Boulding, and Sharp *et al.* Other proponents may assess this decision as validation of Sharp's concepts. For whatever reasons, each has determined it to be in their national interests to forego MBD in lieu of a national paramilitary police and/or coast guard. Thus, the absence of MBD is not evidence of CBD adoption.

Schelling's work in *game theory/bargaining* continues to serve as the foundation/basis for negotiating security treaties/agreements and developing collective defense strategies. Boulding's insight into the *destructive* effects of MBD indicates that it still has a place but is best when combined with integrative power to produce a greater synergy. It is reasonable, then, to conclude that diverting resources from MBD to domestic economic programs and using integrative power to bargain for allied military assistance would be favorable. If States commit to the level of CBD education/planning/training suggested by Sharp and ensure the necessary resources, then CBD might work. Currently, the States without MBD rely on multiple protectors via collective treaties/agreements or by a single protector via separate agreement.

How can CBD be better used?

Of the 195 sovereign States, none have currently adopted anything like CBD. Suggesting *how* CBD can be *better* used is thus conjecture. If CBD is employed as Sharp suggested – as a legitimately-organized, government-orchestrated effort – incorporating Schelling's and Boulding's ideas/principles, CBD could likely facilitate an increase in *productive/economic power* and validate its efficacy. Should *economic power* become stronger, the State's ability to influence regional/international partners and deter potential aggression might also increase.

What are the main challenges in implementing CBD?

Implementing *any* type of nonviolent political activity amidst today's volatile, global context is a challenge, CBD not the least. Two challenges deserve special discussion:

Challenge 1: Fulfilling existing security treaty obligations during transition. The CBD transition process must consider existing/emerging security obligations; tangential to this is notifying treaty/agreement signatories of the State's intent. During transition, the overall military strength of the alliance may be weakened.
Challenge 2: Developing/negotiating an economic power-related quid pro quo. Treaty/agreement members will not question another member's defense system; however, some *quid pro quo* resource in lieu of military forces would likely be required. The strength of every treaty/agreement lies is *acceptable* burden-sharing – what that means to the other signatory members is a moot point.

Schelling's discussions on *threats* and *bargaining* (1966, 1980) are probably more germane today than when written. Violations of sovereign territory by other States and transnational criminal groups are too numerous to recount here. Economic problems abound worldwide causing popular unrest, human suffering, poverty, and discontent with no end in sight. The current list of *Top-10 Poorest Countries*, according to World Bank and Global Finance Magazine (2017), includes (from poorest to less poor): Central African Republic, Democratic Republic of the Congo, Burundi, Liberia, Niger, Malawi, Mozambique, Guinea, Eritrea, and Madagascar. Not surprisingly, each has regular military forces (MBD). *What might be the impact on domestic services/quality of life were a transition to CBD occur? Is there any empirical evidence proving that eliminating the military would either directly or indirectly result in elevating the quality of life as Boulding suggested?* Sadly, there is none.

While security treaties/agreements generally ensure military assistance when warranted, membership is not free. Treaties/agreements have economic components; all operations require resources. This is precisely where Boulding's *productive/economic power* can best serve the interests of all charter parties.

Boulding (1989) described *integrative organizations* as those *not driven by profit* – like alliances/coalitions. If his insights/perceptions are valid, then perhaps States might consider resolving security challenges by *leasing* support (i.e., agreeing to fund the *total* proxy operation on a case-by-case basis). *Could this be a cheaper/more efficient option than maintaining a full-time military?* The impact of allied intervention on behalf of the threatened State, however, also presents challenges:

> A major source of the integrative power of a community or organization is the degree to which the personal identity of the members involved is

bound up with their perception of the identity of the community or organization as a whole.

(p. 173)

If Boulding's assessment is valid, then the challenges associated with CBD might likely be the degree to which the State's national values/interests align with the stated values and interests/purpose of the supporting alliance/proxy. If leadership concludes that the *benefits* of treaty/agreement membership or proxy protection are worth the *cost*, then the conditions are set for CBD. Schelling (1966) suggested that States choosing to outsource defense/deterrence no longer have a say in *how* the proxy acts; whether through coercion or brute force. Either of these may contradict the State's existing ethos. Mohandas Gandhi reminded us that a nation's culture resides in the hearts and soul of its people. If this is true, then, at what point might the populace drive leadership into adopting CBD?

In this extract, Sharp (1990) addresses tactics/techniques for defending against internal oppression and external aggression without mentioning *outsourcing*. Even Sharp (agreeing with Schelling) concluded that the challenge lies in *deterrence*:

> First, the weapons system needs to be sufficiently strong and well enough prepared to have a high probability of deterring internal usurpation and international aggression ... to convince potential attackers not to attack because the consequences could be unacceptably costly to them, including the failure to gain their objectives. Deterrence is a crucial part of the much broader process of *dissuasion*: to induce potential attackers to abandon their intent to attack as the result of any of several influences, including rational argument, moral appeal, distraction, and non-provocative policies, as well as deterrence. However, a major problem exists. Dissuasion may fail, and no deterrent can ever be guaranteed to deter. Consequently, the results of the failure of deterrence and the use of one's chosen weaponry must be survivable and remediable. Second, if and when deterrence fails, the weapons system must be able to defend effectively.... The means used to defend must be capable of neutralizing and ending the attack but must not destroy the society being defended. The defense capacity must be able to cause the attackers to desist and withdraw, or to defeat them, and to restore the society's prior condition of peace, autonomy, and chosen constitutional system.

(p. 3)

Schelling, Boulding and Sharp all recognize the challenges presented by dissuasion/deterrence. Despite the negative aspects, each posited that the *benefits* justify the *cost*. Whereas Schelling and Sharp might have viewed CBD as a strategic-level, economics-driven initiative benefitting all, Boulding urged an approach that reaches to the very ethos of the State: the word, *cost,* must include the *impacts* on existing national values/interests and public perceptions/opinions, if any.

Are there any inspirational case studies?

Neither Schelling nor Boulding suggested any case studies relevant to this topic; Sharp (1990), highlighting certain conditions, offered the following:

> We do have some limited resources in the search for such nonmilitary alternative means of deterrence and defense. Largescale non-cooperation and defiance have already, ... been improvised for defense against foreign aggression and internal usurpations. These cases are not usually well known, and their potential significance for defense has rarely been examined seriously. Yet they exist, thereby establishing that an alternative to military and paramilitary means for national defense is possible under at least certain circumstances... . Can there be an effective post-military defense policy capable of providing deterrence and defense while avoiding the dangers of modern war?
>
> (p. 6)

States having MBD already know the challenges associated with security treaty/agreement obligations. Coalition/alliance operations are difficult and are fraught with inherent cross-cultural and political constraints (e.g., language/dialects, conflicting political guidance, ambiguous *status of forces agreements*, [18] basing rights, logistics support, [19] funding, medical support, communications frequencies, equipment interoperability, rules of engagement, duration of operations, etc.).

Conclusions

The seminal teachings underlying Christianity, Islam, Hinduism, Judaism, and Buddhism regarding *moral law* (i.e., what we *ought* to do) continue to inspire/influence every generation; each urges reflection on how *destructive power* continues to adversely impact mankind. The findings/conclusions of the authors discussed herein attest that tension, unrest, and prejudice still/will exist across not only every State but also within populations whose ancestral lands were borderless. Schelling, Boulding, and Sharp continue to educate/influence anyone interested – urging review of the pros/cons of MBD and the potential cost/benefits gained by redirecting military-allocated funds to domestic services/programs. As more States review/assess their available resources, the better CBD may appear.

Dissuasion/deterrence and a counterattack capability continue to present an altogether different problem for CBD advocates. Nonviolent political activities alone may not deter an *irrational*, unrelenting enemy determined on total occupation (maybe even annihilation) and populace/resources control, regardless of the cost. As Sharp posited (1990), CBD can only work as a *whole-of-society approach* – not simply *whole-of-government*. While it is theoretically true that CBD will free more resources for non-military priorities, it will never guarantee the proliferation of domestic services/programs.

Although Schelling, Boulding and Sharp provided sound arguments/conclusions, logical and fiscal rationale, and even practical methodologies for converting to CBD, another determinant needs mentioning – *Geography*. This is not the same internal, *natural determinant* that was mentioned previously by Jablonsky (1997) or "lust/resource wars" over valuable natural resources explored by Le Billon (2005).[20] This is geography in the context of *proximity to credible adversaries* (i.e., countries not only communicating threats but also possessing the power to project/inflict such threats).

Do theories related to CBD remain valid if *proximity to adversaries* is introduced into the discussion or can it be refined to a *one-size-fits-all* concept? Consider this scenario in the current context of geo-politics/economics: Russia, Iran, China, and the USA, as recognized world/regional powers, pursue their national political objectives amidst a few, long-standing regional/religious conflicts (e.g., Iran-Israel, China-Taiwan, India-Pakistan, and North Korea-South Korea). Next, visualize a slight rearrangement of the Earth's tectonic plates and another perspective appears. Imagine the USA bordering North Korea, Russia and Iran – with Israel just 90 miles to the south (see Figure 10.1).

Is there any conjecture on how regional stability might change if the USA were to adopt CBD? Next, assume all existing security treaties/agreements remain valid. Finally, consider *how* the USA might defend its sovereign borders

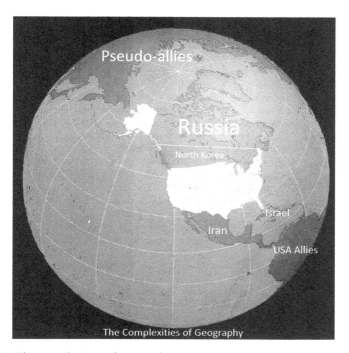

Figure 10.1 The complexities of geography

using *good intentions, faith and the other CBD tools and weapons of communications* cited by the experts.

Ensuring territorial integrity is unquestionably a State's top priority; without a secure environment, mankind's aspirations are hindered. Considering the principles/conclusions posited by Schelling, Boulding and Sharp, a CBD system capable of addressing all likely scenarios is possible, but it will require outsourcing some degree of security. The current spate and types of global fratricide frighten every legitimate leader. As members of the general populace, we are obliged to ask our elected leaders: *Is CBD capable of resolving ethnic/tribal, racial or religious-based violence and deterring likely contingencies?*

Remember the sage advice of British Field Marshal Sir William Slim (1990 [1952]):

> You are an ally too, and all allies look just the same. If you walk to the other side of the table, you will look just like that to the fellow sitting opposite.... There is only one thing worse than having allies – that is not having allies.
>
> (p. 12)

Notes

1 The characteristic spirit of a culture, era or community as manifested in its attitudes and aspirations. Many dictionaries also include traditions, history, patrimony and predominant ethnic beliefs/practices in the definition.

2 "Power is the ability to influence the behavior of others to get a desired outcome. Historically, power has been measured by such criteria as population size and territory, natural resources, economic strength, military force, and social stability" (Armitage & Nye, 2007).

3 "This concept does not imply that the state is the only actor actually using violence but rather that it is the only actor that can *legitimately* authorize its use. The state can grant another actor the right to use violence without losing its monopoly, as long as it remains the only source of the right to use violence and that it maintains the capacity to enforce this monopoly" (Muno, 2013). Since legitimacy, as perceived by the populace, is the operative word here, the use of *illegitimate force* does not refute this concept. For example, criminal organizations (defined here simply as organizations having violated either domestic or international law) may succeed in undermining order without challenging the State's monopoly and thus establish themselves as a *de facto*, parallel, and area-specific source of rule in some areas (Muno, 2013).

4 *Military-based Defense (MBD) System*: a traditional defense system using either a constitutionally-based or legislatively-authorized, government-sanctioned, trained, organized, equipped and funded/sustained military for the defense of the nation-state.

5 In the USA, the term commonly-used is *civilian-based defense*; in Europe, *civilian defense* or *social defense*.

6 Examples of social institutions include economic, governmental, educational, family and religious institutions. Social institutions comprise groups of people who have come together for a common problem-solving goal. These institutions have defined sets of norms and structures that support society's survival.

7 The Oxford English Dictionary has defined *weapon* in several iterations to mean, *inter alia*, an instrument, which is or may be used as a means of attack or defense;

and "a means of gaining an advantage or defending oneself in a conflict or contest." Thus, the term, *weapon of communication* is most appropriate in any discussion of nonviolent tactics.

8 For further information and examples of each, see Sharp, 1973).

9 *Light weapons*: "weapons designed for use by two or three persons serving as a crew, although some may be carried and used by a single person. They include, *inter alia*, heavy machine guns, hand-held under-barrel and mounted grenade launchers, portable anti-aircraft guns, portable anti-tank guns, recoilless rifles, portable launchers of anti-tank missile and rocket systems, portable launchers of anti-aircraft missile systems, and mortars of a caliber of less than 100 millimetres" (United Nations General Assembly, 2005, par. 6). *Weapons of Mass Destruction*: "Missiles, rockets and other unmanned systems capable of delivering nuclear, chemical, or biological weapons, that are specially designed for such use.... Related materials: materials, equipment and technology covered by relevant multilateral treaties and arrangements, or included on national control lists, which could be used for the design, development, production or use of nuclear, chemical and biological weapons and their means of delivery" (United Nations Security Council, 2004, p. 1).

10 Strategic communications (i.e., communications (all media types) created and disseminated at the national level to inform or otherwise influence the populace) is "an umbrella term to describe the activities of disciplines including public relations, management communication, and advertising.... a term used to denote the higher-level concerns behind communicative efforts by organizations to advance organizational mission[s]" (Thorson, 2013, par. 1). "Communication aligned with the company's overall strategy, to enhance its strategic positioning" (Argenti, Howell and Beck, 2005, pp. 83–89).

11 Coalitions provide another method for resolving security-related issues, albeit *ad hoc*. Though not always based on an existing treaty/agreement, coalitions provide a quicker and sometimes more efficient, alternative to resolving security threats. Coalitions are less formal, transitory, generally formed to respond to threats, dissolved once the threat is removed, politically fragile/sensitive, unite nations that are without history of harmonious relations and are generally formed by the willing. Purposes may vary (e.g., diplomatic, security, financial, intelligence, law enforcement, etc.). Examples include US Operations Desert Shield/Desert Storm (Kuwait, 1990–1991); US Operation Enduring Freedom (Iraq, 2003); MERCOSUR/ MERCOSUL (Brazil, Argentina, Paraguay, Uruguay, Venezuela with Chile and Bolivia as associate members); *Alianza del Pacífico* [Pacific Alliance] (Chile, Colombia, Mexico and Peru) and UNASUR (Argentina, Bolivia, Brazil, Chile, Colombia, Ecuador, Guyana, Paraguay, Peru, Suriname, Uruguay and Venezuela).

12 In general, a State's *National Security Strategy* is derived from an appraisal of its national values, interests, threats and policy objectives within the context of the global/ domestic environments. *National Values* represent the legal, philosophical and moral basis for the continuation of the system. National Values provide the basis/sense of *National Purpose* – usually found in the state's founding documents. *National Values* are often publicly expressed in presidential proclamations or laws/statutes. Historical actions/reactions and public opinion often express values as situational, which are modified over time. Values often contradict one another (Yarger & Barber, 1997).

13 In this context, *suitability* refers to the appropriateness of the objective(s) to achieve the overall purpose/goal; *acceptability* refers to the degree to which the populace will accept the concepts/methods used to execute the objectives, and *feasibility* refers to the resources available versus resources required to fuel/support the methods.

14 Although not listed here, Japan's Self Defense Forces constitute a *de facto* military.

15 The UN defines *disarmament* as "the collection, documentation, control and disposal of small arms, ammunition, explosives and light and heavy weapons from combatants and often from the civilian population" (United Nations Peacekeeping, 2016, par. 2).

16 Treaty of San Francisco (Japan) and Paris Peace Conference (Germany).
17 In this context, the ability of a State to project and sustain overwhelming military power.
18 Status-of-forces agreements define the legal status of foreign personnel/property in the territory of another nation-state. The purpose of such an agreement is to establish rights/responsibilities between supporting nation-states and the host government on such matters as criminal and civil jurisdiction, the wearing of the uniform, the carrying of arms, tax and customs relief, entry and exit of personnel and property, and resolving damage claims.
19 Before deploying military forces, the alliance and participating coalition members will want firm assurances regarding which areas of logistics the host State will provide and which supporting States should bring.
20 Le Billon (2005) provides compelling evidence that "resources are likely to remain the economic focus of most belligerents in years to come." As States become more acutely aware, every criminal organization requires resources. "Even if 'conflict resources' come under greater regulatory pressure, there is a likelihood that criminal networks and unscrupulous businesses will pursue trading, especially those already involved in arms trafficking," thus creating the true *nexus* of criminal enterprises.

References

Albert Einstein Institution (1973). *198 Methods of Nonviolent Action*. Available online at http://www.aeinstein.org/nonviolentaction/198-methods-of-nonviolent-action/

Argenti, P.A., Howell, R.A. and Beck, K.A. (2005). The strategic communication imperative. *MIT Sloan Management Review*, 46, 3, Spring 2005. par. 2. Available online at http://sloanreview.mit.edu/article/the-strategic-communication-imperative/

Armitage, R.L. and Joseph S. Nye, Jr. (2007). *CSIS commission on smart power: a smarter, more secure America*. Available online at http://csis.org/files/media/csis/pubs/071106_csissmartpowerreport.pdf

Bogdonoff, P. (1982). *Civilian-Based Defense: A Short History*. Omaha, NE: Association for Transarmament Studies. Available online at http://pbogdonoff.home.igc.org/cbdhist.html

Boulding, E. (1988). *Building a Global Civic Culture: Education for an Independent World*. Syracuse, NY: Syracuse University Press.

Boulding, K. (1989). *Three Faces of Power*. Newbury Park, CA: Sage Publications.

Conflict Research Consortium Staff (2005). *Conflict Research Consortium Book Summary: Three Faces of Power by Kenneth E. Boulding*. Available online at www.colorado.edu/conflict/peace/example/boul7514.htm

Fowler, H.W., Fowler, F.G. & Allen, R.E.(1990). *The Concise Oxford Dictionary of Current English*. Oxford:Clarendon Press.

Hart, B.H. (1968). Lessons from Resistance Movements – Guerilla and Non-Violent, in Adam Roberts (ed.), *Civilian Resistance as a National Defense: Non-violent Action against Aggression*, rev. edn. Mechanicsburg, PA: Stackpole Books.

Jablonsky, D. (1997). National power. *Parameters*, Spring, pp. 34–35.

Le Billon, P. ed. (2005). Geopolitics of 'Resource Wars': Resource Dependence, Governance and Violence. *Geopolitics*. London, UK: Frank Cass Publishers.

Lewis, C.S. (1952). *Mere Christianity*. New York, NY: Harper Collins Publishers.

Muno, A. (2013). *State Monopoly on Violence: Political Science and Sociology*. In *Encyclopedia Britannica*. Available online at www.britannica.com/topic/state-monopoly-on-violence

Powers, R.S., Vogele, W.B., Krueger, C. & McCarthy, R.M. (1997). Protest, power, and change: An encyclopedia of nonviolent action from ACT-UP to women's

suffrage. Available online at https://books.google.com/books?id=xmlWr4aAt4EC&p
g=PA534&lpg=PA534&dq=transarmament+kenneth+boulding&source=bl&ots=
Zb1L_-Hqjm&sig=Wj7WvTnCqg6dKUwQKVC2DgZnafM&hl=en&sa=X&ved=
0ahUKEwjYjIHo-vvRAhVFVWMKHXyjDEgQ6AEIKTAC#v=onepage&q=transa
rmament%20kenneth%20boulding&f=false

Schelling, T.C. (1966). *Arms and Influence*. New Haven, CT: Yale University Press.

Schelling, T.C. (1980). *The Strategy of Conflict: With a New Preface by the Author*. Cambridge, MA: Harvard University Press.

Schelling, T.C. (1984). *Choice and Consequence: Perspectives of an Errant Economist*. Cambridge, MA: Harvard University Press.

Sharp, G. (1973). *The Politics of Nonviolent Action, Part One: Power and Struggle*. Manchester, NH: Extending Horizons Books.

Sharp, G. (1973). *The Politics of Nonviolent Action, Part Two: The Methods of Nonviolent Action*. Boston, MA: Porter Sargent Publishers.

Sharp, G. (1985). *Making Europe Unconquerable: The Potential of Civilian-Based Deterrence and Defense*. Pensacola, FL: Ballinger Publishing Company.

Sharp, G. (1990). *Civilian-Based Defense: A Post-Military Weapons System*. Princeton, NJ: Princeton University Press.

Slim, W.J. (1990 [1952]). Higher Command in War. *Military Review*, May, pp. 10–21.

The North Atlantic Treaty Organization (1949). *The North Atlantic Treaty*. Available online at www.nato.int/cps/en/natohq/official_texts_17120.htm

The World Bank and Global Finance Magazine (2017). *World Development Indicators*. Available online at http://data.worldbank.org/products/wdi-maps

Thorson, K. (2013). *Strategic Communication*. Available online at www.oxfordbibliograp hies.com/view/document/obo-9780199756841/obo-9780199756841-0007.xml

United Nations (1945). *Charter of the United Nations*. Available online at www.un.org/en/charter-united-nations/

United Nations (1999). *United Nations Treaty Collection, Treaty Reference Guide*. Available online at www.unicef.org/french/crc/files/Definitions.pdf

United Nations General Assembly (2005). *International Instrument to Enable States to Identify and Trace, in a Timely and Reliable Manner, Illicit Small Arms and Light Weapons*. Available online at www.un.org/events/smallarms2006/faq.html

United Nations Office of the Special Adviser on the Prevention of Genocide (2010). *Genocide*. Available online at www.un.org/en/preventgenocide/adviser/pdf/osapg_booklet_eng.pdf

United Nations Peacekeeping (2016). *Disarmament, Demobilization and Reintegration*. Available online at www.un.org/en/peacekeeping/issues/ddr.shtml

United Nations Security Council (2004). *Resolution 1540 (Proliferation of Weapons of Mass Destruction and their Delivery Systems by non-State Actors)*. Available online at www.un.org/en/ga/search/view_doc.asp?symbol=S/RES/1540%20(2004)&referer=http://unrcpd.org/wmd/1540-2/&Lang=E

United Nations Treaty Collection (1999). *Treaty Reference Guide*. Available online at http://untreaty.un.org/English/guide.asp

Yarger, H.R., & G.F. Barber (1997). *U.S. Army War College Methodology for Determining Interests and Levels of Intensity. Directive Course 2: War, National Policy & Strategy*. Carlisle Barracks, PA: U.S. Army War College.

11 Systemic violence in Syria and the usefulness of political economy

Stéphane Valter

Introduction: the ingredients of violence

The driving hypothesis is that any nationwide reconstruction project will probably not be enough to promote reconciliation, since the eventual demobilization of combatants is only partially connected to concrete and negotiable issues. Multiple factors impede the transition from war to peace: a domineering and violent environment which is pervasive in the culture, society, economy, politics, religion, etc., in addition to an exacerbated sense of masculinity and honour. The encumbrance of (real or imagined) religious obstacles to peaceful solutions is indeed tremendous due to a history of sectarian *odium theologicum* (which Islamist fighters have been reviving). This paper analyses the various forms of violence – upheld by both concrete issues and constructed differences – carried out by the different categories of people involved in the Syrian war: "regular" soldiers; (mostly Alawite) elite troops, security services, and militiamen; rebels from the (mostly Sunni) "moderate" armed opposition; local and international Islamist al- Qa'ida-related fighters; the terrorist organization of the Islamic State (IS); Kurdish combatants.

Many of these individuals and categories have a vested interest in continuing the fight, and therefore, this paper can only predict the probable failure of political economy-connected solutions in what appears to be a cause gone wrong. So, why include a negative example in work on non-violent political economy? Because analysis remains indispensable even if the solutions are still unrealistic. Today's Syria constitutes assuredly an example of a specific culture of violence, partly related to political economy in the sense that socio-economic cleavages play an undeniable role, yet alongside ideological and sectarian dynamics which are sometimes irrational in the sense that objective assessments are frequently distorted by largely imagined existential threats.

The plague of sectarianism has often built organic barriers between people, to the point that minorities feel threatened by the Sunni majority. Thus, for example, members of the ("ruling") Alawite community tend to view the war as existential more than political: a threat to their very existence, not to mention the loss of power.[1] This (partly) explains the unleashing of brutality against (mostly) peaceful Sunni protesters in the spring of 2011 and later, who rapidly turned into armed rebels. In addition, a rigid interpretation of Islam (i.e. of some ruthless Koranic passages and merciless prophetic acts) has formatted the minds of many Sunnis who have therefore always analysed political conflicts through sectarian lenses.[2] Consequently, for Sunni Islamist and jihadist rebels, who constitute the bulk of the armed opposition, mercy for "political" opponents, perceived as wicked individuals and deviant believers, remains the exception, and cruelty the norm. Yet, it remains obscure how these sectarian cleavages, which are usually more polemogenous than socio-economic, managed to impose themselves on the concerned players.

Whereas the use of strength – as a politically legitimate phenomenon – may aim at calming down conflicts, violence in the Syrian war has been destructive and unlawful, from all sides, to the point that strength can only be linked to social order insofar as rules have been imposed by brute force. If men are unambiguously the main agents of violence,[3] victims include all beings because of random repression, which has generated resentment beyond repair. If masculinity plays an undeniable role in the unleashing of violence, it has to be questioned whether Syria is fundamentally different from other cases. In addition to the fact that masculinity remains a difficult concept to define (muscles and hairiness? aggressiveness and domination?), one should wonder whether it plays a clearly identifiable role in the dynamics of Syria's violence.[4]

From an axiological point of view, understanding the Syrian war obliges one to consider all offenders, rogues, and criminals who thrive on unruliness and chaos, and whose motives are idleness (the "mother of all vices"), frustration, revenge, greediness, and sadism (under the erroneous guise of political or religious claims). This applies to both regime soldiers and rebel fighters. The words of the experienced Italian reporter Domenico Quirico, taken hostage in Syria (2013) by Mafia-like factions of the so-called "moderate" armed opposition, have to be recalled (Quirico and Piccinin da Prata 2014): "I met the country of Evil." And since the Syrian territory has become a battleground for external forces – which are the only actors powerful enough to impose a solution, be it unfair – the civil war must also be viewed via the stakes of regional conflicts and international crises. Finally, there can be no reconciliation without the trial of war crime perpetrators. In spite of recent negotiated de-escalation zones, all of the preceding factors determine a level of violence that hinders peaceful solutions and renders political economy analysis non-satisfying.

Historical, cultural, and political violence

If revolt can be analysed as a reaction to insufferable socio-political constraints, violence may also be viewed from an anthropological perspective. Without attempting to present a comprehensive theory about the cultural roots of violence in Syrian society, one – significant? – example may suffice. It happened in Damascus, in a microbus (beginning of the 1990s), with the usual uncomfortable promiscuity. A sturdy paratrooper started to openly masturbate and nobody dared say a word, in collective apathy, neither the veiled ladies nor the elderly people (who usually enjoy moral authority in civilized contexts). Since the armed forces were (and still are) the only structure where rural young men could (and can) make a living, and thus compensate for their limited education and technical skills, many professional soldiers hail from the Alawite community. Even if the paratrooper was not from this military cast, there remained a deep-rooted fear of facing up to an element of the untouchable security apparatus. But the most striking was the affective frustration tormenting this man because of the institutional dehumanization process imposed on this cog of the repressive system. Collective stupor and societal atomization were obvious signs of systemic cultural violence.

What characterizes Syrian society can be summed up as affective frustration and sexual dissatisfaction (because of moral constraints); interiorized fear *versus* extraverted violence (immunity of the secret services); influence of bloody Islamic sacrificial rites; application of punishments in the name of a superior norm (Islamic law or state security). Since these factors have not changed, the finding of a non-violent solution to the war, given the economic strain, remains distant. Other insidious features relate to a violent environment: dirty cities, dull countryside, unemployment, corruption, a housing crisis, normative expressions of religion, a state of emergency (theoretically abolished in April 2011), external threats (imperialism, terrorism), etc. Geographic violence has also existed through sectarian ghettos: in Damascus, some places are predominantly Alawite, for security concerns and sectarian dynamics (like 'Ish al-Warwar – north, Mezzeh 86 and Hayy al-Wurud – south-west suburbs). The impact of all these cultural, physical, and social elements on the nature of violence – which generates irresistible aspirations for (often irrational and armed) change – needs reflection.

Violence is deep-seated because of the many inter-sectarian massacres throughout the ages (Winter 2010), and it was only the French mandate (1920–1946) which decisively lessened – through coercion – community tensions. After the Baathist takeover in February 1963, minorities definitely broke off their ancestral marginalization since the new regime included many officers from the edged-out communities, who started their ascension within the state's apparatus, which generated Sunni dissatisfaction. This growing frustration created a severe political crisis which culminated in February 1982 when an Islamist insurrection flared up in Hama (with the killing of Alawites, Baathists, and Christians) before being crushed by the regime's forces: maybe up to 20,000 casualties in about two weeks. The background for revenge was therefore very fertile when the March 2011 protests started. After the regime's indiscriminate repression, historical grievances, long-silenced political complaints, and accumulated sectarian hatreds all resurfaced, to a probably unknown level. The interference of the Lebanese Hizbollah, Iranian military, and Iraqi militiamen, viewed by the opposition as occupiers collaborating with a despised regime (and as hordes of Mongol invaders), has irreversibly accentuated the split between Sunnis and Shiites. The increasingly sectarian character of the Syrian war, as well as the decade-old confrontation between Iran and Saudi Arabia have thus rendered Sunnis and Shiites irreconcilable foes.

The causes of violence may be viewed in a regional perspective (yet without subsuming an invariant Arab identity): punishing by force, instead of educating through reason, seems natural because of the stress caused by socio-economic predicaments (poverty, illiteracy, etc.), political constraints (oppression), and cultural factors (conformism and traditions). This pervasive context of violence may be described by the pair of Arabic words: *zalim/mazlum*, or oppressor/ oppressed, from the top of the social hierarchy down to the bottom. Any attempt at imagining a scale of universal violence, through epochs and areas, would probably be futile. If Italian noblemen from the fifteenth to sixteenth centuries felt no guilt at murdering people, they usually had a sense of culpability when killing in a dishonourable manner, but in a context of civil war, notions of honour, respect, and mercy have vanished from the inferno.[5]

Those who suggest that Syrian people were, before the war, peaceful and civilized have been misguided since they underestimated the latent level of violence, which has been expressing itself since March 2011 through the savagery of the state's security agencies, the conversion of unemployed people into pro-regime thugs (the sadly famous *shabbiha*), and the indiscriminate killing of civilians (with missiles and chemicals). This brutality has been matched – on a lesser scale – by the opposition's rockets, the execution of Alawites and so-called collaborators and the use of civilians as human shields. The Syrian regime has functioned for decades on the economy of violence: using terror once and for all. But since the March 2011 uprising, violence has become unpredictable: between random governmental repression and domineering rebellious factions, no one feels safe. Since the military have exerted excessive brutality to curb protest and rebellion, the Sunni population usually considers all Alawites as potential threats (in spite of military defections within this community). The same is roughly true concerning Alawite (and minority) civilians *vis-à-vis* rebel groups, which have highjacked the revolution. Revolt against a repressive system has thus degenerated into mutiny against the elementary rules of political contest and into murderous sectarian dynamics.

Systemic militarization and community cleavages thwart efforts towards any negotiated solutions. The governmental forces (regular and reserve) amount to some 250,000 military, while the core is constituted of professional Alawite officers and soldiers: now probably less than 50,000 (because of death, absconding, and desertion). The dreaded security services are largely composed of Alawites (tens of thousands) whereas mainly Alawite pro-government militias consist of some 100,000 people.[6] One must add Shiite foreign volunteers and mercenaries: around 40,000 from Iran, Iraq, Lebanon, Afghanistan, and Pakistan, plus Russian advisers and soldiers. Conversely, the armed opposition is mostly Sunni, which creates an insuperable barrier in front of any political solution. Many power-wielding groups are Islamist, when not jihadist, and little remains of the nationalist-turned-religious Free Syrian Army (FSA) whose ranks have been depleted by the attractiveness of spirited and equipped Islamist factions (related to al- Qa'ida or IS). Finally, the number of (mostly jihadist) foreign fighters has soared (up to 40,000 from 110 countries for IS). The military situation is complexified by sectarian and ethnic demography: whereas Sunnis form more than 70% of the population (Arabs and Kurds – between 10 and 15% – included), Alawites are around 12%, to whom must be added "friendly" communities: 1.5% of Ismailis, 3% of Druses, 1.5% of Murshidites,[7] plus neutral Christians (more than 10%). Such a heterogenous demographic cocktail seriously jeopardizes any agreed-on solution.

Masculinity, Koran, and sexuality

The *modus operandi* for expressing violence may vary, although self-perception and assessment of brutal masculinity remain similar since the oriental pattern of patriarchy – influenced by an exacerbated tribal sense of collective honour (Dukhan 2014) – has imposed determined behaviour, although the extent to which masculinity may impede non-violent solutions remains a hypothesis. The Tunisian historian Hichem Djaït (Djaït 1974, 195–228) dubbed it the "Arab basic personality": males are supposed to stand for the group's honour, women's chastity (in particular) being sacred, whereas rape – the supreme physical and symbolic wound inflicted upon enemies – has been a prevalent feature of the conflict. Another hypothesis is that the longer a civil war goes on, the more chances there are that the "lower" classes will reinforce (because of strenuous socio-economic conditions?) brutal codes of interaction. Whatever the reasons, prisoners are few: those who surrender are generally abused, tortured, and killed, by both the regime and the opposition (with the possible exceptions of Hizbollah[8] and the FSA).

Another hypothesis that postulates the difficulty to attain non-violent solutions lies in some bellicose passages of the Koran as well as in some brutal prophetic acts, which both constitute a-historic models for (Syria's and beyond) reactionary Sunnism.[9] For example, reports have been released of public executions, by Islamist groups (especially the IS, but not only), because of (supposed) revolt against God's will or disrespect towards the Prophet, masculinity codes having to reject leniency in such situations. For philosophers like W. von Humbolt (*The Heterogeneity of Language*) and I. Kant (*Critique of Pure Reason*), each linguistic system, as an expression and vector of past experiences, refers to specific perceptions of oneself and others. In this perspective, we can surmise that the Koranic text has controlled the thinking process of generations of Muslims since it has sacralised its own scriptural content together with the Arabic language,[10] guarded them against the alteration of time, and petrified them under the weight of an imagined norm (which is very strictly interpreted in the case of Islamists).[11]

The first Muslim community's fears were expressed in a Koranic language full of threatening exhortations which became rooted in the next generations' psychology,[12] so that they would not put the revealed text into question and always deem themselves beneath God's expectations. The Koran contains indeed a lot of symbolic and physical violence (like IX, 29). Moreover, the "divine" revelation presents itself as inimitable (XII, 13; X, 38; II, 23), enshrined within the celestial

Archetype (XLIII, 4), originating from God and all-encompassing (many verses). Although the Koran states just once (XXXIII, 21) that the Prophet is the pre-eminent model, his warlike example (contained in the *sunna*) has assuredly stimulated Islamist and jihadist violence. Muhammad thus indulged himself sometimes in cruelties in the heat of military action, like after the battle of the ditch (*khandaq*) when he cold-bloodedly ordered the decapitation of some 600 to 700 men from the Banu Qurayza Jewish tribe (in 627). One of the executed men was wearing an orange-red tunic (*hulla shaqhiyya*, like dates when their tawny colour turns red)[13] (Al-Waqidi 1993, vol. 1, 512–13), which could be paralleled by some gruesome executions carried out by the IS.

After the Khaybar oasis's takeover (628–629), Muhammad acquiesced to the torturing of the Jewish chief Kinana, apparently to know where he had hidden his valuables, before commanding his execution. Yet, the Prophet generally showed clemency, and except felony, the only thing he could not tolerate was someone bantering with his status of messenger. Correlatively, summary executions have been carried out by Islamist militias (the al- Qa'ida franchise Nusra Front, the IS, etc.) under accusations of blasphemy that frontally opposes the revealed Text's sacredness and the veneration due to the Messenger (particularly when speaking *ex cathedra*). The preceding examples show unambiguously that many patterns of violence derive from creed and history, i.e. identity and memory, and can therefore not be negotiated, when they are not themselves drivers of brutality.

The Syrian regime, from the late president to his son Bashar, has always tried to present itself as respectful of Islam. Yet, it has always been perceived by traditional Sunnism as dangerously secular (because of Baathist ideology) and offensively schismatic (because of the Alawite creed, plus the over-presence of Alawites within the security apparatus). Aggravating circumstances are the (relative) liberty enjoyed by Alawite (and more generally non-Sunni) women, who wear no head veil and stroll around freely, plus – sometimes – the consumption of alcohol. Such "deviant" ways of life are perceived by narrow-minded believers (and Islamist fighters) as intolerable offences against God's commandments, which deserve "legal" punishments: expeditious justice and summary executions. On the other hand, the security services have repressed dissenters cruelly, though with a lay conception of the sacred: namely, the regime's stability.

Concerning the treatment of captives, some of the Prophet's and the first caliphs' deeds have probably been taken by many Islamist rebels as examples which legitimize their atrocities (Valter 2014). At the beginning of the pre-dication, some compassion prevailed towards captives (LXXVI, 8–9), but after the victory against the polytheists at Badr (624), the attitude became more bellicose (VIII, 68/67–72/71). Just after Badr, Bilal, the first muezzin, required that a captive be put to death; similarly, other prisoners were executed, and some injured people were finished off. Yet, in a *sura* probably revealed some time after Badr, a passage (XLVII, 4–5/4) recommends, half-heartedly, to spare prisoners for future haggling. Moreover, the Koran does not forbid slavery, and the Prophet himself possessed a few female slaves as concubines.[14] During the (preventive) expedition against the Banu Mustaliq rebellious tribe (627), for instance, the female captives were offered to the warriors as refreshments. Although the Prophet showed sometimes magnanimity and pragmatism, the actual prevailing models draw their inspiration from a history-inspired savageness impermeable to mitigation.

A salafist sheikh of Jordanian origin, Yasir al-'Ajlawni, recently issued a legal opinion (*fatwa*) declaring licit the rape of Alawite women on the basis of the Koranic concept of bondage (*mulk al-yamin*). These forced concubines would even, according to him, enjoy the women slaves' legal and "protecting" status.[15] But a group of Syrian Muslim scholars (the *Rabitat al-'ulama' al-suriyyin*) adopted a convoluted stance on the lawfulness of slavery with regard to pro-regime militiamen's women. After reminding that Islam aims more at emancipating slaves than at enslaving free people, they opined that reducing regime supporters' women to bondage contravened law and interest more than the contrary, according to a casuistry that does not declare servitude illegal and immoral, but could nevertheless encourage some (remote) national reconciliation.[16]

The debate about the "legal" sanctions against rapists is illuminating: the "moderate" FSA's official site shows reticence at executing at once, by shooting, any person guilty of rape since some scholars argue that this punishment must be reserved to fornicators; so, the armed rapist should rather undergo the harsher chastisement of *hiraba* (the Koranic penalty for organized crime[17]), but with no amputation, the immediate application of the prescribed penalty being incumbent upon the sheikh who accompanies the rebels. The FSA site distinguishes between two types of rape: the premeditated one, the purpose of which is to tarnish honour and take revenge, must be publicly punishable according to the *lex talionis* (*qasas*). The other, which results from the satisfaction of a sexual drive in a moment of "psychological and religious weakness", is not related to any precise sanction. Moreover, three types of sexual aggression have been identified by religious scholars: fornication; rape under threat, eventually sanctioned by *hiraba*; rape under armed constraint, punishable by *hiraba*. [18] But according to testimonies, even "moderate" FSA elements sometimes resort to rape. Thus, punishing with both severity and equity the widespread abuse of women will have to loom large on the agenda of any future transitional justice if confidence is to be restored and violence halted.

IS fighters' attitude towards enemies' women is peculiar: savage masculinity (humiliation, rape, torture) with formal respect of the Islamic law (understood in an inhumane way). When they capture women hailing from minority communities (Alawites, Christians, Yazidis, etc.), they enslave them before raping or selling them.[19] Thus, imposed sexual intercourse and human trade cannot be carried out outside a "prescribed" legal framework (Khadduri 2006). In spite of the IS's demise, it is dubious that in such a context of generalized violence, driven by commonplace brutality and unacceptable jurisprudential justifications, where honour has been sullied and life ruined, reconciliation will be easy, even under economic incentives or some truth-and-reconciliation process. If the emblematic violence perpetrated by IS fighters – and Islamist militants more generally – derives from general patterns of human barbarism (and as reactions to ignominies committed by the regime), it is also legitimized by cruel examples of the Prophet's tradition (Juárez Becerra 2014).

Historic/legal incitements to extreme violence

IS's strategy (and other jihadist groups' to a certain extent) has aimed at instilling terror, through brutal force inspirited by a religious legacy only perceived with fanaticism: the tactic in Iraq and Syria has relied on the lethal exaltation of jihadists plus on the insurrectionary expertise of ex-Baathist officers in order to create an atmosphere of fear (via exemplary executions) and infuse total submission.[20] Whereas IS's nihilist agenda has neglected recognized borders, other jihadist fighting groups have positioned their military operations within the sole Syrian national territory, which may pave the way for eventual agreements based on what remains of patriotism or, at least, on shared interests. Before its downfall by late 2017, IS was a centralized terrorist structure whose self-declared "caliph", Abu Bakr al-Baghdadi, possessed some theological credentials (through a doctorate prepared in Baghdad) which may have inspired his religion-stirred pathology (also fuelled by social, political, and psychological frustration, like most of IS fighters). An appalling form of IS's violence consists in the way hostages are, once useless for ransom or blackmail,[21] ceremonially executed. Punishment by fire is symptomatic. A video released in February 2015 showed the terrible execution of a Jordanian pilot whose war-plane had been shot down: he was locked in a cage and burnt alive. Another ghastly video (June 2015) showed the ceremonial drowning of supposed spies (dressed in orange outfits) imprisoned in a cage.

Noticeably, the famous polygraph al-Tabari (d. 923) gives in his *History* details about the first caliph, Abu Bakr (al-Siddiq). Confronted to a revolt originating from different tribes (some of them had rival prophets) which contested the political and fiscal centralism of Medina, he fought "apostasy" with cruelty (even if he was sometimes accommodating). Tabari (no date, vol. 3, 251) cites a letter from Abu Bakr to his officers: "I order that nobody be fought nor slain before being reminded of [the commands coming from] God's Apostle. [...] War will be waged against whom will refuse [...] and my soldiers will burn them, exterminate them, enslave women and children." In another letter, Abu Bakr declares (*ibid.*, 252): "My generals will accept nothing but submission (*islam*). [...] Who will be impervious to my orders will be fought, and [...] they will be liquidated by fire and steel." A tradition mentioned by Tabari (*ibid.*, 258) indicates that the first caliph was famous – in a positive way from an Islamic point of view – for leading devastating military campaigns. When recalling the battle of Buzakha (north of Medina), Tabari gives these minutiae (*ibid.*, 262–263): Khalid b. al-Walid, "the Sword of Islam", under Abu Bakr's instructions, carried out ferocious reprisals to revenge atrocities committed against Muslims. Khalid burnt alive rebellious people, bound others hands and feet before crushing them with stones, pushed some off the summits of cliffs, threw others into wells head first, and riddled the remnant with arrows. These "Islamic" examples of pitiless punishment doubtlessly serve as justifications – in addition to sadism – for jihadist (especially IS) fighters when they combat regime soldiers and repress opponents.

Whereas Abu Bakr al-Siddiq's cruelty responded to a brutal environment and uncertain future, his actions have remained a behavioural model for Islamists, who have always considered the teachings of Islam as non–chronological by definition and nature since, for them, the "divine" message can only transcend historical periods and social conditions. Contrarily, Abu Bakr al-Baghdadi's criminality can only be explained as a pathological expression of frustration and hatred. Anyway, with such entrenched mental models, jihadist rebels (and IS in the first place) can hardly compromise and find negotiated solutions. But regime soldiers and thugs have also been involved in mass torture and killing, and prisoners have been starved, raped, burnt alive, etc. Here, there is no "Islamic" model, the only motives being efficiency and perversion. In the desperate search of de-escalation and negotiation, the question of whether religion-linked savagery may be easier to alleviate than regime "secular" and industrial brutality remains unclear.

Many feuds occurred in the Levant between Sunni and Islamic minorities, especially after 1305 when a *fatwa* was promulgated by a Sunni (Hanbali) theologian, Ibn Taymiyya. He considered the Alawite "religion" to be a jumble of outrageous doctrinal deviancies, and thus regarded the Alawite community as deserving the capital punishment. He anathematized Alawites (plus Ismailis and others) and called for their extermination on the ground of both conspiracy with the Christian crusaders and apostasy. Some of his *fatwa*'s passages (Friedman 2010, 188–197) call for collective murder:

> These people called Nusayriyya,[22] they and the other kinds of Qarmatians,[23] the Batinis,[24] are more heretical than the Jews and the Christians and even more than several heterodox groups. [...] These [Nusayris] should be fought as long as they resist, until they accept the law of Islam. [...] Their fighters should be killed and their property should be confiscated.

A similar *fatwa* was issued in 1638 by Nuh Afandi al-Hanafi al-Hamidi, the Ottoman empire's *shaykh al-Islam*:

> Keep in mind that these renegades, oppressors, and debauched people combine all the forms of impiety, infringement, and obduracy as well as the manifestations of depravity, Manicheism, and heresy. Those who tolerate their godlessness and heterodoxy, whereas it is incumbent [upon the believers] to fight them and permissible to kill them, are infidels like them. [...] It thus falls [to the believers] to eliminate these execrable, irreligious,

and profligate people. [...] It is allowed to reduce their women to bondage since the servitude of the apostate [...] is licit.

With such – still effective – fanatical discourse, non-violent solutions are remote since fighting "heretics" remains a legal duty for Islamists.

Analogous accusations have been levelled against Alawites (who have over-reacted to the – real or imagined – Sunni threat by committing numerous atrocities) and identical chastisements inflicted upon them by jihadists. The plentiful *fatwas* emanating from the Wahhabi clergy, which supports the armed rebellion (except IS, a threat to the Saudi kingdom's stability), carry the same heinous rhetoric. Among jihadists, IS's viciousness is the fiercest: some 1,500 (mostly Shiite) cadets were slaughtered at Camp Speicher, near Tikrit in Iraq (June 2014), after they were exhibited like sacrificial sheep. Another massacre was committed at Tabqa, in a military air base located in northern Syria, when some 220 captured government soldiers were grue-somely killed in a filmed mass execution (August 2014). Some "primitive" weapons seem to be considered by the executioners as genuinely Islamic, like knives and swords, in addition to "archaic" ways of execution like throat slitting, beheading, crucifixion, which does not prevent jihadists – and IS in the first place – from relying on technology to save time (machine guns and even chemical weapons). How could Alawites (and other minorities) not feel threatened by such horrors?

For many civilians stuck between the devil and the deep blue sea, the regime is as bad as Islamist groups. The IS has represented – until its recent collapse – an attractive, well-equipped, and efficient structure for some marginalized Sunnis around the world, who joined this terrorist organization to assert a polymorphous pathological virility: parading among scared civilians, shooting prisoners, decapitating hostages, capturing and raping women. On the other side, for Alawites, other Islamic minorities, and Christians, moved by existential fears, the regime stands as a rampart against religious fanaticism, even if nobody nurtures any illusion about the violent and corrupt nature of the system. But for many Sunnis (yet not all), the sectarian nature of the regime plus its bru-tality constitute a tremendous menace to their very security. So, it is hard to imagine how remote political compromises and meagre economic incentives could reverse the actual trend of violence, largely anchored in cultural, histor-ical, and religious destructive dynamics.

Epilogue

Any solution out of the war remains connected to local players' perceptions and international sponsors' interests, in particular to many GCC countries which want to give a sectarian stamp to the political conflict between Riyad and Teheran. Wars may end because of a lack of resources, and the history of international relations shows, since the 1648 treaty of Westphalia, that big powers are capable of imposing unfair peace onto peoples.

For Moscow, in addition to the preservation of its new and hardly acquired influence in the region, the paramount threat consists in the eventual downfall of the Syrian state's institutions, which would open the door to international Islamist terrorism. In such a scenario, jihadist terror would certainly spread towards Russia. For Europe, stabilizing the refugee crisis remains one of the top priorities, while Washington is prone on defending its regional allies and its own strategic interests through the containment of terrorism and (uncontrolled) instability. For Teheran, keeping afloat an ally close to Hizbollah is an essential aim. Israel, for its part, witnesses the mayhem as long as no security threat spills over its borders. Implementing a truce before reconstructing the country therefore means that external actors agree to restrain their local allies, with a common agenda based on power sharing (that nobody wants) and material benefits (that are still unobtainable).

For Ankara, the most dangerous enemy remains the PKK, the Kurdish Leninist organization whose military confrontation with the Turkish armed forces has killed around 30,000–40,000 people from all sides since 1984. While the PKK has been endeavouring for years to create an independent state in eastern Turkey, it now strives to carve out an autonomous enclave in northern Syria. It is assuredly true that PKK's violence has been a natural response to the "official" terror exercised by the militarist Turkish state, now administered by an authoritarian Islamo-nationalist government. Yet, this does not clear the PKK of its own responsibilities: it has been a criminal organization, and may probably still be considered as such, in spite of the founder's pretentions to have changed (while in jail) his ideology from popular guerrilla warfare to libertarian socialism and democratic confederalism. Even if such a claim sounds dubious (and inconsistent), the PKK-affiliated Syrian PYD has implemented an interesting form of rule in northern Syria (Rojava), with local pluri-ethnic and "democratic" councils. Yet, it seems that this "democratic" administration is in reality rather authoritarian, certainly because of critical war conditions. In any case, the success originates from a rather homogenous population, common dislike of central Baathist rule, and shared fear of jihadist terror, elements which are not present in other parts of Syria.

Does religion constitute a moral – albeit strenuous – path towards (re) conciliation? Denominational barriers between communities would probably testify to the contrary, insofar as the conflict is not entirely political. Accumulated hatred between communities renders dialogue a distant aim, even a chimera, in the absence of impartial transitional justice. Can political solutions be found when no group seems desirous of engaging in genuine concessions? Furthermore, contrarily to other situations with a reconciling process based on wealth redistribution, Syria is now largely destroyed and possesses little natural resources to attract investors. In addition to that, the war economy benefits powerful groups (through smuggling and monopolies), related to the regime or the armed opposition, which prefer a lucrative yet violent *status quo* to an unprofitable peace.

Culturally, patterns of masculinity will globally remain the same, and abuse of women will only engender revenge. Apart from the – largely patriarchal –

Kurdish movements, one may question how gender relations have been affected by the war. Women have been involved in the fighting (especially Alawite auxiliaries and Kurd militants), in socio-economic activities because of a shortage of men, and in a modification of traditional moral codes (high divorce rates, etc.) due to chaos (extreme widowhood). But has the new role of women profoundly reshaped the social relations between genders, in a sense that could contribute to the appeasement of the conflict? Apart from the Kurds, changes have been limited in scope and women still do not hold leading political or military positions from which they could facilitate the reconciliation process.

Very probably, economic tensions due to the war have accentuated existing patterns of domination, with the possible exception of women's emancipation in a few cases. Indisputably, war-related economic hardships have put more stress on the vulnerable, who are deprived of empowerment and protection. The pre-war unfair class relations have deteriorated: crony capitalists dominate the production and distribution process in collusion with officers and war lords. Besides, the authoritarian regime is unable (and/or unwilling?) to control its military and militiamen who pay themselves directly on the remains of a crumbling economy. Even if the war is largely perceived as existential, the conflict has become entangled in a fight for material gains, and reversing these debased trends will need strong economic incentives plus the eradication of unlawfulness.

As Hanna Arendt showed in different circumstances, an exacerbated sense of superiority, correlated with perversity, leads to the banality of evil: those who have organized and carried out killings are sociologically "normal" (Arendt 2006). This denatured virility would originate from an incapacity to communicate and think from the others' point of view. What is significant is that all warring factions in Syria – with rare exceptions: maybe the Kurdish organizations in Rojava (although one should not view things too ideally) – have repressed free expression and refused plurality.

In a still inconceivable reconciliation process, what would be the best manner to attenuate violence? The French philosopher Montesquieu (1689–1755) suggested that the major political virtue is the courage to forget the past, especially when it is laden with suffering. Yet, amnesia may contribute to the reproduction of violence. Rousseau (1712–1778) used to say (for example, in *Émile*) that the prime reward of justice is the feeling that we are putting it into practice. However, is it possible to forgive unpardonable and indefensible crimes? If one considers the exposure of children to violence (like victims, unintentional spectators, or even perpetrators of crimes), combined with the devastation of the educational system and the disintegration of moral codes, there is legitimate space for despair.

Assuming that a reconciliation project will mollify sectarian resilience and placate accumulated hatred is possible. After Palmyra fell to the IS (May 2015), the Syrian novelist Mustafa Khalifa recalled his excruciating detention in the city's sadly famous prison:

> I encountered my worst tormentor while I was walking in the street. [...]
> He hugged me and I hugged him back, and honestly, I felt no grudge or

hatred, which was a surprise. All that I felt then was how much he was confused and ashamed. [...] Any inmate would see his tormentor as a victim, which he indeed is.[25]

This stirring remark suggests that extreme and vicious forms of violence could lead under certain circumstances – for those who believe in redemption – to an inversion of domination patterns: the lines between revolt and repression could therefore be blurred, men being confronted to their conscience alone. Hence, ethical awareness and pardon – as far as human beings can be humanist – would probably serve as the most efficient tools for the enforcement of non-violent solutions.

Notes

1 Alawites form a medieval split from mainstream (Imami) Shiism, and have always been despised by conservative Sunnis.
2 The passages from Koran and *sunna* just aim at showing that they do not over-determine Islamist militants as much as they fuel the minorities' existential fears.
3 As the war drags on, women have become more involved, as victims or (rarely) combatants. Therefore, one may (partly) question the validity of the masculinity paradigm as a dominant structuring process.
4 In spite of local cultural peculiarities, masculinity – as a socio-political dynamic – is not restricted to the Middle East, since even western democratic countries have allegedly virile leaders, like Silvio Berlusconi and Donald Trump, not to mention, in less democratic contexts, Vladimir Poutine, Recep Tayyip Erdoğan, Rodrigo Duterte, and the like. Amazingly, in the case of Syria, president Assad cannot be considered as the paragon of virility (contrarily to his brother Basil – the heir – who died in a car crash and whom he was obliged to succeed) whereas the society is highly patriarchal.
5 Some nine million persons are displaced (out of 22), with about 2.5 million abroad.
6 Some 150,000 soldiers, intelligence officers, and militiamen have been killed since March 2011, half of them being Alawites.
7 An almost centennial scission from the Alawites.
8 Hizbollah militiamen are known for their discipline.
9 Yet, it cannot be demonstrated – since it is unprovable – that Koran and *sunna* prevent warring players from concluding peace.
10 The revelation's privileged idiom, according to the (probably first) verse revealed on the subject: XX, 113.
11 The Arabic cultural and linguistic renaissance only took place by the end of the nineteenth century.
12 As far as we can subsume the existence of a collective psychology.
13 Dressing victims in orange could also, of course, be an exorcizing method for surmounting Guantanamo's agonizing experience.
14 For example, "*Ma malakat aymanu-kum*", or "(A captive) that your right hands possess", IV, 3.
15 *A Salafi Shaykh Permits the Capture of Women in Syria and Sexual Intercourse with Them*, (in Arabic), 24.3.2013, available online at www.youtube.com/watch?v=8Rg4rUBo LIo (accessed on 8.5.2013).
16 Available online at www.islamsyria.com/consult.php?action=details&COID=379 (accessed in Summer 2013, since been deleted).
17 V, 37/33–38/34. The possible Koranic penalties are banishment, asymmetrical amputation, execution, crucifixion.

18 Available online at http://syrianarmyfree.com/vb/showthread.php?t=32578 (accessed in Summer 2013, since been deleted).
19 When the Yazidis, erroneously dubbed Satan's worshippers, were besieged (summer 2014) near the Sinjar mountain, entire villages escaped in the arid, barren, and scorched hills, preferring to die out of thirst and starvation instead of falling captives to the jihadists.
20 Christoph Reuter, *The Terror Strategist: Secret Files Reveal the Structure of Islamic State*, 18.4.2015, available online at www.spiegel.de/international/world/islamic-state-files-show-structure-of-islamist-terror-group-a-1029274.html (accessed on 12.5.2015).
21 Onur Burcak Belli & *alii, The Business of the Caliph*, 4.12.2014, available online at http://www.zeit.de/feature/islamic-state-is-caliphate (accessed on 13.12.2014). The IS has appeared to be a reliable partner after agreements have been reached on the price. But this falls short of providing perennial solutions for reconstruction.
22 A depreciatory term for Alawites (which indicates a kinship with Ali) since it refers to a 9th century eponymous Iraqi propagandist.
23 A tenth to eleventh century dissidence from Ismaili Shiism.
24 A generic term designating all Shiites, and especially those who rely on allegoric readings of the Koran.
25 Imad Karkas, *The Shell: Mustafa Khalifa on Palmyra's Infamous Prison*, 28.5.2015, available online at http://syrianobserver.com/EN/Interviews/29240/The_Shell_Mustafa_Khalifa_Palmyra_Infamous_Prison/ (accessed on 30.8.2015).

Bibliography

'Abbud, Salam (2002). *The Culture of Violence in Iraq* (in Arabic). Köln/Beirut: Dar al-Jamal.
Al-Khatib, Muhammad Kamil (no date). *One Hundred Years of Suffering* (in Arabic). Beirut: Manshurat 0021.
Al-Waqidi (1414 [1993] and 1418 [1997]). *Al-Maghazi* (in Arabic), 2 volumes. Qomm: Maktab al-i'lam al-islami.
Angelova, Ilina (2014). "Rebel-Held Suburbs of Damascus: Resilience Mechanisms in the Face of Chemical Attacks." *Arab Reform Initiative (Policy Alternatives)*. Available online at www.arab-reform.net/rebel-held-suburbs-damascus-resilience-mechanisms-face-chemical-attacks
Arendt, Hanna (2006). *Eichmann in Jerusalem: A Report on the Banality of Evil*. New York: Penguin Books.
Bocco, Riccardo (1995). "'Asabiyât Tribales et États au Moyen-Orient. Confrontations et Connivences." *Monde Arabe Maghreb-Machrek* 147: 3–12.
Bozarslan, Hamit (2015). *Révolution et État de Violence. Moyen-Orient 2011–2015*. Paris: CNRS Éditions.
Bucaille, Lætitia (2013). "Femmes Combattantes." *Critique Internationale* 60: 7–88.
Chouet, Alain (1995). "L'Espace Tribal Alaouite à l'Épreuve du Pouvoir. La Désintégration par le Politique." *Monde Arabe Maghreb-Machrek* 147: 93–119.
(Al-)Dawoody, Ahmed (2011). *The Islamic Law of War. Justifications and Regulations*. New York: Palgrave Macmillan.
Djaït, Hichem (1974). *La Personnalité et le Devenir Arabo-Islamique*. Paris: Le Seuil.
Dukhan, Haian (2014). "Tribes and Tribalism in the Syrian Uprising." *Syria Studies Journal* 6/2. Available online at http://ojs.st-andrews.ac.uk/index.php/syria/article/view/897
Friedman, Yaron (2010). *The Nusayri-Alawis: An Introduction to the Religion, History, and Identity of the Leading Minority in Syria*. Leiden: Brill.

Ghassûb, Mayy, and Emma Sinclair-Webb (2000). *Imagined Masculinities: Male Identity and Culture in the Modern Middle East*. London: Saqi Books.

Hannoyer, Jean (ed.) (1999). *Guerres Civiles. Économies de la Violence, Dimensions de la Civilité*. Paris/Beirut: Karthala / CERMOC.

Juárez Becerra, María José (2014). "Radical Islamists: Islam's Rashidun or Hijackers Groups?" *Retos Internacionales* 5/11: 103–118.

Keane, John (1996). *Reflections on Violence*. London: Verso.

Khadduri, Majid (2006). *War and Peace in the Law of Islam*. Clark, NJ: The Lawbook Exchange.

Le Gac, Daniel (1991). *La Syrie du Général Assad*. Bruxelles: Éditions Complexe.

Leverrier, Ignace (2014). "Les 'Lettres de Syrie' de Joumana Maarouf En Librairie." Available online at http://syrie.blog.lemonde.fr/2014/04/08/les-lettres-de-syrie-de-joumana-maarouf-en-librairie/

Quirico, Domenico, and Pierre Piccinin da Prata (2014). *Le Pays du Mal. Otages en Syrie. 152 jours*. Paris: L'Harmattan.

Seurat, Michel (2012). *Syrie, l'État de Barbarie*. Paris: Presses Universitaires de France.

Tabari (no date). *History*, (in Arabic), 11 volumes. Cairo: Dar al-Ma'arif.

Valter, Stéphane (2003). "La Réplique à Ibn Bâz (1912–1999) de 'Abd al-Rahmân al-Khayyir (1904–1986)." *Bulletin d'Études Orientales* 55: 380–381.

Valter, Stéphane (2012). "Rivalités et Complémentarités au Sein des Forces Armées: le Facteur Confessionnel en Syrie." *Les Champs de Mars* 23: 79–96.

Valter, Stéphane (2014). "La Justice Chariatique en Syrie 'Libérée': Un Modèle Juridique Consensuel?" *Confluences Méditerranée* 90: 155–173.

Van Dam, Nikolaos (1996). *The Struggle for Power in Syria. Politics and Society under Asad and the Ba'th Party*. London: I.B. Tauris.

Winter, Stefan (2010). *The Shiites of Lebanon under Ottoman Rule, 1516–1788*. Cambridge: Cambridge University Press.

12 How to break the spell? Sources of violence and conflict in an oil rent based economy

A case study of Iraq and the Autonomous Region of Kurdistan

Silvia Nicola

Introduction

Instead of establishing liberal, free market-based and democratic institutions, as post-interventionist wishful thinking twice propagated, respectively in the 1990s and the mid-2000s, Iraq has been caught up in different spirals of extreme violence, instability and destruction. Despite this apocalyptic scenario, the West may, however, believe to have found a beacon of light in the midst of the Iraqi quagmire and its political labyrinth in the form of the Autonomous Region of Kurdistan.

While reliant on *de facto* self-governance since the early 1990s, the Autonomous Region of Kurdistan in the northern part of Iraq received a drastic developmental boost by its formal legal recognition through the new Iraqi constitution of 2005. Subsequently, it also managed to assert its interests against the central government on numerous occasions; the most significant contentious issue between central and regional government being the extended rights of self-determination the Kurdish Regional Government (KRG) later gained in the management of natural resources (mainly oil and gas) and thus in the steering of its economy and regional administration (Nicola 2017).

Seeking exponential economic growth and international support, the KRG engaged in pursuing solo-run international oil exports, and developing its economy through rentier-like measures, and the sustained increase in armament of its security forces and civilians alike. Likewise, economic growth has accompanied also the rhetoric of the central Iraqi government. This leitmotif being, however, only a desperate means of postponing additional political and foremost social conflicts from erupting.[1] Pursuing an oil rent based exponential economic growth is, however, luring the KRG into a trap as well, since such a consolidation of a single economic sector is far from being sustainable. On the contrary, it poses the risk of keeping the Autonomous Region of Kurdistan stuck in the spirals of violence Iraq has been entangled in for decades.

But what are the links between (armed) conflicts, natural resources, and political economy? And to what extent can political economy become non-violent? With no clear academic definition of a non-violent political economy, this paper aims to identify potential sources of violence and conflict with regard to the political economic sphere in order to formulate recommendations for action for the transition of the sector towards a more non-violent political economy.

In terms of the structure of this chapter, the analysis of the intimate relationship between conflict and resources will, first of all, rest theoretically on discussing the socially constructed character of the historical and political process of transforming nature into a commodity. Secondly, the conflict sources with regard to the usage and management of fossil fuels will be identified empirically[2] through the comparison of Iraq and Iraqi-Kurdistan's relationship towards oil and gas resources. Finally, besides summing up the discussed evidence, the conclusion will also offer a brief overview of potentially useful actions in overcoming the sources of violence and transforming the economy to a more non-violent version.

State of research

While the current market economies are based on the principles of a growth paradigm, this idea has been continuously criticized since the early 1970s. The foundation of the growth principles was formulated as an analogy to the postulates of mechanics, based on the law of energy conservation through transformation, and the maximization rule. As a result of this, the limits of growth were merely hypothetical. In the 1970s, however, Georgescu-Roegen (1975: 349) unmasked the belief, that "man will forever succeed in finding new sources of energy and new ways of harnessing them to his benefits" as a myth, since according to the second law of thermodynamics regarding entropy "every action, of man or of an organism, [...], any process in nature, must result in a deficit for the entire system" (ibid.: 354).

Consequently, the idea of limitlessness of both growth and energy sources (except perhaps solar energy and even that not indefinitely) is not only false, but also extremely dangerous in its consequences for mankind. This danger arises from an ecological point of view, due to the careless exploitation of natural resources leading to pollution, soil degradation, etc., but also from an ethical perspective, since current and earlier generations have consumed higher amounts of the scarce resources available and at a greater pace than future generations will be able to, thus influencing the "distribution of mankind's dowry among all generations" (Georgescu-Roegen 1975: 374), which, given the finite nature of resources, is irrefutably disadvantageous for all future generations.

With the idea of *Limits to Growth* (Meadows 1972) reaching the public consciousness, various economists have tried to offer damage-reducing alternative theories and interpretations (such as Low-Growth (Victor 2008; Binswanger 2009) or Steady State models (Daly 2008)), without bringing about a paradigm shift. Nevertheless, as the Sustainable Development Commission (2009: 8) has put it, there is as yet no credible, socially just, ecologically sustainable scenario of continually growing incomes for a world of nine billion people. [...] [S]implistic assumptions that capitalism's propensity for efficiency will allow us to stabilize the climate and protect against resource scarcity is nothing short of delusional.

While there has been – and probably still is – without a doubt a strong resistance in fundamentally changing the way societies, economy and most of all international markets have been working for the last couple of decades, the number of critical voices is not only on the rise but also enjoying more public awareness. This critical movement[3] has especially gained momentum since 2008, when the First International Conference on Economic De-Growth for Ecological Sustainability and Social Equity was held in Paris. Since then, the term "degrowth" has also entered academic journals and fueled both scientific debate and the pursuit of alternative ways of living (D'Alisa et al. 2015: 1–17).

While the series of conferences and academic exchange, started in Paris, is being successfully continued and the philosophy of degrowth further elaborated, the term "non-violent political-economy" remains less prominent. Non-violent political economy is a hard to define term, which could be comparable in its purpose with the similarly abstract and normative concept of peace. While there is no academic consensus either about the definition of non-violent political economy, or its limits, there are, however, different theoretical streams which place themselves under this aegis, such as the already discussed perspectives of degrowth, the Economy of Gifts, *buen vivir* or *sumak kawsay*,[4] Buddhist or Ghandian Economy.

Despite these developments, degrowth and non-violent political economy still have a limited total outreach. This becomes most strikingly visible in the Middle East, a region in which economy bows to only one (but false) deity: growth. This belief of economic growth as an overall savior is also being supported by the academia[5] in the region. Said academia, however, engages in – at least – a theoretical critique of the oil-based rentier economies of most MENA countries. Nevertheless, this also implies that an overwhelming majority of literature in oil abundant countries and on Iraq will still defend a growth-centric approach.

While H. Mahdavy (1970) firstly introduced the notion of a "rentier state" in the 1970s, Beblawi (1987) further developed the concept and focused closely on the market dimension and thus on "rentier economies", where an economy supports itself from rents – often received from selling natural resources. While criticism of the Arab economic model and state system has induced the idea of economic diversification, it appears that even in times of global de-carbonization discourses, there are still not enough financial and thus lucrative incentives for the oil-rich Middle Eastern countries to renounce their rent-based mentality (Tagliapietra 2017). Beyond the repetitive call for economic diversification, Esfahani (2006) sees – as many other growth critics too – a solution to the low and volatile economic growth in the region in a more bottom-up approach, meaning a higher involvement of the population. Nevertheless, he implies that the flaw of the rent-based economy would lie in the deficient use of the obtained rents, without questioning the whole economic apparatus and the abnormalities of a rent-based mentality.

With regard to the state of research dealing with the case under scrutiny, the literature on the Autonomous Region of Kurdistan has been flourishing in the last two decades, focusing preponderantly on the KRG's independence aspirations. Nevertheless, the access and management of the oil resources, as well as other economic activities, are seen as preconditions for the fulfillment of these aspirations (Natali 2010, Rahim 2013). Interestingly, the political economic literature on the central Iraqi oil sector completely neglects taking the KRG into account (Tuzcu 2011; Al-Saadi 2010). Comparisons between the two governmental entities are being made mainly with regard to single economic aspects such as the optimization of the process of monetizing fossil fuels or the legal debate surrounding the two different modes of contracting international oil companies (IOCs), as it will be seen in the empirically oriented part of this chapter. Needless to say, this string of comparative literature has evolved only after 2005 and has been strongly co-shaped by substantiated but interest-led reports from IOCs and associated think tanks.

Theoretical framework

This chapter conceptualizes non-violent political economy by using a negative definition based on the absence of violence or lack of fear from violence in the political-economic sphere, in how political institutions, environments and economic systems influence each other. Given the finite nature of energy and resources, this chapter focuses particularly on the role of government with respect to its power in managing resources. The theoretical conceptualization used for this chapter aims to point out different sources of violence or of conflict and switches its focus from the actor, who might be subject to violence (either state, society or individual), to the object of contention and potential use of violence, namely: the scarce resources.

The theory-oriented approach starts by using what Philippe Le Billion coined as a "conflict lens" and examines, in a political ecological fashion, the complex mechanisms of the relationship between humans and their environment. Furthermore, Le Billion claims that resources are not apolitical but are politicized. Therefore, resources participate in the shaping of various patterns of conflict and violence, through their specific historical, geographical, and social characteristics. Moreover, "among these qualities, their territorialization, as well as physical, economic and discursive characteristics come to define resources both materially and socially in dialectic relationship with institution and practices" (Le Billon 2004: 2).

While conflict must not always have a negative connotation, the processes of dealing with contentious issues have far-reaching consequences even beyond the original object of dispute. In this chapter, forms of conflict escalation are not limited to the obvious open usage of direct, physical violence, but also include violence in its structural and symbolic dimension, as described by Galtung (1990). Under these circumstances, mismanagement, corruption, patronage, racism, etc. subsumed by Le Billon as "unrealized potential" would be paradigmatic examples of structural violence.

Environmental determinism

A first source of conflict, which has the potential to escalate into violence, would be the processes allowing the transformation of nature into a commodity, since, according to Zimmerman (1951). "Resources are not, they become". Nevertheless, the distribution of resources is by nature unequal across the globe and among nation-states. This fact might nurture a "quasi-environmental determinism", which depicts distributional struggles according to the debate regarding "resource scarcity" versus "resource abundance".

Given the rich oil reserves of Iraq, the country is being challenged by a so called "resource course". Natural resource abundance is seen by some authors, such as Collier (2000), as susceptible for war. While this hypothesis remains very debatable, there is not as much dispute when it comes to the argument that the abundance of natural resources leads to poor economic growth and weak governance (Auty 2001, Sachs and Warner 2001), these two outcomes being often related to a greater likelihood of conflict (de Soysa 2000). Phillipe Le Billon (2004), however, points out that this perspective is leaving out an important aspect – the socially constructed nature of resources – since there is enough empirical evidence where even oil has been mobilized in peaceful development (for example in the case of Norway). Nevertheless, this depends to a great extent on the nature of the political and economic system.

The socially constructed character of resources is furthermore not only a political process but a historical one as well, with deeply political actions and consequences, which begin the very moment the transformation of nature into a commodity is initiated. This process contains three major sources of potential for conflict and violence: first, the framing of property rights and access to the disputed resource. Second, the management of its exploitation, as well as its distribution through exportation. Third, and most importantly, the allocation of the profits obtained thereby.

Geographical conditionalities

The first stage of the process, involving access and property rights, is closely shaped by nature (point or diffuse) and geography (proximate or distant to the state's capital). The combination of these two characteristics fuels different kinds of conflict and forms of violence (Le Billon 2004). Nevertheless, the mere existence of resources will not automatically transform the population living close by into warlords, rebels or armed secessionists. The political process of identity articulation will, however, have a strong impact on this. The articulation of identities means the way a demarcation line between one's own group and another is being drawn during an interaction, in order to push through egoistical interests to the detriment of the other[6] (Tilly 2005).

The second part of the economic process of transforming nature into a resource deals with exploration or production. In the case of oil, this stage requires the availability of large-scale infrastructure not only at the exploration sites, but also pipelines or refineries. Geography becomes also relevant when it comes to internationally commercializing a resource. In the case of oil and gas, it is useful to have direct access to the ocean, while landlocked entities depend on cooperation with neighboring countries to bring their commodities to the world market.[7]

Historical path dependency

Nevertheless, the process stage most prone to conflict remains the last one: addressing the further transformation of the resource into a monetary benefit and the subsequent need for revenue distribution or allocation. In the case of resource-rich countries, it is not uncommon to build an entire economy around the export of the abundant resource, based on the false assumption that a strong extractive sector would benefit the economic and political development of other industrial branches (so-called staple theory of (export-growth).[8] Contrarily, opposite results have been recorded, with many resource-rich countries being affected by the so called "Dutch Disease", a situation in which the resource sector develops disproportionately in comparison to the other non-resource sectors by concentrating all efforts on rent-seeking activities (Ebrahim-Zadeh 2003).

These developments shed light on two potential sources of conflict and violence: first, the fixation on growth and the deceptive causality between development and growth as the only possible way to improve the economic, political and social well-being of one's citizens, and second, the deficient use of the revenues obtained from the trade of the abundant resource. Developing a sole economic branch cannot address societal, environmental or political grievances or accommodate sudden changes, such as a major price-drop of the exported resource.

Bad governance

While resource abundance *per se* is not the cause of poor governance, weak institutions and authoritarian tendencies, the misuse or just the unintended but still inadequate use of rents (Esfahani 2006) do have the potential to lead to higher risks of political instability, conflicts, and violence. These risks are even further aggravated by a lack of transparency and participation possibilities. In comparison to other sectors or even other resources (such as coffee, crops, etc.), oil or gas-based activities only create very few job opportunities. This leads to high unemployment rates, as well as to a concentration of ownership in the hands of the political elites responsible for the extraction and export activities. Aggravating, is also the fact that the value increase of commodities such as crude oil often happens only outside the country of extraction (UN 2018).[9]

Financing governments to a large degree through a so-called "unearned income" (Moore 2004) has eroded social ties and limited the chances for the ruling elite to engage with its citizens in a non-violent, solution-oriented claim-making process. While not pushing effectively for an economic diversification, the practices described above do tend to open doors for the formation of informal, unofficial economies based on smuggling and other partially illegal activities. These are mostly detrimental to the already marginalized groups and provoke even higher degrees of social inequalities (Le Billion 2004).

Conclusively, the section above has shown where potential sources of conflict and violence with regard to political economy might be lurking. The so-called "growth-mania" which has influenced our understanding of a liberal-capitalist market has ignored ecological and environmental concerns for decades, while fueling an unsustainable mass-consumerism based on the belief in energy transformation and infinite resources. At the same time, it has nurtured a historical process regarding the transformation of nature into resources, while accepting side-effects such as pollution, degradation or deprivation (Klein 2014). Besides these environmental concerns, which are in themselves far from being apolitical, this process has made the transformed resources into highly political, contentious claim-making objects.

The case study: Iraq and the Autonomous Region of Kurdistan

The theory-deduced sources of violence throughout the process of transforming nature into a resource and further monetizing it into a highly disputed commodity can be observed exemplarily in the case of Iraq and its autonomous region, Kurdistan. While the environmental determinism and the geographical conditionality might have served for an already unequal basis, the following section will show that particularly man-made (both ill-conceived and ill-intended) decisions have aggravated and heated up the spirals of violence in the country.

Environmental determinism

According to the latest figures of the Organization of Petroleum Exporting Countries (OPEC) from 2015, it is believed that Iraq is one of the most resource-abundant countries in the world when it comes to global proven crude oil reserves. With its estimated conventional crude oil wells of approximately 145 billion barrels, Iraq ranks fourth globally[10] (OPEC 2016). Nevertheless, as discussed above, the mere presence of potential or proven reserves of natural resources, such as oil and gas (at an impressive depth beneath the earth's surface), does not automatically sentence a country to recurrent conflicts and spirals of violence. However, the way in which collective actions are taken regarding these reserves is potentially contentious (Nicola 2017).

Geographical conditionalities

So-called "environmental determinism" further influences the aspects of geographical conditionalities: firstly through the demarcation of borders and the building and consolidation of Iraq as a nation state.[11] It has been this specific social and political process which has led to the allocation of such tremendous wealth to a single political entity. Following the reasoning of Le Billion, the location of the reserves within the country plays a further crucial role as a source of potential conflict and might even fuel – in the Iraqi case – secessionist aspirations. These independence ambitions have been most strongly articulated by the KRG on 25 September 2017, when the citizens residing on the territory of the Autonomous Region of Kurdistan[12] have been asked in a unilaterally organized referendum if they wish to become citizens of an independent state: Kurdistan. Despite a huge approval rate among KRG citizens, resembling dictatorial election results, the referendum has pushed the KRG into isolation following harsh sanctions imposed by the central government and supported actively by Iraq's neighbors and indirectly by an apparent indifference of supposed Western allies.

While there is no longer a point in prettifying the existence of these independence aspirations, it is hard to demonstrate that this secessionist process has been nurtured only by the existence of oil wells in the region administrated by the KRG. On the one hand, the Kurdish independence movement can be traced as far back as the end of the eighteenth century, when today's territory of Iraqi-Kurdistan was part of the Ottoman empire (Natali 2010), while Iraq started exploring oil wells only in the late 1920s (Tuzcu 2011). On the other hand, the active exploration of oil wells in the Autonomous Region of Kurdistan, which started in the early 2000s, has demonstrably led to the consolidation of the KRG (Nicola 2017) and boosted their capacity of actively promoting both state-building as well as nation-building mechanisms, which were thought to provide a concrete base for a potentially successful secession. Nevertheless, the latest concrete attempt of the KRG in this direction – the referendum – utterly failed.

The political and social connotations together with processes of identity activation[13] seem more suitable to explain the mechanisms for Iraqi-Kurdistan's attempt to secede from Iraq, while the oil reserves do play a role in their separatist ambitions and thus fuel conflicts. Oil has accounted for countless violent episodes between the two actors in the past. An example of identity politicizing is the language used by the US Energy Information Administration (World Energy Council 2013) when describing the geographical location of crude oil resources:

> Iraq's resources are not evenly divided across sectarian-demographic lines. Most known hydrocarbon resources are concentrated in the Shiite areas of the south and the ethnically Kurdish region in the north, with few resources in control of the Sunni minority in central Iraq.

The mere existence of hydrocarbon resources is being linked to sectarian and ethnically fueled strife as well as to control and access concerns, making social and political power concerns the "real" source of conflict.

Furthermore, geography also becomes relevant when it comes to transporting and exporting the resource through potential access to sea routes. In the case of Iraq, the rich southern oil wells are in the immediate proximity of the Persian Gulf, while the Autonomous Region of Kurdistan, taken as an entity by itself, is landlocked. This means that it depends on other infrastructure (pipelines or roads for trucks) to be able to bring crude oil across the border to the nearest port. Reliable neighbors are important too. The further a resource has to be transported from a distribution point to the end consumer, the higher the risk of violent intervention by unauthorized third parties becomes. In this case, even lightly-armed, relatively unskilled individuals can cause a high degree of damage and disruption by attacking vital road junctions or pipelines. This has recently been the case with IS fighters, who have paralyzed the transport of oil through Iraq's main pipeline connecting the northern field around Kirkuk with the port of Ceyhan in Turkey. The IS has used the captured oil to finance its illegal activities (Wong 2014).

Historical path

While the question of access to natural resources may apparently derive from geographic conditionalities regarding the location of a resource, the processes through which these resources are being transformed into a commodity, accessed, and explored are shaped not only by political power struggles, social interactions or cultural practices, but also by historical path dependencies. All of these aspects are flowing into the political economy of a resource-rich country.

In the case of Iraq, these processes go back to the 1920s, when the foundation of today's oil and gas sector was laid[14]. These processes have been subsequently influenced by power struggles within the political elites, as well as by the different economic discourses and developments at an international level. While in the aftermath of World War II, in 1949, there were only seven major IOCs[15] in possession of wells accounting for 88% of traded oil, the oil exporting countries "nibbl[ed] away at the control" of the IOCs throughout the 60s and 70s (Levy 1982). It was in the wake of this trend and during the peak of the Cold War that the nationalization process of the Iraqi oil industry was conducted and finally completed in 1972. Both power and profits were slowly moved to the state through the establishment of national oil companies (Tuzcu 2011).

However, instead of distributing the obtained wealth equally among all Iraqi citizens, this wealth has been misused by the political elite and especially, Saddam Hussein, who took control of the country in 1979 to consolidate his "personal dictatorship". In an attempt to extend his domestic political power regionally, Saddam engaged in an economically draining war with Iran from 1980 to 1988, at the end of which he only accumulated exorbitant levels of debt. The severely financially stricken economy did not get a chance to recover, since only two years later Saddam plunged into the next war through the annexation of Kuwait. The subsequent sanctions imposed by the international community together with the physically devastating war for the restoration of Kuwait's sovereignty nullified decades of human development with disastrous consequences for the life expectancy, basic health, or education possibilities of the citizens (Fürtig 2016).

Saddam's actions with regard to both war strategies and management of the oil sector had far-reaching consequences stretching until the present time: on the one hand, the economy was crippled to such a level that the measures adopted by the Coalition Provisional Authority (CPA), in charge of the reorientation of the country after the intervention and the resulting fall of Saddam in 2003, were doomed to failure from their inception. Many criticized these measures, based on their rejection of the so-called "shock doctrine", imposing an aggressive form of neo-liberalism according to which democracy will allegedly grow based on the opportunities created by free-market and competition. Privatization, especially of the nationalized oil sector, was seen as an attempt to rob the Iraqi people of the wealth they were supposedly entitled to (Klein 2007).

Regardless of the philosophical debate if capitalism is boon or bane, the level of destruction of the economy has been so severe that there was basically no market to respond to the "shock doctrine". This fact had been grossly underestimated. Additionally, Iraqis would have been unable to compete internationally. Furthermore, while the connection between the US-led interventions of both 1991 and 2003 and Iraq's oil-richness has been made more than once, with a subtext implying causality, this link remains far from being unequivocally proven.

On the other hand, without a new Oil and Gas Law, which had been drafted by the government according to neo-liberal standards but which did not pass through parliament, it meant that the industry is still regulated by pieces of legislature which were adopted during the 1970s and 80s – a dark time of the Baathist dictatorial regime, when the oppression of the Kurds in the north of the country had reached genocidal levels. This also stands contradicted by the new Iraqi constitution from 2005 which acknowledges through the new alignment of the country the autonomy and extended rights of the Kurds.

This discrepancy is sharply criticized by the KRG and even instrumentalized to a certain degree, as the KRG minister of natural resources of that time, Ashti Hawrami, described the Iraqi state oil companies as "an instrument of the power of Saddam Hussein in the 1980s to get all the money" (Kern and Reed 2014: 1). While the Iraqi constitution states that oil belongs to all the people in Iraq, the KRG, haunted by the traumatic experiences of the past, fears the concentration of power over the oil marketing activities in the hand of the central government. Thus, the historical path dependency left a twofold bequest: on the one hand, historically grown conflicts and on the other hand, a dilapidated economy, which would need – under "perfect" economic conditions – years to recover.

Driven by both fear of the past and the wish for independence, the KRG unilaterally passed an Oil and Gas Law on a regional level, retracting itself from the rule of the 1970s and 1980s legislature and embracing an apparently new economic orientation. Instead of the Technical Sharing Contracts (TSCs) traditionally offered by the central government to international oil companies (IOCs) for their technical support and know-how, the KRG has tried to attract investors to its still under – or even unexplored areas by offering Product Sharing Contracts (PSCs), in which foreign contractors benefit directly from the amount of crude oil drilled in exchange not only for know-how, but also for infrastructure, international recognition, and help with the commercialization of the resource (Nicola 2017).

The new law seems to be liberal, market-oriented and investor-friendly through numerous benefits for the IOCs such as small or non-existent corporate taxes, or high investment return rates compared to the stiff, out-of-date legislative conditions at national level (Nicola 2017). It also resembles the calls for privatization rejected by the central government and feared by the opponents of the Washington Consensus. Nevertheless, there is an important difference rebutting this critique. The IOCs pursuing the creation of a solid oil and gas industry in Kurdistan – most probably driven more by profit-oriented than development-oriented reasons – are engaging in a historically underdeveloped and almost unindustrialized region with poor infrastructure and medical health services. This poses far more challenges and economic risks than investing in the already explored and proven wells in the south of Iraq and requires a certain commitment.

At the same time, the involvement of IOCs is often related to a plea for greater transparency, accountability and the fighting of corruption. Subsequently, it can be claimed that the KRG has the opportunity of building an oil sector without the historical baggage of mismanagement and greed, in the spirit of economic freedom and reflected collective self-determination. On the other hand, the lack of experience puts the KRG into a bad negotiation position without any leverage in front of extremely powerful IOCs (Klein 2014). The KRG's demonization of the central state is the only driving factor behind these negotiations. While the KRG benefits from international recognition as a reliable partner in terms of its economic cooperation with IOCs, this increases the risk of the internal power disputes between regional and federal government also being internationalized.

Bad governance

Besides the already disadvantageous historical circumstances under which the Iraqi oil and gas sector developed, many sources of conflict and violence arise, additionally, from the highly inefficient use and distribution of oil revenues. The oil sector of Iraq's largely state-run economy provides more than 90% of the government's revenues (World Bank 2017). While this might give an idea of wealth related to the impressive abundance of resource, the oil business has not been a viable source of broad-based economic development in Iraq. Not only does the Iraqi oil sector not contribute to the country's accumulation of wealth but the current state of business is depleting it, as the oil wealth is being consumed unsustainably and without investing in the creation of human or physical assets.

The Systematic Country Diagnostic of Iraq, last published by the World Bank in February 2017, goes to the heart of the problem by acknowledging the multi-causality around Iraq's political economy failures: "The economy wreckage of wars and sanctions, combined with the dissolution of the country's key institutions, meant that growing oil revenues in the post-2003 period reinforced the status quo rather than becoming an impetus for reform" (World Bank 2017: 13). The short-sighted rent-seeking activities are no longer enough to even fund the functioning of the administration. In 2016, Iraq spent 50% more money than it had collected: $77.87 billion expenditure compared to the $52.43 billion revenue (CIA 2017). These dis-satisfactory figures occurred during a year in which the GDP increased considerably, given the economic conjuncture and recovery of the international oil prices after the shocking fall of prices in 2014.

This limited example helps to illustrate how vulnerable an oil-based economy is, not only due to the volatility of the prices in the sector, but also due to the high dependency on one single resource. At the same time, such an increase in the GDP does not constitute real economic growth, but an artificial result of extrinsic conditions, without the generation of additional assets or value. Relying only on oil revenues has led to a neglect of the non-oil infrastructure and has kept capital investment away from the private sector, which is currently weak and incapable of generating enough jobs for the rapidly growing Iraqi population with its preponderant youth bulge. Discrepantly, the oil sector, while attracting most of the government's attention, only provides around 1% of all employment opportunities (World Bank 2017).

Under these circumstances, the public sector has evolved to be the largest formal employer with around 40% of Iraq's work force on its pay roll (World Bank 2017). This ineffective anomaly also holds true for the KRG. In both regional and central Iraq, the number of ministries, state-owned enterprises and individuals employed through patronage and nepotism is disproportionately high and a burden on the budget. Nevertheless, this practice does not accommodate the growing needs of the population, but can be understood as a paradigmatic example of the incapacity of the administration to nurture a proper relationship between the state and its citizens, both due to a lack of taxation instruments as well as deficient public services (UN 2013).

While it is claimed that the national oil reserves belong to the people of Iraq, it seems that its exploitation and subsequent value and wealth generation do not bring benefits – neither in terms of capital accumulation nor personal growth – for the majority of the people, but only for a selected few. Interestingly, despite different historical path dependencies between the central and the regional governments in terms of damage following the destruction and violence since the 1980s, the same "entrepreneurial" culture of patronage, corruption and selective access to easy and "unearned" money is being nurtured by both the KRG and the Iraqi government, based on the active concentration of power in the hands of an archaic political elite, and the intentional erosion of participatory means for the broad population.

Conclusion

As it has been seen in the preceding discussion, the process of transforming natural resources into tradable resources, such as oil, is intrinsically connected to the evolution of numerous conflicts, which vary in the degree of their violent manifestations. Nevertheless, the political, ecological, theoretical framework described here by the usage of paradigmatic examples has made the decisive contribution that it is not the resource *per se* which is solely responsible for the emergence of a violent political economy, but rather the social construction of oil, which depends on intertwined dimensions such as its abundant character determined to a certain extent by the environment, geographic conditionalities, the historical context, as well as the characteristics of the political and economic institutions managing the oil sector and governing the distribution of the revenues obtained.

Iraq's involvement in wars and armed conflict for more than three decades now, from the Iran-Iraq war of the 80s to the latest battles against IS, have indubitably shaped all aspects of both daily life and political, social, and economic institutions in Iraq. While the hydrocarbon resources are not the sole cause of the country's inability to break the spiral of violence, this chapter has shown a wide range of sources of conflict or violence which are related to the activities, processes and interactions of petroleum operations. The oil and gas sector in Iraq has become a liability instead of the desired motor for development, stability and eventual wealth.

One deceptive characteristic of the Iraqi political economy is its growth-orientation when a higher GDP is obtained through higher oil prices or through a greater amount of exploited and exported crude oil. Aside from the ecological recklessness of this thinking and its unsustainable character, a non-violent political economy can and should be built on minimal extraction of fossil fuels, where the oil and gas sector serves as a stepping stone for the diversification of the private sector, including services and other industrial branches. There are enough examples from both industrialized and emerging countries, which show that both diversification as well as the de-carbonization of economy are possible, even after years of strife.

This potential and imperative is acknowledged even by institutions obsessed with capitalist growth, such as the World Bank (2017: 113), which sees the agricultural sector as vital for a reformation of Iraq's violent political economy, since "unlike most of its oil-rich neighbors, [Iraq] has a population large enough to contemplate skills specialization" through its considerable agricultural resources. At the same time, especially living in a de-carbonization era, the use of clean energy sources – predominantly solar, given the climate and geographical conditions in Iraq – could also ease further challenges such as the growing electricity demands, which are currently only being addressed through insufficient and costly subsidies.

According to Tagliapietra (2017), there are still not enough incentives to motivate Middle Eastern political elites to transition away from fossil fuels, and actively choosing not to exploit these resources, even when realizing that the current wells will most probably be depleted in the next 100 years. Non-violent political economic ideas and scenarios are good and solid options, even if utopian, to conceptualize such incentives. In her 2014 book Naomi Klein describes the positive example of Ecuador, where a fund has been created, which should replace or re-compensate for the revenues which would have been obtained if a particular resource would have been exploited, but that was not tapped into due to environmental concerns. There is a serious amount of research needed to examine to what extent a similar solution might be also suitable for Iraq and the Middle East. To what extent is it possible to create an international organization resembling the General Assembly, which would administrate a shared money pot designated to distribute fund assets for the developing of alternative energy sources in the case of a partial (but substantial) or a complete guaranteed renunciation to the exploitation of fossil fuels. How can keeping fossil fuels in the ground be incentivized without being paternalistic?

If humankind has demonstrated that it is able to overcome extremely violent human-induced catastrophes such as World War II, this also means that it is not impossible to grow out of an unsustainable carpe diem mentality and to take responsibility also for the generations to come. Nevertheless, history has also shown that this process is a long-term project. The only difference is that we do not know if there is enough time left.

Notes

1 Examples of such unaddressed pressing social issues are: the overall growing population, the numerous educated but jobless young people, rapidly accelerating electricity demands, the global trend of mass consumerism, etc.

2 The examples provided are paradigmatic and by no means claim to be exhaustive.

3 The support of the degrowth philosophy can be reinforced by different considerations: either based on the acknowledgement of the undeniable limits of growth, based on the belief, that despite economic stagnation, wealth must be maintained even without growth, or based on the wish of a revolutionary "liberation from capitalism" and the pursuit of an egalitarian form of society (D'Alisa et al. 2015: 1–17). For the sake of transparency towards the reader, it has to be mentioned that the author has been socialized in a European democratic spirit, which is strongly linked to the history of growth and free-markets. Having enjoyed the benefits of a welfare state, which "has bridled the most problematic effects of free market", while ensuring a strong social integration (Deriu 2012), the author acknowledges the gravity of ignoring the limits to growth, without sharing to the same extent the endeavors of a revolutionary transformation of society.

4 For a more detailed discussion of the concepts "growth", "economy of gift", "buen vivir", and "conviviality" and other similar philosophies compatible with a non-violent political economy, see: D'Alisa et al. 2015.

5 This can be seen, exemplarily, when looking at the research promoted or funded by the Egypt-based Economic Research Forum (ERF 2017), a "foreign NGO dedicated to promoting high quality research that contributes to inclusive and sustainable development in the ERF region (consisting of the Arab countries, Iran and Turkey)". Despite a global strengthening of unconventional oil sources, a worldwide de-carbonization rhetoric or a weakened global oil demand, the ERF organizes events around the optimization of growth ("Structural Change, Resource Misallocation and Growth Dynamics in the MENA Region" or "The Political Economy of State Business Relations and of Growth in the MENA Region").

6 As an example, despite the fact that there have been historically grown contentions between Kurds and Turks, Turkish business people engaged in economic activities in the Autonomous Region of Kurdistan have often underlined their shared Islamic heritage as a common basis for pursuing – in this case – a shared interest: obtaining profit. In this way, the demarcation line – previously traced along ethnic considerations (Kurds, Turks) – has been newly articulated in such a way, that it delimits Islamic people (Kurds and Turks) from non-Islamic groups, while erasing the ethnic differentiation.

7 The importance of this geographical conditionality has become evident during the crisis in the Autonomous Region of Kurdistan following the independence referendum held without the consent of the central Iraqi government. In a coordinated action to collectively punish the KRG, all neighbors have closed their borders so that formal economic exchange has been hamstrung.

8 While this so-called staple theory of (export-)growth might have proven true in the Canadian case, it did not yield the expected results when used in other economic and political contexts.

9 While crude oil is being exported from Iraq or from the Autonomous Region of Kurdistan, it is only in the refineries, where the resource is being transformed into the end-product ready for consumption. At the point of writing this article, there are no refineries known to the author in the Autonomous Region of Kurdistan. While Iraq used to also rely on a downstream infrastructure, this has been almost completely crippled by the ongoing violence and direct physical destruction lasting to varying degrees for over 30 years now.

10 The first three places of the ranking are occupied by Venezuela (with approx. 300 billion barrels), Saudi Arabia (with approx. 270 billion barrels) and Iran (with approx. 160 billion barrels) (OPEC 2016).

11 The demarcation of today's borders of Iraq as a nation state has been deeply influenced by the colonial imposition of the secret Sykes-Picot treaty, which decided over the partition of the territory of the Ottoman Empire among France and Great Britain following the end of World War I. For a deeper analysis of the treaty's impact on Iraq and the Autonomous Region of Kurdistan, see Fürtig 2016.

12 Not only citizens residing on the territory administrated by the Autonomous Region of Kurdistan were allowed to cast their vote, but also members of the diaspora – people of Kurdish descent living in other parts of the world – and people living in disputed areas such as Kirkuk, which are – at least *de jure* – under the rule of the central state.

13 For a detailed account on the articulation of the collective identity asserted by the KRG, see Nicola 2017.

14 The national process of oil explorations cannot be separated from the realities created on the ground by the colonial powers of that time, the British influence being observable even regarding this particular topic with the Anglo-Persian Oil Company of 1909 developing itself later on into today's British Petroleum (BP) (Levy 1982).

15 These seven major IOCs were: Exxon, Mobil, Socal, Texaco, Gulf, BP, Royal Dutch Shell (Levy 1982).

References

Al-Saadi, S.Z. (2010). Political Economy of Iraq's Growing Oil Power. A Crucial Phase, *Culture and Conflict Review*, Spring, 4, 1.

Auty, R.M. (ed.) (2001). *Resource Abundance and Economic Development*. New York: Oxford University Press.

Beblawi, H. (1987). The Rentier State in the Arab World, *Arab Studies Quarterly*, 9, 4, pp. 383–398.

Binswanger, H.C. (2009). Wege aus der Wachstumsfalle, *Vorgänge – Zeitschrift für Bürgerrechte und Gesellschaftspolitik*, 186, 2, 23–27.

Collier, P. (2000). *Economic Causes of Civil Conflict and their Implications for Policy*. Washington, DC: World Bank.

de Soysa, I. (2000). The resource curse: are civil wars driven by rapacity or paucity? In M. Berdal and D. Malone (eds), *Greed and Grievance: Economic Agendas in Civil Wars*. Boulder, CO: Lynne Rienner.

Daly, H. (2008). *A Steady-State Economy*. London: Sustainable Development Commission.

Deriu, M. (2012). Democracy with a future: Degrowth and the democratic tradition, *Future* 44, pp. 553–561.

D'Alisa, G., Demaria, F. and Kallis, G. (eds) (2015). *Degrowth: A Vocabulary for a New Era*. Routledge: New York.

Ebrahim-Zadeh, C. (2003). Back to Basics – Dutch Disease: Too Much Wealth Managed Unwisely? *Finance and Development*, 40, 1.

Esfahani, H.S. (2006). *A Reexamination of the Political Economy of Growth in MENA Countries*. University of Illinois at Urbana-Champaign.

Fürtig, H. (2016). *Geschichte des Irak. Von der Gründung 1921 bis heute*, 3rd edn. München: C.H. Beck.

Galtung, J. (1990). Cultural Violence, *Journal of Peace Research*, 27, 3, pp. 291–305.

Georgescu-Roegen, N. (1975). Energy and Economic Myths, *Southern Economic Journal*, 41, 3, pp. 347–381.

Kern, N. and Reed, M. (2014). Iraq, Turkey and the New Kurdistan Pipeline Deal, *Foreign Reports Bulletin*, Middle East Policy Council.

Klein, N. (2007). *The Shock Doctrine. The Rise of Disaster Capitalism*. London: Penguin Random House.

Klein, N. (2014). *This Changes Everything. Capitalism vs. The Climate*. London: Penguin Random House.

Le Billon, P. (2004). The Geopolitical Economy of 'Resource Wars', *Geopolitics*, 9, 1, pp. 1–28.

Levy, B. (1982). World Oil Marketing in Transition, *International Organization*, 36, 1, pp. 113–133.

Mahdavy, H. (1970). Patterns and Problems of Economic Development in Rentier States: The Case of Iran. In Cook, M.A. (ed.), *Studies in Economic History of the Middle East*. Oxford: Oxford University Press.

Meadows, D.H. et al. (1972). *The Limits to Growth*. New York: Universe Books.

MooreM. (2004). Revenues, State Formation, and the Quality of Governance in Developing Countries, *International Political Science Review*, 25, 3, pp. 297–319.

Natali, D. (2010). *Kurdish Quasi-State: Development and Dependency in Post-Gulf War Iraq*. New York: Syracuse University Press.

Nicola, S.L. (2017). *Adding 'oil' to the fire? International Economic Cooperation and the Dynamics of Contentions. The Case Study of the Autonomous Region of Kurdistan*. FI

Working Paper No. 9, Felsberg: edition 1. Available online at www.fibw.eu/images/ dokumente/WP-9-2017-Nicola-Kurdish-Oil.pdf (accessed April 2, 2018).

OPEC (2016). *Annual Statistic Bulletin 2016*. Available online at www.opec.org/opec_web/static_files_project/media/downloads/publications/ASB2016.pdf

Rahim, D. A. (2013). Kurdish National Security: At the Era of Oil and Gas (Master Thesis), George C. Marshall European Center for Security Studies/ Universität der Bundeswehr München.

Sachs, J. D. and A. M. Warner (2001). The Curse of Natural Resources, *European Economic Review*, 45, pp. 827–838.

Sustainable Development Commission (2009). *Prosperity Without Growth? The Transition to a Sustainable Economy*. London: Sustainable Development Commission. Available online at www.sd-commission.org.uk/publications.php?id=914 (accessed February 3, 2018).

Tagliapietra, S. (2017). The Political Economy of Middle East and North Africa Oil Exporters in Times of Global Decarbonisation, Working Paper Issue 5, Bruegel.

The United Nations Interagency Framework Team for Preventive Action (2011). *Conflict Prevention in Resource-Rich Economies*. Available online at www.un.org/en/land-natura l-resources-conflict/pdfs/Resource%20Rich%20Economies.pdf (accessed April 2, 2019).

Tilly, C. (2005). *Identities, Boundaries and Social Ties*. Boulder: Paradigm Publisher.

Tuzcu, M. (2011). Has a New Political Era Changed Iraqi Economy? Challenges for a Late Rentier State. Master of Arts in Law and Diplomacy Thesis, The Fletcher School, Tufts University.

UN (2018). Available online at https://unstats.un.org/unsd/energy/yearbook/default. htm (accessed April 1, 2019).

US Central Intelligence Agency (2017). *The World Factbook – Iraq*. Available online at www.cia.gov/library/publications/the-world-factbook/geos/print_iz.html

US Energy Information Administration (EIA) (2013). *Country Report – Iraq*. Last Updated April 2, 2013.

Victor, P. (2008). *Managing Without Growth – Slower by Design not Disaster*. Cheltenham: Edward Elgar.

Wong, E. (2014). Insurgents Blow Up an Iraqi Pipeline, *New York Times*, November 3.

World Bank (2017). Iraq. Systematic Country Diagnostic, February 3, 2017, Report No. 112333-IQ.

World Energy Council. Available online at www.worldenergy.org/data/resources/country/iraq/oil/ (accessed April 1, 2019).

Zimmerman, E. (1951). *World Resources and Industries*, revised edn. New York: Harper and Row.

Index